T0340301

Understanding, Defining and Eliminating Workplace Bullying

Workplace bullying is a severe and pervasive problem around the globe and in particular in the United States where no meaningful steps have been taken to address this problem. This book will help readers to understand and to define workplace bullying to be able to prevent, detect, remedy and eliminate workplace bullying. Readers will gain an understanding of the forms, causes and effects of workplace bullying. Readers will also be able to understand the current gaps in U.S. law and become familiar with more effective international laws to address workplace bullying. Finally, the reader will be presented with the potential paths to put an end to workplace bullying in their own workplace and in workplaces across the globe.

Jerry A. Carbo is a Professor of Labor Relations and Business and Society in the Grove College of Business at Shippensburg University. He is also a practicing attorney in the State of West Virginia. He has over 20 years of experience as a manager, attorney, advocate and researcher dealing with workplace harassment and bullying.

"In this comprehensive study, Professor Carbo explores the problem of workplace bullying at the individual, organizational, national and international levels. Within this multi-perspective framework, the book is impressive in its analysis of the scope of workplace bullying and the depth of its individual and systemic impact. The proposed solutions, based on a human rights model, will surely invigorate the debate over how to best address the problem of bullying at the workplace."

Risa L. Lieberwitz, Professor of Labor and Employment Law,
Cornell University, USA

Understanding, Defining and Eliminating Workplace Bullying

Assuring dignity at work

Jerry A. Carbo

Routledge
Taylor & Francis Group

LONDON AND NEW YORK

First published 2017
by Routledge

2 Park Square, Milton Park, Abingdon, Oxfordshire OX14 4RN
52 Vanderbilt Avenue, New York, NY 10017

Routledge is an imprint of the Taylor & Francis Group, an informa business

First issued in paperback 2019

British Library Cataloguing-in-Publication Data
A catalogue record for this book is available from the British Library

Library of Congress Cataloging-in-Publication Data
A catalog record for this book has been requested

ISBN: 978-1-4724-8244-0 (hbk)
ISBN: 978-0-367-88201-3 (pbk)

Typeset in Bembo
by Apex CoVantage, LLC

Contents

List of illustrations   vii

Preface: protecting employees' human rights   ix

SECTION 1
Understanding workplace bullying   1

1 An introduction to bullying and its impact on workers
   and workplaces   3

2 What does workplace bullying look like?   11

3 Workplace bullying is a terrible problem: why is it so
   important to address workplace bullying?   22

4 Why does bullying occur and endure?   33

SECTION 2
**Workplace bullying can be addressed but is not in the
United States**   45

5 Gaps in the U.S. employment law: workplace bullying can
   be, but is not being, addressed   47

6 Evidence from abroad: steps can be taken to eliminate
   workplace bullying   70

SECTION 3
Ending workplace bullying   83

7 Defining the problem: a transformative definition
   of workplace bullying   85

8 The potential for micro level solutions   107

  9 Employer-based solutions   114

 10 Concerted activity as a solution   129

 11 The need for a strong law and strong enforcement   144

 12 Conclusion   159

    References   163
    Index   169

Illustrations

Figure

4.1   Workplace bullying life cycle   43

Tables

2.1   Types of workplace bullying   19
3.1   Some examples of the effects of workplace bullying   28

Preface: protecting employees' human rights

The purpose of this book is to emancipate workers from the binds of their bullies and to help readers of this book to engage in emancipating targets of workplace bullying, themselves or others, from the torment. In order to do so, the reader must have a full understanding of workplace bullying. To gain this in-depth understanding of the problem of workplace bullying, we must let go of traditional notions of study and exploration. These types of studies are bound by the same systems that allow for and even create workplace bullying. Instead, we must engage in a deeper, more critical analysis of workplace bullying. We must be willing to explore bullying not just as an individual problem or even organizational problem, but we must also be willing to explore it as a systemic problem. We must be willing to look in a deep and meaningful way at the causes and effects of workplace bullying, and then to explore true solutions to this problem. Such an analysis fits well within a critical exploration of bullying, whether it be from a critical sociology, management or legal analysis. As a result, this book will follow such a critical analysis.

Adler suggests that, as part of critical management studies (CMS), one of our key questions is to ask critically in the name of whom and what. This book will be critical in the name of workers and the protection of their human rights. Human rights are rights one has by virtue of the simple fact of being a human. These are rights we all hold regardless of race, color, religion or any other status and they are rights that we hold wherever we go – in our communities, in our nations and in our work. These rights go beyond the mere ability to survive, and instead include those things needed to live the life of a human being. The key to human rights is of course the enforcement and protection of these rights for all. Enjoyment of these rights are what make us human in the first place. Human rights exist not only as the requisites for health but to fulfill those needs for a life worthy of a human being.[1] Those whose human rights are violated live in a manner that is less than human, a circumstance that tears at the very fabric of their being, and would even bring into question the purpose of their being. Unfortunately, according to Professor James Gross, the concept of human rights, particularly workers' rights as human rights, has never been an important influence in the making of U.S. labor law or labor policy. Even beyond the borders of the United States, international human rights organizations, human rights scholars and labor organizations and advocates have given little attention to workers' rights as human rights.[2]

However, the lack of legal recourse or recognition of these rights in employment laws does not in any way excuse the violation of human rights, nor does it make acceptable the lack of exploration of these rights to begin to apply these in our own legal system. In fact, while current U.S. employment laws fail to address these rights, historically, the United States has recognized the existence of these rights. The recognition of these rights is exemplified in Thomas Jefferson's eloquent passage from the Declaration of Independence:

> We hold these truths to be self-evident; that all men are created equal; that they are endowed by their creator with [inherent and] inalienable rights; that among these are life, liberty and the pursuit of happiness; that to secure these rights, governments are instituted among men.[3]

The message in the Declaration of Independence is clear – we must endeavor to define and understand human rights so that we can protect and assure these rights for all. It could be argued that the very purpose of any form of government is to protect these human rights. Unfortunately, for workers today, this focus on human rights is lacking, particularly so in the United States.

According to Rene Cassin, a French legal scholar and Nobel laureate, "dignity, liberty, equality and brotherhood" form the foundation of human rights.[4] According to the Vienna Doctrine, "all human rights derive from the dignity, and worth inherent in the human person."[5] Dignity "plays an important role in ensuring a standard for the protection of civil and political rights and social and economic rights in Europe."[6] So dignity seems to provide at least a good starting point for understanding human rights and a good starting point for the protection of such rights. As I will discuss throughout this book, workplace bullying strips targets of this dignity.

Dignity can be defined as "the quality or state of being honored or esteemed."[7] There are many different conceptions of the meaning of dignity. For instance, Toth suggests that the right to work, to equal pay, to just and favorable working conditions and to freedom of association may all be included within the definition of dignity as it relates to work.[8] From a sociological standpoint, "dignity has been defined as a sense of self-worth."[9] In other words, dignity is the state of having value, and in this case value as a human being. Not only is this state of having value a human right, but it is one of the foundations for all human rights. Human rights are about more than protecting our physical lives; they are about protecting the meaning of our lives, and dignity lies as at least part of this foundation of human life. It is this value as a human being that must be protected both at the workplace and outside of the workplace.

To gain a further understanding of this value we can look at Maslow's hierarchy of needs. Maslow's theory helps us to understand what people need to live as human beings. Maslow's hierarchy suggests that human *needs* are many and varied. These needs include not only the basic needs, such as the need for food and water (physiological needs), but also include higher-level needs such as esteem, acceptance and, ideally, self-actualization.[10] Maslow himself recognized these needs as a legitimate basis for human rights.[11] Other human rights scholars have also agreed that Maslow's work at least sets out a number of those things that should be included in human rights.[12]

Building from these studies, philosophies and experiences many doctrines of human rights have been developed across the globe. The most important of these may indeed be the Universal Declaration of Human Rights as mentioned earlier. However, The International Covenant on Economic, Social, and Cultural Rights, International Covenant on Civil and Political Rights, and even the Declaration of Independence, the Bill of Rights and the Declaration of the Rights of Man and other treaties and covenants and conventions, provide guidance as to what should be included as human rights.

These treatises recognize that human rights apply within our workplaces. For instance, in the Universal Declaration of Human Rights a number of the articles deal specifically with work, including articles 23 and 25.

> Article 23 (1): Everyone has the right to work, to free choice of employment, **to** *just and favourable conditions of work* and to protection against unemployment.
> Article 25: Everyone has the right to a standard of living adequate for the health and well-being of himself and his family, including food, clothing, housing and medical care and necessary social services.[13]

Fear of job loss and the resulting social outcomes – inability to meet basic needs – often trap targets in hostile working environments that are permeated with bullying and intimidation. As we can see from Article 25 of the UDHR, if human rights were truly being enforced, nobody would ever have to endure that fear and thus the hostile environment. Targets could walk away from these hostile environments and still be assured their basic needs would be met. However, we do not live in such a system – clearly not in the United States and more and more not across the globe. Instead, people are dependent on their work to meet their basic needs. Each and every day, they know that without their jobs they are just a short time away from struggling to meet the most basic of their needs. Each of us goes to work in a system where in the best of times, we know that 1 in 20 members of the U.S. labor force are ready and willing to take our jobs and that more people will be entering that labor force each day. We know that employers can easily decide to uproot our jobs and move them across the country or across the globe. We also know that if we lose these jobs, at best we will get a short-term partial replacement of our lost income through unemployment insurance. As a result, the vast majority of working people do whatever they can to hold onto the bit of security they have by maintaining their jobs. Even when workers face some of the most severe forms of bullying, targets are often left with the only rational choice of staying and enduring the behaviors.

Our current system of employment in the United States and much of the westernized world fails to uphold human rights in the workplace. Subjugation to a hostile environment such as that created by workplace bullying is a clear violation of Article 23 and the right to just and favorable working conditions. Yet, in the United States, there is no protection for employees from being bullied and harassed in the workplace. We fail to assure the safe and health working conditions and fail to assure the physical and mental health of workers in the United States that is assured as a right under the United Nations Covenant on Economic, Social and Cultural Rights.[14] Instead, the psychological well-being of employees is damaged in the degrading, intimidating, controlling and hostile working environments created by workplace bullies.

As we move to a global economy, protecting human rights becomes even more difficult and more relevant to the workplace. Within the context of the increased power of international economic organizations such as the World Trade Organization (WTO) and the increased power of multi-national corporations (MNCs), "a morality founded on some set of human rights principles may well be the only effective way to confront the divisions by class, race, ethnicity and gender within the contemporary global setting."[15] As we rely on and focus more on markets to solve societal problems, we become less able to address human rights. "[M]arkets foster efficiency, but not social equity or the enjoyment of individual rights for all."[16] Failure to enforce a human rights standard leaves employees at the whim of the employer and markets to meet even their most basic needs.

As the global economy becomes more and more of a private market based on the U.S. economic model, and as social safety nets are removed from governmental systems, access to this standard of living comes only through work.[17] As more people around the globe work for other people and engage in work for large MNCs, the protection of even these fundamental needs becomes more and more important. Because meeting this standard of living will only come through gainful employment, the right to such employment becomes an imperative human right. Further, the protection of human rights while at work likewise becomes imperative.

A human right to work and to just and favorable conditions of work goes beyond the right to earn a living necessary for one's survival. As Donnelly appropriately states, work is also important to the attainment of goals necessary for human dignity.[18] These goals may also be described as higher-level human needs (the needs necessary to live as a human being) and can again be described by reference to Maslow's hierarchy of needs, specifically Maslow's needs for esteem, growth and self-actualization.[19]

To meet these needs there must not only be a focus on the right to work itself, but also to certain conditions of work. Workers do not become any less human when they "clock-in" to their work. Therefore, people have the same human needs and rights when they are working as when they are outside of their employment. The opportunity to meet these higher-level needs is also a human right; these needs must be met in order protect the right to dignity;

and these rights must at least in part come through the institution of work that plays such a large role in human existence. When human rights are violated inside or outside of the workplace, the decision is made that some should live as less than humans. If higher-level needs are violated in the workplace, then the human right to dignity is violated at work.

The protection of this right to dignity in the workplace must become a focus of our public policy. Laws should be analyzed based upon whether they uphold this foundation of human rights as well as the rights enumerated in the Universal Declaration of Human Rights and other widely accepted conventions. Employer practices, union activities and worker interactions should be analyzed in much the same way. Workers' rights and human rights in the workplace have been ignored for far too long in the U.S. legal system and in organizational research. "Human rights evolve in reaction to new or newly recognized threat to human dignity."[20] Workplace bullying is an example of such a newly recognized threat to human dignity.

The exploration of how workplace bullying violates these human rights and how bullying should be addressed to assure and protect these rights will be undertaken in the remaining chapters of this book. This analysis will be conducted from the stories of targets of workplace bullying shared with me during various forms of qualitative research including in-depth interviews, focus groups, written narratives and participant observation, as well as my experiences as a manager, advocate, attorney and activist. This information will be intertwined with research from other experts in the field of workplace bullying. By looking at all of this primary and secondary research, I hope that I will be able to provide the reader with first a better understanding of how to define workplace bullying in such a way as to include all acts of bullying. I then hope to provide the reader with deeper insight into the phenomena including the causes and effects of workplace bullying. Once this understanding is gained, the ultimate goal of this book is to provide the reader with potential solutions. These solutions include micro as well as macro level solutions and provide suggestions in terms of how each solution could be implemented. The phenomenon of workplace bullying is simply too large for any one book, researcher or even legislature to tackle on his/her/its own. The reality is that in order to end workplace bullying and to protect the human rights of all workers, we need a movement. I hope that after you have read this book, you will become a part of that movement.

This book is meant to serve as a guide to help targets, organizations and advocates to understand workplace bullying so that we can eliminate bullying from the American workplace and assure dignity for all working people.

Notes

1 (Donnelly, 2003).
2 (Gross, 2004).
3 (Jefferson, 1776, p. 21).

4 (Ishay, 2004, p. 3).
5 (The United Nations, 1993).
6 (Toth, 2008, p. 277).
7 (Anon., 2004, p. 201).
8 (Toth, 2008, p. 277).
9 (Toth, 2008, p. 282).
10 (Jones & George, 2007).
11 (Donnelly, 2003, p. 13).
12 (Donnelly, 2003, p. 13).
13 (The United Nations, 1948) (My emphasis).
14 (The United Nations General Assembly, 1966).
15 (Sjoberg, et al., 2001).
16 (Donnelly, 2003, p. 201).
17 See Noreen Hertz, *The Silent Takeover: Global Capitalism and the Death of Democracy* (Harper Collins 2003), and Naomi Klein, *The Shock Doctrine: The Rise of Disaster Capitalism* (Metropolitan Books 2007). In both of these books, the authors outline the spread of an extreme form of capitalism preached by the Chicago school economists that consists of eliminating all social safety nets and the privatization of all businesses, including traditional governmental roles. Both books also describe the role of the WTO and IMF in spreading these practices through the placement of these conditions on loans.
18 (Donnelly, 2003).
19 (Jones & George, 2007).
20 (Donnelly, 2003, p. 222).

Section 1

Understanding workplace bullying

The phenomenon of workplace bullying is still not completely understood. There are still today too many myths and misunderstandings about bullying. In my research and in my time conducting training on workplace bullying, I have heard the following myths:

Myth: Bullying is simply a childhood phenomenon that kids experience in schools and on playgrounds.

Fact: Bullying is something that impacts millions of working adults, every day in workplaces across the globe.

Myth: Enduring bullying will make the target stronger.

Fact: Bullying has devastating effects on targets, bystanders, families, friends, communities, organizations and society.

Myth: Bullying is just a normal part of the workplace.

Fact: Bullying is a violation of the most fundamental of human rights, it has no place and no value in the workplace.

Myth: Targets are just whiners and weak.

Fact: Targets are often the strongest people in a working environment. Targets come from all walks of life, all different positions in organizations.

Myth: The U.S. legal system protects against workplace bullying.

Fact: The U.S. legal system fails to address workplace bullying. There is no law that directly addresses workplace bullying and no tort action that effectively addresses workplace bullying.

Myth: Laws to address workplace bullying would create a civility code.

Fact: While there is nothing at all wrong with a civil workplace, statutes against workplace bullying do not create such a code, instead they protect employees' rights in the workplace.

These as well as other myths about workplace bullying will be addressed throughout this book. In the first section of this book, I hope to provide the reader with a better understanding of workplace bullying. I provide the reader with an introduction to workplace bullying and some of the research in workplace bullying in the opening chapter. In Chapter 2, I provide the reader with a description of workplace bullying and examples of workplace bullying tactics and behaviors. From there, in Chapter 3, I lay out the effects of workplace bullying on targets, witnesses, families, communities, society and the organizations themselves. Finally, in Chapter 4, I hope to give the reader a bit of understanding of the causes of workplace bullying by describing the life cycle of workplace bullying from my experiences as a researcher, manager, advocate and activist.

1 An introduction to bullying and its impact on workers and workplaces

Sara had been successful her entire career. She could not understand why at this point in her life she was facing bullying from her colleagues and her supervisor and felt like her career was on the line. As a professor, she was a prolific publisher, had won numerous teaching awards and served on more committees than any of her colleagues. However, she found all of her colleagues were ganging up on her, her dean had engaged in bullying her and pressuring her to make changes to her classes, including changing student grades in her classes, and now she was afraid her department would deny her tenure. She had approached her union leadership, but they refused to address any issue between union members. For Sara, the working environment became so bad it began to impact her health and she began to lose sleep and weight and began to feel tired and listless. She decided she would have to get out. For Sara, like so many other targets of bullying, her torment only ended when she left her employment.

Sara is definitely not alone in her story and her story is no longer unique. The reality is that even by conservative estimates, each and every day millions of Americans are bullied in the workplace. The reality in the American workplace is that the vast majority of workers will be exposed to workplace bullying in one way or another – as targets, witnesses or even as bullies. For the targets of workplace bullying and the witnesses to these actions, the results of the bullying can be devastating.

Targets of bullying are held hostage by their bullies. They are controlled, manipulated, exploited and tormented. Targets are marginalized and degraded and targets as well as bystanders are often frozen by fear. Targets are stripped of their esteem and their dignity. Targets often find themselves unable to concentrate, unable to work and unable to relate to others as a result of their bullying. Targets of workplace bullying suffer psychological distress and illnesses, and even physical illnesses, including high blood pressure and heart disease from the bullying at work. For some targets, the bullying has a violent end in death from these diseases, workplace violence, workplace homicide or suicide. Targets often see their relationships with family members and friends break down. Communities lose valuable members and contributors who have fallen victim to workplace bullies. Targets, their friends and families, their organizations and society as a whole all suffer as a result of bullying in the workplace.

For targets of workplace bullying, the bullying leads to loss of esteem, shaken confidence, it impacts their ability to work and their ability to function outside of work. For many targets, the bullying leads to long term psychological damage, and even physical illnesses. Many targets of bullying suffer from PTSD symptoms and even find themselves contemplating suicide or acts of workplace violence. According to Gardner and Johnson, "bullying causes stress-related illnesses that shatter many careers. Anxiety, stress and excessive worry head the list of health consequences for targets, thereby interfering with their ability to be productive at work."[1] Keashley and Neuman found that "exposure to bullying is associated with heightened levels of anxiety, depression, burnout, frustration, helplessness, negative emotions such as anger, resentment and fear, difficulty concentrating, and lowered self-esteem and self-efficacy."[2] Bullying has also has been linked to symptoms consistent with post-traumatic stress syndrome, suicidal thoughts and attempts. There is also clear evidence that some victims of bullying end up committing suicide. According to Davenport and colleagues, "For the victim, death – through illness or suicide – may be the final chapter in the mobbing story."[3] Bullying may be "a more crippling and devastating problem for employees than all other work-related stress put together."[4] Further, many of these symptoms appear before the target even identifies their tormentors' behavior as bullying.

These devastating outcomes are also extremely widespread. A Michigan study by Keashley and Jagatic found 59% of respondents had "experienced at least one type of emotionally abusive behavior at the hands of fellow workers."[5] An Australian study found the over 99.6% of research respondents in K12 had experienced workplace bullying and half of the respondents had experienced **32** or more bullying behaviors in the workplace.[6] Hornstein suggests that 20% of the American workforce faces workplace abuse on a daily basis and 90% will face it at some point in their careers.[7] Studies of workplace harassment indicate that the percentage of targets of the broader phenomenon of bullying (which includes harassment) would be over 70%.[8] When we step back and consider how many current American workers have experienced bullying during their careers the number is shocking – over 50 million by the most conservative of measures.[9] This does not account for the underreporting of workplace bullying due to ineffective and under-inclusive measures and the ineffective self-report method which will be discussed later. Bullying occurs in all different workplaces and targets come from varied backgrounds, demographics, personalities, experiences, expertise, job ability and most every other trait or behavior. The reality is that any workplace and any worker are susceptible to bullying at almost any time. Further, the reality is that if you are in the American workforce and even if you just picked up this book by chance, you will in your career almost definitely be a party to workplace bullying – as a target, witness or even as a bully.

Bullies come in all shapes and sizes. In the United States, bullies are most often in formal positions of power in the U.S., but co-workers and even direct reports can engage in bullying. Bullies come from every demographic background imaginable – male, female, black, white, Asian, Native American,

Hispanic, any age, color, religion and national origin. Bullies also engage in bullying in many different ways – from schoolyard type of threats, to ostracizing, teasing, withholding of information, or using company policies to torment their targets. While most bullies intentionally engage in bullying, for some they may not even realize their behaviors are bullying.

Bullies are not the only perpetrators in these behaviors. In order for bullying to occur, organizations must at a minimum fail to take steps to prevent these actions, but more often than not they create environments that allow, support or even promote workplace bullying. Many organizations protect the bully and even utilize the bullies' abilities to control their targets. Bullies who are otherwise "top performers" are often praised and protected while their targets are blamed and marginalized. Other organizations provide tacit approval of these behaviors through inaction or a misunderstanding of bullying. Far too many organizations provide support and allow for bullying by standing in the way of laws that could help to prevent, detect, remedy and eliminate these behaviors in the workplace.

Society as a whole, while a victim of bullying, is also not without blame. We often times glorify bullies (just consider *Hell's Kitchen* and *The Apprentice* and the behaviors of the main characters on each show and the marketing of these bullying behaviors). We also glorify or at least accept the behaviors that are so often bullying – extreme level of control over employees' lives by employers, the exploitation of the workers, even the degrading of workers in the pursuit of profit. Too often we blame targets for their own torment (excusing bullying because the worker was lazy or unproductive or annoying or different) or we tell the target to toughen up – it is work after all and people who are working in today's economy should just be "happy they have a job" (and rarely does it matter when today is or what the economy looks like to hear that phrase thrown around). Finally, it is the current social system that allows bullying to occur, targets to feel ashamed and prevents targets from having reasonable escape paths from their tormentors. We support systems that reward the opportunistic bullies and turn a blind eye towards the tormenting bully.

Despite the severity and the pervasiveness of workplace bullying, most targets have little or no recourse. Too often in today's system of commerce targets are trapped in the bullying environment. They are unable to simply pick up and find another job. Further, if the bullying has crushed their esteem, they are less likely to be able to find other employment or even feel confident enough to search for other employment. Resiliency training is also not a viable solution. For targets of bullying, it is not an issue of toughening up. In fact, most of them are already tough and have endured a lot in their careers to become successful, success that is often stripped from them by the workplace bully. Organizations are more likely to exacerbate the problem than they are to lend any meaningful assistance to employees. There also is no right to legal recourse for targets of workplace bullying in the United States. The law provides protection against only the harshest forms of bullying where intent and psychological damages are both clear and severe, or where the target can prove that the bullying was based on a protected status under federal or state equal employment opportunity laws.

In my career as an academic, attorney, union leader and researcher over the past 20 years, I have seen workplace bullying destroy the careers and more importantly the lives of targets. I myself have also experienced workplace bullying as a target and experienced damage to my career and my life as a result of such bullying. I have also unfortunately seen workplace bullying become more and more prevalent in American workplaces. Perhaps because of this pervasiveness, bullying behaviors seem to be gaining acceptance. I hear workers and future workers accepting behaviors that would have been considered bullying less than a decade ago as just a "normal" part of work. I even hear career advisors tell these individuals that they should consider themselves "lucky just to have a job," and in essence not to worry about these behaviors as they are "just a part of work." Both of these outcomes are the result of workplace bullying being ignored for far too long. No human being should have to endure workplace bullying in order to earn a living. While there are clearly more books and articles addressing workplace bullying today than nearly two decades ago when I started my career in this area, there is still little that has been done to effectively address the problem of bullying in the American workplace. Rather than addressing the problems of workplace bullying, we hold onto mistaken beliefs that get in the way of addressing the problem.

We often mistakenly minimize the problem. We ignore how bullying in the workplace violates human rights and destroys the lives of targets and witnesses. We therefore fail to see the importance of addressing workplace bullying. This mistaken belief leaves targets on their own and casts doubts (unfounded doubts) on the need for meaningful legislation.

We mistake the causes of workplace bullying and rather than seeing bullying for what it is – a phenomena that is supported, promoted or at the very least allowed by employers. We continue to hang onto the mistaken belief that employers and employees alike are equally opposed to bullying in the workplace, and therefore solving the problem rests with enlightening employers – both in regards to the presence and the solutions for workplace bullying. This outlook on workplace bullying is damaging – it has allowed bullying to spread and in many of its forms to become an accepted part of the workplace. Rather than addressing workplace bullying, the vast majority of employers ignore the problem and legislators do likewise either via a desire to "support" these employers or due to the unfounded belief that the employers will address the issue.

We mistakenly see bullying as a merely a micro level or individual level problem. We fail to recognize how workplace bullying is a systemic, macro level problem that requires a macro level solution. Because we tend to focus on the target, the bully or the organization, we tend to focus on micro level solutions – self-help, employer programs or even counseling for specific bullies – that leave the majority of targets of bullying unprotected, or organizational level solutions that have simply not come to fruition. We oftentimes assume we have adequate employment laws and fail to recognize how these laws leave the vast majority of targets of harassment and bullying with no meaningful recourse. As a result, we fail to push for the types of legislative reform needed to protect the human rights of American workers.

The realities are that workplace bullying is not a minor problem. It is pervasive. We could really at this point consider it to be an epidemic in the American workplace. Workplace bullying is severe – the effects on targets, workplaces, communities and society are devastating. The employer community knows (or should know at this point in time) about workplace bullying and they have known about this phenomenon for long enough that at this point if they were truly going to address the issue voluntarily, it would not be as rampant as it is today. The fact that bullying continues to be more and more common in national surveys and that these same surveys show that employers are ineffective at addressing workplace bullying shows that employers are complicit either through malfeasance or misfeasance. Bullying is a systemic problem. We have created a destructive system of highly competitive, frantically paced, individualized capitalism that supports bullying behaviors and bullies at the expense of targets. There are no current adequate legal remedies to workplace bullying. Workplace bullying has failed to be addressed in the courts, in the legislatures, by employers and too often even in unionized workplaces. The legal system, judges, legislators and even union leaders are just as complicit both through failure to act as well as through bad actions. In fact, when we look at the role of judges, we see them extending the opening for opportunities for bullies to engage in bullying rather than addressing the types of status-based bullying they could clearly eliminate through legal interpretations of the EEO laws.

While, the U.S. legal system ignores or even exacerbates the problem of workplace bullying, HR departments and even union leaders often do the same. HR Departments, save a select few, either completely ignore the problem, or make the problem worse for targets of bullying.[10] Union leaders who do not take this problem seriously, or worse yet who might place part of the blame on targets, create even worse problems by sending the message that their members are fair game to be bullied by management.[11] The reality is workplace bullying is a severe, devastating and pervasive problem that causes incredible amounts of lost productivity, absences, illnesses, psychological damage and trauma, loss of esteem and even death through illnesses, suicides and workplace homicide. Workplace bullying is an affront to human decency and a clear violation of human rights. The target of workplace bullying is stripped of their human right to dignity, a basic foundation of all human rights. They are stripped of various human rights recognized in international documents including the Universal Declaration of Human Rights (UDHR) such as the right to just and favorable working conditions and the right to physically and psychologically safe working environments. Yet, for the vast majority of targets of workplace bullying, there are no real viable options for recourse.

For the past 18 years, I have focused my work on addressing workplace bullying in one way or another. I first began to explore workplace bullying as a law student when I read the terrible district court decision in *Burns v. McGregor*.[12]

The judge in this case decided that the plaintiff could not have been offended by rather severe sexual harassment because she had, prior to the harassing behavior, posed nude in an adult magazine and had "pierced and bejeweled nipples." The judge's unjust treatment of this target of workplace harassment (which was later overturned) led me to explore whether this type of treatment was common. When I shared this concern with many of my male colleagues in law school, they seemed to think the issue was unimportant and often agreed with the district court, "blaming" the target for having posed in nude and "bringing on the workplace harassment." Perhaps it is not coincidental that, around this same time, one of the largest U.S. law firms – Baker and McKenzie – was hit with a sexual harassment lawsuit and paid out over $7 million in damages to a single plaintiff.[13] It became clear that, even in the legal profession, harassing behaviors seemed to be a common if not perhaps an accepted practice.

I continued to explore workplace harassment and after law school, as a master's student I studied the arguments in the Fargher and Ellerth Cases which were in front of the Supreme Court of the United States (SCOTUS) at that time. At both a personal and legal level, I could not understand how the lower courts could have in essence excused these employers from managing the conditions in their work environments. I also began to notice that the media was minimizing workplace harassment, much the same way they had minimized personal injury claims. Perhaps the most shocking instance the media's inaccurate portrayal of a sexual harassment occurred in reporting a case at Miller brewing as simply being a case of a discussion of a sitcom taken out of context.[14] These instances all began to lead me to the conclusion that not only was harassment a problem in workplace, but that societal view was exacerbating the problem.

Shortly after all of these cases, I began my career in human resource management (HR or HRM). Part of this career entailed implementing workplace harassment systems in two Fortune 50 companies. As a member of the HR team in these organizations I trained investigators, trained managers and trained the entire workforce on our policies, their rights and their responsibilities. I also began to investigate numerous claims of workplace harassment and, over the next several years, saw the impact of harassment from the perspective of management. I also saw a marked difference between how harassment was handled in the union setting versus a non-union setting. In the union setting, harassment was always an important issue, there was no determining if the harassment was based on a protected status before anything would be done. The union stewards and leaders protected their members against all forms of harassment. However, in the non-union setting it became clear that management took a legal minimalist stance, and they were only willing to deal with unlawful harassment, despite my best efforts to convince them otherwise. Even the so-called business case against workplace harassment or bullying was not enough to fully convince the employer to address all forms of harassment. This was perhaps the first time I really began to think about the difference between unlawful harassment and generalized harassment or bullying.

In my time in HR, I also saw first-hand how "top performers" were protected by employers against allegations of workplace harassment. At one workplace, a female marketing professional was nearly driven out of the workplace when she reported the sexually harassing behavior of the sales director. Despite the clear evidence that the sales director had continuously approached the female marketing professional, had used sexually explicit terms in reference to her and had bragged about this to other workers, the GM refused to even allow a full investigation, constantly putting up barriers as I attempted to investigate the incident. After initiating an investigation, I received direct threats; I attempted to pursue retaliation measures and then ended up having the very individual I had been investigating assigned to conduct my performance review (part of 360-degree review) by one of the managers who had threatened me during the course of the investigation. Yet this same employer had no problem engaging in a detailed investigation that led to the termination of employment of a mid-level employee who looked up porn on his company computer while in the office on an early Saturday morning before any other employees were even in the building (while inappropriate, this behavior did not impact any other worker in the office, unlike the actions of the Sales Director). Of course, even in this investigation, when computer records were reviewed and it was found that several male employees had been spending time on porn sites, only a few were selected for discipline, while excuses were made for those who were perceived as being more valuable to the company.

When I moved into my own private practice of law and into academia, the divide between harassment claims that were actionable and those that were not became clearer and clearer. I began to see that not just many, but perhaps most instances of workplace harassment fell outside of the legal parameters/definitions of harassment. Most people who came to my office for representation over issues of harassment did not complain of harassment based on any of the protected statuses under the federal laws or the state laws in West Virginia. Their claims tended to be of a general form of bullying and harassment falling outside of the status-based protections and simply not severe enough to rise to the level of intentional infliction of emotional distress. The divide had nothing to do with the harm to the targets, but most often existed due to the U.S. legal focus on discrimination rather than the right to dignity in the workplace.

Through these experiences, I came to four clear revelations. First, workplace bullying clearly violates targets' human rights. Second, I have a deep desire to address and eliminate workplace bullying in any way that I am able. This includes all forms of workplace bullying and comes from my deep desire to protect workers' human rights in the workplace. Third, the gaps in coverage for targets of workplace bullying are simply unacceptable and in order to really meet my goal, I would have to push for meaningful improvement in the legal system. Employers are not doing enough, I cannot do enough as an attorney because the legal system is not doing enough, and while several unions I worked with took the issue seriously, too many other unions and union leaders fail to do so. Fourth and perhaps most critically, the problem of workplace bullying can be solved.

We can take steps to prevent, remedy, detect and eliminate workplace bullying. Steps have been taken in other countries to begin to root out this problem. We can learn from these models in other countries and build on them to do even better. We also have models here in the United States from which to learn and expand. We have models of addressing workplace harassment, a sub-category of bullying. We also have models of how advocates and unions have taken steps to address workplace bullying. We even have models of organizations who have voluntarily taken steps to address bullying in their workplaces.

With these four revelations, and the experiences I had in workplace harassment I was honored to be appointed to the EEOC Select Task Force on the Study of Workplace Harassment. In the meetings of this group and through the additional testimony provided to this task force, my concerns about workplace harassment and bullying were confirmed and expanded. It was clear that, in the 30 years since the Meritor Savings Bank case, employers had not taken nearly enough steps to eliminate workplace harassment. It was also clear that targets of workplace harassment were targeted for so many different reasons – including all of the protected class statuses.

It is these four revelations and my work on this task force that have led me to write this book. What I hope to bring to the reader are my experiences as an attorney, advocate, researcher and manager. I hope to help the readers of this book to understand workplace bullying, understand why it is such an important issue and most importantly to understand the steps each and every one of us can take to help to eliminate this problem from the American workplace. This is not a research book for academic press, but neither is it simply a self-help or trade book.

Notes

1 (Johnson & Johnson, 2001, p. 28).
2 (Keashly & Neuman, 2004, p. 346).
3 (Davenport et al., 2002, p. 33).
4 (Einarsen, 1999, p. 16).
5 (Keashley & Jagatic, 2003, 35).
6 (Dan Riley, 2011).
7 (Hornstein, 1996).
8 (Feldblum & Lipnic, 2016); (Hornstein, 1996).
9 (Namie & Lutgen-Sandvik, 2010).
10 (Namie & Namie, 2009).
11 (Carbo, 2015).
12 (Burns v. McGregor, 1993).
13 (Gross, 1994).
14 (Pellegrino, et al., 1999).

2 What does workplace bullying look like?

As Elizabeth returned to her office, she could not even express her frustration. No matter how well she prepared for her meetings with the President of the university, he threw something different at her, took different steps to make her feel small and stupid, and left her deflated and defeated. In terms of performance measures, he would always have a new and different target, and then act as if she should have known about the new expectation even at times claiming to have spoken with her about the new demands. He continued to find excuses to keep her department a program rather than a school, assuring that she would be viewed as lower than the other program leaders – "deans" – as she remained merely a director. On some days, he would make her wait for an hour outside of his office while he took care of important business during their scheduled meeting times, on others he would call emergency meetings half an hour early knowing she would not be able to get to campus in time to attend. If he could not find a policy to thwart her efforts, he would convince the board to develop a new one. The tactics were constantly changing, but the results were always the same.

The tactics, tools and behaviors of workplace bullies are many and varied. In fact, bullies will often use many different tactics against the same target as we see in the case of the university President tormenting Elizabeth. The bullies' tactics are so varied that we may never have a definitive list of bullying behaviors. Fahie and Devine (2014) divide the types of bullying into two categories – derogation and exclusion and pressurized and oppressive management regime – with numerous sub-categories under both for a total of 14 categories of bullying.[1] Within each of the various tactics, bullies also rely on various sources of power to bully – from information, to referent, to formal, to relationship power, bullies exploit any type of power they can find. The bullies themselves also come from all walks of life. While most bullies in the United States hold formal positions of power over their targets, I have also seen peer bullying and even bullying from direct reports. While a bully must have some source of power to be able to bully, it does not have to be a formal source of power. Bullies are male and female, black, white, Asian, Hispanic, gay or straight. The reality is that bullying comes from a multitude of sources and takes a multitude of forms.

Much of my research has focused on understanding and defining workplace bullying. I have conducted numerous qualitative interviews of targets of workplace bullying, have asked respondents to complete surveys describing the bullying they have experienced and asked respondents to complete written narratives defining workplace bullying, and engaged in participant observation at a number of work settings. My initial research into this area was conducted while completing my dissertation at Cornell University's School of Industrial and Labor Relations. In that research, I conducted dozens of written narratives and surveys, 16 in-depth interviews and three focus groups. I also have conducted numerous interviews of targets since that time both as a researcher and an advocate. From these research and practice experiences, I have hoped to gain a deeper understanding of workplace bullying in order to be able to define and then eliminate this problem.

Based on my research and experiences, I divide workplace bullying into three categories of behaviors. These categories are based on the tool or weapon of choice of the bully. The first type of bullying, personal level bullying, is engaged in at a micro or personal level. There is no reliance on organizational policies, but that does not necessarily mean the bullying is not linked to policies in that policies allow it to occur or even support the bullying. The tactics are engaged in through direct interaction between the person that is the bully and the person that is the target. This form of bullying includes the use of any form of communication or lack thereof, yelling, berating, talking down to, threatening or ostracizing and ignoring (as well as many other tactics the creative bully might come up with). This form of bullying often includes unlawful forms of harassment such as sexual or race-based harassment.

I label the second form of bullying organizational policy bullying. In this form of bullying, the bully directly uses an organizational policy to torment their targets. This bullying does not include the reasonable application of reasonable organizational policy. Instead, this form of bullying entails the use of organizational policy as a tool of torment. Often times the bully engaged in organizational policy bullying uses ambiguous or subjective policies in a manner to demean or degrade the target. This form of bullying often includes unfair evaluations, overloading with work tasks, assignment of menial tasks, or taking away the voice of the target by stripping them of autonomy. Bullies who have the power to implement organizational policies often use this form of bullying.

The third type of bullying is bully by proxy. In this type of bullying, the bully uses others to engage in the torment of their targets. This might be by forcing the proxy to use a policy against the target, it might be through creating a mobbing environment where others join the bully, or it might be by allowing and promoting the proxy to engage in bullying behaviors that are personal or organizational policy behaviors. Many bullies engage in all of these forms of bullying and many targets experience all forms. There is also a thin and blurred line between these forms of bullying. The idea behind these categories is not to require that any form of bullying fit into a box, it is meant to show the vast array of tactics and behaviors that bullies will turn to in order to torment their targets.

Personal level bullying – Interpersonal communications and behaviors

My research into workplace bullying made it clear very early on that bullying takes many forms. There are some forms of bullying that appear to be much more common than others. When I have conducted surveys (often as a first step to identifying potential qualitative research participants) I have consistently found that around 50% of the survey respondents report that they had information withheld from them at work. Likewise, 50% of respondents have indicated they have had gossip spread about them at work, have been ignored at work, or even have been shouted at now and then. Sexual harassment and racial-based harassment and bullying are also extremely common with just under half of the female respondents indicating they have been the targets of unwanted sexual attention and more than 50% of minorities reporting mistreatment due to their race.

Personal level bullying often takes one of two extreme forms – either ostracizing the target or berating, yelling or screaming at the target. Vanessa and Julie, two targets of bullying experienced both extremes. Both Vanessa and Julie were university administrators when I interviewed them. Vanessa was ostracized by all of her co-workers in her department. Her co-workers and even direct reports in her department would intentionally talk about going to lunch without inviting Vanessa. They would only speak to her when absolutely required and refused to acknowledge her presence at any other time. They even held department meetings without informing her of the time or location of the meetings. The disrespect she received from her department also seemed to spill over to peers in other departments. In one instance, she was publicly yelled at and berated by a peer level administrator when she asked for a file from the co-worker. This bully not only yelled at Vanessa, but also continued to follow her down the hall in front of students, faculty and administrators as Vanessa left the office. This was not an atypical behavior from this bully and not once did the university address this behavior other than to promote the bully into higher positions of authority. Vanessa seemed to experience bullying from all levels as she also had information withheld by a direct report that negatively affected her work performance. For Vanessa, she was never sure what tactics her bullies would utilize. On one day, they even resorted to taking a bite out of an apple Vanessa had on her desk and then leaving it on the desk for her to see.

Julie experienced some of the same bullying tactics. Julie was also ignored by her co-workers, who refused to acknowledge her when she came into work each day (even after she would greet each co-worker). She explained she would make a point to always say "Hello" or "Good Morning" to each of her co-workers, but each and every time she was greeted with silence. At first, Julie thought that perhaps her co-workers were just busy or did not notice she had greeted them, but over time she noticed she was the only one who was ignored and no matter how clear she made her greeting it was always ignored.

Julie also said that she felt physically intimidated during staff meetings as her supervisor and one co-worker in particular would lean in or even lean over her when she had raised concerns about plans or policies. She also had been ignored on many occasions by her supervisor during these meetings. She shared examples of bringing up ideas during these department meetings with no response and then her supervisor would later bring up the same idea and take credit for the idea.

Kelly, another research participant, managed an office for an optometrist. Kelly explained that it was common for her supervisor to yell at her and her co-workers. Often times this bully would engage in personal attacks and berating of employees for issues completely unrelated to work. The bully would call workers names and use inappropriate language to describe them. The bully would also often "snap" at workers if they asked a question about work or the office. Jennifer, a full-time student and part-time food service worker in a nursing home experienced bullying of a different form early on in her career. Jennifer described a co-worker in a food services company physically threatening her by flexing her bicep and shaking her fist at her. Jennifer's bully began targeting Jennifer because she felt Jennifer worked too fast. Jennifer's bully seemed to seek her out in the workplace to glare at Jennifer.

Personal level bullying behaviors of a sexual nature also are common personal forms of bullying. Of the interview participants, Mary, Maria, Katherine, Jennifer and Julie all reported harassment of a sexual nature. Julie was exposed to sexual innuendos and undertones and even inappropriate touching in a university setting. Katherine and Jennifer both described these types of experiences as wait staff at the same local restaurant with a working environment wrought with sexual harassment, where female workers were regularly objectified and groped. Mary and Adrienne, worked in the office of small employers, both described repeated advances by the male owners of the small businesses in land use and manufacturing where they worked.

Personal bullying also includes the spreading of rumors. Sara had rumors spread about her by colleagues and supervisors. Mary shared that her supervisor had spread rumors to her male co-workers that she was promiscuous and cheated on her husband. Patrick, a faculty member, had rumors spread about him that he was tough to work with and was sexist.

Workplace bullying often takes the form of interpersonal communications. Bullies often engage directly with their targets through intimidation, shaming, ostracizing, spreading of rumors and other forms of interpersonal torment. It does not take long for one who studies workplace bullying to see these types of interactions. Most working people in the United States will see or experience these forms of bullying. We can equate these types of bullying behaviors to traditional definitions of bullying that might be most familiar to us. The personal bully in the workplace often looks like the stereotypical schoolyard bully in the types of tactics they employ (although at times they may be a bit more sophisticated than the schoolyard bully and other times not). However, personal bullying is just one of the common forms of bullying we see.

Organizational bullying – Use of policies/practice to bully

Organizational bullying was very common for research participants in all forms of my research – including the qualitative interviews, the narrative definitions, and my own participant observation of workplace bullying. Research respondents including targets described the use of scheduling, task assignment, shift assignment, performance evaluations and investigation policies as tools of workplace bullying. Targets reported that bullies would often implement specific policies that they would use to bully their targets (sometimes all of their direct reports). In one case, a restaurant owner instituted a "dress code" for all servers to be "Poky-Perfect" in their attire and their hygiene. Those who were not would be singled out or left out and their co-workers would be encouraged to point out any flaws in their attire, jewelry, make-up, hair style and even physique. For another bully, a morning seat check was used to "keep his employees in line" as he would circle the room each day right at 7:30 assuring everyone was in their seat, even if they had to leave other work to get back to their desks and even if they had come into work much earlier than the required seat check moment.

Organizational bullying also occurs in the way established policies and procedures are implemented. In one organization, leaving "troublemakers" off of committees or removing these "troublemakers" from committees was a bullying method of choice for a university President. The official university policy gave the President the final say over the composition of the committees. However, until this bullying president joined the organization, the policy had never been used to punish employees by committee assignment or lack thereof, and in fact committee composition had been left to the discretion of the faculty. Several research participants had been removed from committees by this university President when they brought up concerns around policies implemented or suggested by the President, or when they questioned decisions made by the President. Greg, an associate dean with an accounting background and expert in public budgeting, was removed from the budgeting committee when he brought up concerns about a budget proposal from the President's office. A business faculty member was removed from a faculty evaluation committee when she suggested a minor change to the President's proposed system. According to one participant, members of every committee on campus were eventually left with the choice of rubber stamping and confirming the President's decisions, or seeing their committee disbanded or themselves removed. The faculty members in particular were dependent on these committees for their career advancement. Service on these committees was part of the evaluation as well as the promotion and tenure process. The President of course was well aware of this and had selected an extremely effective tool to bully the faculty into submission. This bully President assured that faculty and staff had no true voice in their university.

Denial of leave was another example of "bullying" through policies. Maria, a research participant and hotel employee, was denied leave the one time she asked for a day off in her two years of employment with the hotel. Maria explained that she felt like her new supervisor did not like her and she was never sure why. Maria felt it might be because of her national origin (being an immigrant from South America) or due to her religious beliefs, but she always felt like he gave her a hard time about everything she did. She never thought that the first time she requested to take a personal day to attend a wedding he would also use his ability to deny her leave. Not only did Maria's employer deny her leave, but he then embarrassed her when she returned from taking unapproved, unpaid leave as a result of the denial of the leave by posting in large letters on the scheduling board that she had been suspended. Even in the Army it seems that policies can be used to bully. Jim, a former soldier and another research participant, identified the unfair application of organizational policies in the military as more abusive than the ranting and insults during boot camp. Jim's CO denied Jim leave even when everyone in his squad was granted leave. Bryan, a big box retail worker, worked with a bullying supervisor who would change his schedule to include times Bryan had indicated he was unable to work due to classes or commitments at home.

Work assignments and overload are also common forms of bullying. Often times this will include taking away meaningful work, like the committees mentioned earlier. In addition to seeing this with the university committees, I have also seen bullies target other workers by taking away meaningful work and assigning menial tasks. This occurred with Lea, an HR assistant. When Lea's first supervisor left for a better position, the supervisor who took her place decided to bully Lea. One step she took was to take away Lea's favorite work and to instead assign filing from a different department as part of Lea's job tasks. At another employer, Katy had been a successful manager of an internal program until her bully was hired to run her school. After he was hired, he began harassing her and when she complained her job description was completely modified to take away any type of authority and to replace all of her meaningful work with purely administrative tasks.

Other bullies move their targets into dangerous or uncomfortable work. In one facility, a supervisor, Jim, would place his targets down in what was referred to as the hole. The jobs down in the hole entailed working with an odorous glue and insulation. Workers in the hole would often leave for the day with rashes, hives and severe headaches. Jim most often targeted two specific workers for this assignment to the hole. The first was a direct report who had refused his sexual advances and the other was her best friend who had helped her to file a complaint against Jim. Bryan's bullying supervisor would always pull Bryan off of his cashier station and assign him to retrieving carts and sweeping and cleaning the outside of the store. The supervisor always targeted Bryan for these unwanted assignments, only changed Bryan's schedule and never allowed Bryan to work the cashier job he preferred and worked when other supervisors were on his shift.

In addition to bad work, extra work is also often times used as a form of bullying. Greg, the assistant dean removed from the committee was also bullied by his dean. The dean tended to rely on overloading Greg with assignment after assignment, assuring he could never accomplish any of the assignments completely and that he felt a constant pressure to get things done. The work needed to be completed and needed to be assigned, but it was clear to the target, his co-workers and even the bully that the amount assigned to him was unfair and completely overloaded him. In many cases, this overloading of work assignments by the dean was due to the fact that she had been overloaded with assignments from the provost or president of the university. Specifically, this faculty member mentioned that the new president expected so much more out of the dean that her response was to put so much more on him. It became a case of a trickling down of bullying through workload.

Julie's supervisor decided to limit all non-work discussions during working hours. This policy was enforced even when there were no students around. Again, this could be interpreted as simply a workplace policy, but in this case, it appeared at least to the target to be bullying via workplace policies. Suzanne was consistently given the worst assignments by her supervisor in a K12 setting. She conducted home visits and was given the toughest cases, with the toughest travel schedule. Her bully also was constantly micromanaging her work and looking over her shoulder, even showing up at clients' homes unannounced – a practice that was at least informally avoided to assure that the clients would not feel uncomfortable. Robert explained how a new performance management system was put into place to in essence drive out those who disagreed with the President at his university. The performance management system was developed by a committee after the President had disbanded two prior committees who developed systems that did not fit his goals. Patrick and Sara also expressed concerns that a faculty evaluation, promotion and tenure system were all used as tools to bully faculty members who were not liked by their deans, peers or other faculty around campus.

The withholding of information is yet another common bullying tactic. Kevin, a research participant and intern (at the time) in the financial services industry, explained how an office assistant would withhold information from all of the junior financial advisors to assure they would listen to her and allow her to run the office as she saw fit. Even though Kevin's bully was technically lower on the organizational chart than her targets, they relied on her to provide information they needed, including sales leads and compliance documents. She used her access to information as well as her relationship with the manager at this office to bully the junior employees. She would constantly check material on the desks of the junior advisors (and the intern) to see if they had left any confidential material anywhere on their desks when they took any break (bathroom, lunch, coffee). If they did, she would use this information to threaten them and suggest that she could always report them to the manager if she chose. For Sara, Sally and Patrick, their boss would withhold information about the purpose of meetings – calling them to his office a day or so in advance and refusing to tell them the purpose of the meeting. He would then spring the topic on these individuals when they would show up for a meeting. Sometimes the meeting would be about a simple question that could have been answered in email, sometimes the meetings were to make accusations against them.

Stereotypes of bullying often focus on the interpersonal type of bullying. The bully makes threats or degrading statements about the target. While interpersonal bullying clearly occurs, we cannot ignore bullying that relies on and utilizes organization policies. We cannot accept that bullying through policy is simply practicing sound management or supervision. These are excuses that bullies attempt to hide behind. Organizational forms of bullying do exist and can be damaging to the targets and the organizations. Therefore, any definition of bullying must include these types of practices.

Bully by proxy

Bullies also often turn to others to do their dirty work. Sometimes they will include others in their bullying to create a mobbing environment. For instance, for Julie, her bullying seemed to start with her supervisor. He ignored her during meetings, leaned in towards her to refute any comments she made that he might disagree with and often looked over her shoulder as she worked. However, this bullying spread to her entire department. A male colleague began to engage with her during department meetings in the same manner as her supervisor. He would lean towards her in an intimidating fashion to disagree with her. The entire department began to join in by ignoring her during these meetings and then throughout the day. In this case, the supervisor did not relent on his own bullying behavior, but instead he allowed the rest of his department to join in, to create a mobbing atmosphere.

Other bullies engage proxies to further detach themselves from the actual bullying behavior. Robert suggested that the President at one university had decided to use junior faculty to bully the more senior faculty. The junior faculty were given power to tell the senior faculty what they should be doing in their jobs and the power to roll out the President's performance management system. This sentiment was shared by others in the focus group setting from this same university. In my own experience, a university President used the head of several departments as his henchmen. They would often target individuals who had questioned the President or his decisions. In one case, a director of a successful program was removed from his position by one of these henchmen after questioning the President's commitment to the program. In another case, courses were taken away from faculty who had been involved in a negative performance review of the President. Katherine's bullying boss required all of her employees to engage in judging how "Poky-Perfect" their co-workers were each day. They would be rewarded for pointing out flaws in their co-workers' attire, make-up, hair or demeanor. In my own experience, a university President decided to bully me by engaging a colleague in my department. The President offered my colleague the position of dean as long as he would remove me from the director position of a program. A program that I had developed into the second largest graduate program of its sort in my state, despite repeated refusals from the President to fund the program or to even allow the program to retain some of the funding it was bringing into the university.

Trickle down bullying is another form of bully by proxy. As mentioned earlier, Elizabeth was bullied so often by the university President that she began to bully her direct reports. This trickle down effect also often spills over to outside of the workplace as the target in the workplace takes out their frustrations at home. Julie, as well as other targets of workplace bullying, shared that they would often times become mean at home and a bully at home due to their bully's behavior in the workplace.

Types of bullies

Based on my research and experiences in workplace bullying, not only it is clear that bullying takes many different forms but also that bullies come in all shapes, sizes, colors and positions and use any source of power available to bully their targets. Many targets of workplace bullying who shared their stories with me were targeted by their supervisors. Kelly was bullied by the boss and owner of the office she managed. Greg was bullied by his dean. Other university faculty and staff were likewise bullied by their dean or even the university President. Supervisory bullies can and do use their formal power to engage in bullying. They can implement policies, administer policies, set terms and conditions of work and even use their formal authority to hide or excuse their behavior.

However, bullies are not always supervisors. In my research, there were many examples of bullying co-workers and even direct reports. Both Vanessa and Julie were bullied by their co-workers (as well as their supervisor). Sara, Sally and Craig, all senior faculty members, were bullied by junior faculty members

Table 2.1 Types of workplace bullying

Personal Level Bullying	Organizational Bullying	Bully by Proxy
Yelling	Work overload	Specific policies that require
Physical threats	Impossible tasks	others to engage in bullying
Racial/National origin	Taking away meaningful	type of behavior
epithets	work	Creating an atmosphere of
Teasing	Withholding needed	mobbing
Personal attacks	information	Trickle down bullying
Inappropriate advances,	Assigning menial tasks	
touching and other forms	below one's level of	
of sex-based harassment	responsibility	
Ostracizing/Ignoring	Taking credit for work done	
Rumors/Gossip	by target	
	Refusing to recognize work	
	done by target	

in their Universities. These bullies relied on their relationship power from those in authority to engage in bullying their targets. Jennifer was bullied by her co-worker at the rest home. In this case, Jennifer's bully relied on physical power, physically threatening Jennifer. Even direct reports could engage in bullying. Kevin experienced bullying from a support staff member and he reported that this support staff bullied all of the financial advisors in the office. Vanessa was also bullied by a direct report who withheld information and engaged with the rest of the department in ostracizing Vanessa. For both Kevin and Vanessa, their bullies relied on informational power and perhaps relationship power as well.

Bullies come from all walks of life within organizations. While the supervisory bully is the most common, bullies can also be co-workers and even direct reports. The key for any bully is that they must have some source of power to use against their target. This power does not have to be formal power – it can be information power, relationship power, or even referent power. Bullies don't only rely on various sources of power. Jim's CO, the university deans, the university President and the office managers and owners all relied on formal positions of power. Kevin's bully relied on expert power and informational power. Vanessa was bullied by a direct report who relied on her informational power and withheld such information from Vanessa. The bullies who ostracized Julie and Vanessa also used their referent power to convince others to engage in the bullying. The source of the bully's power is not always obvious. Much like the creativity in selecting tactics, bullies will also be creative in identifying and using various sources of power.

Workplace bullying comes in many different forms. From the prototypical personal type of bullying many of us might think of when we hear the term, to the use and even development of policies as tools to bully, it is impossible to ever list all of the types of bullying that can and may occur in organizations. It is important to list the forms and types of bullying to have a better understanding of the phenomenon, but we must be careful to understand that no list of bullying behavior is complete. Just as we must understand that we can never understand every form of bullying, we also need to be careful to understand that we cannot predict the source of bullying. Bullying can come from any source within an organization. While supervisory bullying may be the most common form and can often be the most damaging for targets, co-workers and direct reports also engage in bullying – sometimes in conjunction with supervisors and other times on their own accord.

Workplace bullying takes many different forms. Bullies often torment their targets through personal level bullying by yelling at them, ostracizing them, ignoring them, shaming them or humiliating them. However, bullies also are likely to turn to organizational policies to torment their targets. Bullies assign targets unwanted work, overload them with extra work tasks, mess with their work schedules, bully them through the use of unfair performance appraisal processes, or take away the targets' voice and autonomy in the workplace. Bullies also engage others to torment their targets. They may do so while standing on the sideline watching the bullying from a distance or by engaging with their accomplice through a form of mobbing of the target. Bullies will rely on any source of power they can find, from formal position power, to informational power, to referent power. Finally, bullies come from all levels of the organization and from every demographic background imaginable. Because bullies come from so many different sources and use so many different tactics, we can never completely list all of the types of workplace bullying. However, this chapter hopefully provides you with an idea of the types of bullying that do occur in the workplace. It is likely that many of you have seen or experienced other bullying tactics and other forms of workplace bullying. As will be discussed in the solutions chapters (Chapters 8–11), the path to addressing bullying is not to identify each and every behavior that should be prohibited, because we can never have a complete list of bullying tactics or behaviors. Instead, the path to addressing and ending workplace bullying is to focus on the rights of every person in the workplace: The rights of targets of bullying to be free from such bullying and the right of every worker to dignity in the workplace.

Note

1 (Fahie & Devine, 2014).

3 Workplace bullying is a terrible problem

Why is it so important to address workplace bullying?

Lindsey could not believe how she was feeling and further could not believe she was about to quit her job. She had always believed herself to be so tough. She was always a tomboy growing up, and had not changed much as an adult. She could not believe how the bullies in her workplace had completely wrecked her. She could not stop the nervous ticks and even the prescription from her doctor did little to calm her nerves. She could no longer stand the stomach pains that came with going into work. She knew if she went into work one more day, she might not make it out. Even though she had no idea how she would pay her bills next month or even next week, she could not make herself get out of bed and head to work.

Workplace bullying is a severe and pervasive problem in the American workplace and really the global workplace. Millions of workers, like Lindsey, suffer every day as the targets of workplace bullying. The outcomes for these targets are extremely severe and for many the outcomes can be even worse than what Lindsey experienced. Workplace bullying is a violent, destructive epidemic that must be addressed.

Effects on targets

Workplace bullying can be devastating to targets' careers and lives. Bullying harms targets' emotional, psychological and even physical well-being. Workplace bullying can cause excessive worrying, anxiety, and stress, to such a level that it even ruins the target's career.[1] Bullying leads to lower self-esteem for targets and often leads to fear and resentment. Workplace bullying has even been linked to post-traumatic stress–type symptoms. Targets of bullying are often pushed to suicidal thoughts or even attempts.[2,3] In addition to suicidal thoughts and attempts, workplace bullying has also been linked to deadly illnesses for the targets.[4] The reality is that bullying may be "a more crippling and devastating problem for employees than all other work-related stress put together."[5] Bullying is an incredible harm that tears targets apart and destroys the targets' human rights leaving them working and often spending much of their life as less than a human being.

As an attorney, researcher and HR manager, I have seen how devastating workplace bullying can be to the targets. The most common effects I have seen have been emotional, psychological and work related. The vast majority of targets I have interviewed, worked with or advocated for have left the organizations where they suffered bullying. I have seen deans and faculty members retire early in a university setting where bullying became rampant. I have also seen tenured faculty members leave their universities to escape their bully despite having to start their tenure clock and process over at a new university. I have spoken with targets who have changed professions as a result of bullying in hopes that bullies might be less pervasive in a different profession. I have seen clients shake, cry and twitch as they shared their experiences with me. On my worst day as an HR Manager, I was informed that one of our employees had committed suicide. I could not definitively link her death to bullying in our place of work, but I knew she had been bullied by management and co-workers and was on medical leave at least in part due to these experiences. While the organization I worked for did try to help her, we may have just been too late.

Job exit is a very common outcome for targets of bullying. Often times this exit is a "voluntary" exit, in that the target is not fired. However, the reality is that this exit is often seen by the target as their last resort to escape their tormentor. One research participant, Kevin, was bullied by a support staff member during his internship in the financial industry. While he ended up with numerous lucrative job offers in that same field, he decided that he would rather see if there was less bullying in other types of work. Another participant, Julie, left friends, family and most importantly her bullies behind when she decided to take a job on the other side of the country. Sara left a tenured position to escape her tormentors. Over the course of my initial qualitative research project on workplace bullying, every single research participant at least mentioned looking for other work. Several targets suggested they were considering early retirement, others mentioned changing organizations and others left their employment during the course of the research. I have also in the years since that research received messages from several of the participants who remained in their jobs, that they have since that time left their tormenting employment and their bully behind.

Targets of bullying who stay in their environment often struggle with their jobs. Kelly explained how the employees in the office she managed were unable to reach their full potential and instead spent their time trying to figure out how to manage the bullying situation. As an HR Manager, I saw numerous examples of employees expending a great amount of effort to avoid the bully in their workplaces. In one organization, in an environment that was largely open door and collegial, all employees would close their doors and hide in their offices when the bullying general manager from the corporate office was in town. In another facility, assembly workers took turns being the "lookout" for a bullying supervisor. In another manufacturing facility, employees in an area supervised by a bully bid on every job that was posted, including lateral and even downward positions to get away from the bully. In yet another environment, managers literally would tell their direct reports to remain out of sight during visits from a GM who was an extreme bully.

In the years that I have studied workplace bullying and advocated for targets of bullying, it has become clear that the effects of bullying could not always be measured in terms of work-related outcomes. Many targets of bullying continue to work very well, and have a great deal of career success (of course they may have had even more had it not been for the bullying). Sara, while she eventually left her employment, was a prolific publisher and won numerous teaching awards all while being bullied. Greg was a well-respected associate dean, extremely popular professor, had a successful business in addition to his job at the university and was often called as an expert witness by local and regional attorneys. Despite this career success and the absence of evidence of bullying based on their job performance, the bullying led to unacceptable consequences to the rest of their lives. These effects included lower morale and motivation, a loss of dignity and esteem, a level of frustration that spilled into other parts of their lives and, for all of these very successful employees, a desire to leave their employment.

The job and career effects that targets of bullying suffer should not be minimized. However, it is often the psychological and emotional impacts of workplace bullying that lead to the worst outcomes for targets. "Humiliation," "anger," "objectification" and "belittlement" are all common feelings and experiences that targets of bullying have shared with me. Many of my research participants, clients and friends who have been bullied have stated that they felt degraded, or felt that they were inept and not worthwhile. Mary, whose boss harassed her about her divorce and proselytized to her about religion, stated that she felt "belittled." Katherine who was told to be "Poky-Perfect" in her appearance as a waitress, stated that she felt objectified, or less than human. One research participant worried that she herself would become mean if she stayed in the bullying environment. Sara shared with me that she had become physically ill as a result of her bullying and had lost so much weight that her doctor became concerned for her health. Sally, another target of workplace bullying and university professor, became so ill that she was forced to take leave for over two years. Maria, a hotel worker compared the effects of her workplace bullying to childhood experiences she had with bullying. She explained that the bullying made her feel isolated, worthless and like nobody liked her. Her bullies both as a child and at work had stripped her, at least in part, of her right to esteem. Lindsey was forced onto medications to try to control her anxiety and a nervous tick she had developed as a result of her workplace bullies, while other targets informed me that they found themselves self-medicating with alcohol and drugs. In addition to the worker who committed suicide while on leave, I have also heard stories of suicide attempts and thoughts from many of the activists I have worked with in this area of study. It is most likely that other targets of workplace bullying I have worked with have had suicidal ideations.[6] The outcomes for targets of workplace bullying are devastating. Even those that do not take on physical manifestations are devastating and destructive.

Effects on family and friends

Targets of bullying also do not always suffer alone. The bullying often has an impact beyond the target with negative effects on their families and friends. Many of the targets with whom I have spoken told me that the bullying they experienced at work spilled over into other areas of their lives. Julie and Mary both explained how the bullying they suffered led to both of them often being "mean" at home even though they both tried their best to leave their experiences at work. Patrick explained how the bullying left him feeling exhausted and unable to do anything outside of work. Interestingly, Susan, one of the targets I interviewed, was the bully of a different target in my research. She actually recognized her bullying of Greg. She said she felt awful about it and had always viewed Greg as a friend. She tried to stop her bullying behaviors, but the impact from her bully led her to bullying Greg and others, often without her even thinking about her actions or realizing what she was doing. Targets have also shared with me that the bullying has hampered their abilities to function as a spouse, partner and even as parents. Targets have shared with me that they often felt insecure or nervous in their communications, even with those with whom they were close. Targets shared having shorter tempers and more anger outside of work and that this would often be deflected onto family members and friends. Several targets explained that they were depressed and just no longer felt like going out or hanging out with friends and family. When we look at the outcomes for targets of workplace bullying – the increased stress, the health outcomes, the increased irritability and even paranoia, it is hard to imagine that the effects would not carry over to family and friends. Julie, Vanessa and Suzanne all mentioned at one point that they ultimately left their bullying environment because they did not want it to further impact their family and friends.

Effects on organizations

We could hope that understanding the severe impact on targets of bullying would convince employers to address workplace bullying. Truly ethical and socially responsible companies would surely address and look to eliminate workplace bullying based on these effects. However, the reality is that the vast majority of employers do not address workplace bullying. Instead, the focus is solely on profits, and the human right to dignity, esteem and any other human right is often not even a consideration. This should be no surprise given the examples of employers putting profit before the safety and lives of miners, meatpackers, warehouse workers and many other employees in "dangerous" jobs.[7] Employers often put profit before the right to education and a childhood by engaging in the use of child labor directly, through subsidiaries or through suppliers.[8] Profit comes before the right to a decent standard of living to every employer who pays less than a living wage.[9] Therefore, for many employers, it will take more than pointing out the human rights violations that occur when workplace bullying is allowed to exist. For this reason, I also find it important to explore the organizational impact of workplace bullying.

Just as workplace bullying can be devastating to targeted employees, the effects can also be quite severe for organizations. Workplace bullying has been linked to two separate airline accidents that resulted from flight crews being afraid to question pilot decisions, or life-threatening and even life-ending medical mistakes in health care environments where the stress and fear from bullying interferes with the practice of medicine.[10] Even where we do not see catastrophic events, the organizational outcomes can be quite devastating. Bullying in the workplace leads to lost work time, reduced organizational commitment and decreased effort at work.[11] Workplace bullying has also been found to lead to higher turnover rates[12] and potentially to increased lawsuits.[13] Bullying has been shown to destroy learning environments in organizations[14] and to lead to a negative environment for teachers and staff in K12,[15] as the aforementioned bullying of nurses has been shown to lead to burnout in nurses and ultimately impact the patients. Workplace stress and workplace bullying cost employers **billions** of dollars.[16]

As an HR Manager, I have seen how a bullying supervisor led to increased administrative costs, increased grievances and decreased morale. One supervisor, Jim, who was particularly known as a bully, had a constant flow of employees bidding out of his area, was never able to find enough workers to fill his area for voluntary overtime, and spent hours in my office trying to resolve grievances. This supervisor was such a problem that the union listed him as their number one bargaining issue. In another organization, I witnessed workers intentionally slacking on work and making mistakes in attempts to make a supervisor look bad. I saw a bullying GM in this same organization drive away several top engineers in a highly critical function in our organization. In my research on workplace bullying, I have seen valuable employees leave organizations, and have heard about mistakes and errors being made because workers were overly concerned with bullying. I have also seen the reduced commitment to organizations from targets of workplace bullying. Every target I have spoken with who felt enough confidence in themselves to find other work was looking for employment away from their bully. As an HR manager, I have witnessed the high turnover rates and absenteeism in areas managed by bullying supervisors. The cost of a single bully in an organization is estimated to be as high as $2 million per year.[17] From a business standpoint, there really is no reason that employers should not address and look to eliminate workplace bullying.

Effects on communities and society

Workplace bullying also impacts other members of communities and societies. When targets experience economic impacts, these impacts spread beyond just the target. When targets are forced to leave their employment, they clearly suffer economic consequences, but so do the rest of us. If the target is unable to pay their mortgage, how does the resulting foreclosure impact the property values in their neighborhood or the interest rates banks charge to make up for the loss? What happens to the income that they were putting back into society, to the local and national businesses that depend on the demand from these targets as consumers? What about the impact of the workers around the targets? How much work do they have to take on to cover for the lost productivity of the targets?

Bullying has also been found to have a direct negative impact on witnesses of the bullying, including loss of sleep and depression.[18] The impact on targets of workplace bullying has also been found to have an impact on their clients and customers as the targets are unable to perform their work in the manner they would absent such bullying.[19] Consider the impact on the patients of the burned out or depressed nurses, doctors or aides, or the impact on students of teachers who are burned out and depressed from the bullying they have experienced. If targets of workplace bullying are depressed and worn out from the day in the workplace, then they are unlikely to contribute to their communities, to engage with the neighbors or to volunteer in community activities. Consider the potential impact of the lost productivity, the lost innovation that we all suffer because of the bullying of targets. Perhaps the researcher who would have found the cure for AIDS or cancer was bullied out of their profession or simply lost his/her ability or will to innovate.

Workplace bullying has broad and severe impacts. For targets of workplace bullying, the bullying impacts nearly every aspect of their lives. They are impacted financially, psychologically and even physically. Bullying is an affront to the target's human rights to dignity and esteem. Too often, the target is forced to leave his/her employment, forced into counseling, medication or, even worse, taking drastic measures such as suicide attempts or even workplace violence. The effects do not just stay with these isolated targets. Their friends, families, co-workers, clients, patients, students and communities all feel the negative effects of workplace bullying. The effects go even further, harming society as a whole. The reality is that there is no reason for bullying to continue to occur because even organizations are negatively impacted by bullying – the very organizations that are responsible for allowing bullying and could effectively prevent, detect and remedy workplace bullying as will be discussed in Chapter 9 of this volume.

Bullying is an epidemic

Given the severity of workplace bullying and the damage it causes to targets of bullying, organizations and society, any level of bullying is unacceptable. However, the reality is that no matter how we measure bullying, it is pervasive. The majority of research has measured bullying in two different ways – the self-report method or the operational method.

Under the self-report method, research participants are provided a definition of bullying and asked if they have been or are being bullied. A second method, the operational method, entails providing research participants with a list of

Table 3.1 Some examples of the effects of workplace bullying

Personal (Target)	Family/Friends	Organizations	Community & Society
Lower esteem	Broken relationships	Turnover	Lost participation from targets
Fear and resentment	Too exhausted to engage	Absenteeism	Lost economic contribution from targets
Exit – Quit or retirement	Bullying of spouse, partner, child	Lack of discretionary effort	Increased health care costs
Turnover intent	Breakdown in communications	Workplace accidents	Addiction and associated problems
Nervous ticks	Diminished relationships	Increased sick leave, workers comp	Foreclosures and evictions
Crying		Time spent on resolving complaints	Unemployment and the associated costs
Distress		Lawsuits	Poverty rates
Medical leave		Billions of dollars in direct and indirect costs	Dangerous workers
Physical illness			Lost innovation
Suicide ideation and attempts			Impact on witnesses
Lower productivity			
Depression			
Anger			
Anxiety			
Paranoia			
Isolation			
Prescription medicaiton			
Self-medication			
Isolation			
Violence			
Addiction			

behaviors and asking them if they have experienced each of these behaviors, how often, and, in some cases, for how long. Two major operational surveys in use are the Leymann Inventory on Psychological Terror (LIPT) and the Negative Acts Questionnaire. Leymann's definition of workplace bullying under the LIPT requires exposure to 1 of 45 acts on a weekly basis for more than six months, a more stringent standard than the NAQ and thus leads to reports of lower frequencies of workplace bullying. Under the NAQ, a participant is defined as a target of bullying if he/she has experienced one of the listed behaviors over the last six months on a regular basis. The NAQ also includes a self-report question.

There is a wide variance in reporting rates of bullying under these two methods. The self-report method consistently leads to lower rates of bullying being reported. In 2001, Mikkelson and Einarsen found that while 2–4% of employees self-reported bullying, 8–25% were classified as targets under the NAQ instrument.[20] Agervold and Mikkelson found an even larger variance, with only 1.6% self-reporting and 13% defined as targets under the operational method. In a study of Finnish professionals with business degrees, 8.8% self-reported as targets, but a rate of over 24% was found using a modified 32-question NAQ.[21] Even more, in one study using an operational method in Australian schools, 98% plus of teachers surveyed indicated they had been exposed to at least one form of workplace bullying.[22] Studies in the United States, even using a self-report method, have found bullying rates of around 30% over a career.[23]

Clearly, there is a difference between the self-reporting of being bullied, and the report of behaviors we might typically consider workplace bullying. When we look to the sub-category of bullying, unlawful harassment in the United States, this gives us an idea of whether the self-report leads to underreporting or the operational method to overreporting. Unlawful harassment in the United States is generally considered a subset of the broader phenomena of workplace bullying. As will be discussed later, harassment must be based on a protected status to be unlawful in the United States, whereas bullying can be defined as generalized harassment. Dr. Mindy Bergman in testimony to the EEOC Select Task Force on the Study of Harassment, stated that the rates of workplace sexual harassment for women in the United States range from a low of 50% to a high of 90% and from 25 to 75% for men.[24] Even at the low end, since unlawful harassment is a subset of bullying, we see that the reports of workplace bullying are significantly underreported under both methods. If harassment rates are this high, then bullying rates must be even higher. This is exemplified in other studies such as one by Riley, Duncan and Edwards where 99.6% of the staff and teachers surveyed in Australia experience workplace bullying, and in fact more than 50% experienced 32 or more of the 44 listed forms of bullying.[25]

As I first proposed in 2010 together with Amy Hughes, the possible, if not probable reason for the difference in response rates is that the definitions of workplace bullying used in the self-report method or the targets' own perception of this definition are too narrow to capture all of the behaviors of workplace bullying.[26] This does not mean that they were not bullied, it just means that they did not perceive what happened to them to have been bullying. However, in many of these cases, it is likely that they were already suffering from the bullying behavior.

In my discussions with targets of workplace bullying, I have also found that they are hesitant to label the behaviors they are subjected to as bullying. One respondent suggested that as an adult it was impossible for him to be bullied. Another stated he would have never thought of the behaviors as bullying because he assumed that was something that kids did. Several respondents indicated that they believed they were too strong to be bullied. Two respondents indicated that they felt like even complaining about the behaviors was unfair and they were just being "whiners." The reality is that, for a variety of reasons, targets do not want to label themselves as targets or much worse as victims.

Seeing underreporting of workplace bullying is not surprising. We see the same type of underreporting and much the same reasons when we look at workplace harassment or even sexual assault. We know that in both instances the reports of behaviors are the proverbial tip of the iceberg and the majority of instances of harassment and even assault go unreported.[27] The fears that the operational methods lead to overreporting seem to be unfounded.

In fact, when we look at the studies of harassment and understand that harassment is one form of bullying, we realize that the biggest issue is that the bullying studies have an underreporting problem. Cortina has found that even when women in the workplace have experienced harassment and unwanted sexual attention, less than one in three will label such behavior as sexual harassment.[28] Not only do targets tend to label the phenomena of harassment and bullying too narrowly, as Raver and Nishii and Hershcovis have indicated, so do researchers in this area.[29]

Further, rather than being concerned that the operational methods might overreport, based on the findings of Bergman, Cortina, Riley and colleagues and my own experiences, there is a strong possibility that these operational methods lead to underreports and the self-report method leads to a severe level of underreporting. The operational methods miss forms of bullying. As discussed earlier, bullying takes so many different forms that we can probably never list all of the different measures bullying might take (I have yet to see a survey that asked whether a co-worker took a bite out of your apple as just one example, yet for one of my research participants, this is exactly what one of her bullies did). Further, for one reason or another, the operational methods all seem to focus on a repetitiveness requirement. This is a mistake that leads to many real forms of bullying being left out. This mistake will be discussed later as I put together a more adequate definition of workplace bullying. Requirements to prove high levels of harm, or to prove general or specific intent also lead to definitions of bullying being under-rather than over-inclusive.

Workplace harassment is extremely pervasive, even more pervasive than the prevalence levels of bullying in the vast majority of studies suggest. This suggests that the cause of the discrepancy between the self-report and the operational method has to do with the problems in the self-report methodology. When using a self-report method, it seems that we get an underreporting of bullying. The operational methods correct some of this problem, but still leave a gap. This gap seems to exist not due to the items on the operational methods, but the strict limitations placed on these – requiring either multiple acts or a repetitiveness of the behaviors. Both of these elements are impediments to rooting out the problem of workplace bullying and both of these will be addressed as we turn to defining workplace bullying. What we are left with is the realization that workplace bullying is pervasive no matter what method we use to report rates of bullying, yet the reality is that we are underestimating just how pervasive this devastating phenomenon really is in the workplace.

The effects of workplace bullying on targets, their families, communities, society and organizations are devastating. The effects are severe and include social, psychological, economic and even physical effects. Bullying violates the most basic of human rights and even the foundation of human rights. While targets suffer, their families and communities share in this suffering. Organizations also pay a high price for allowing workplace bullying. Targets become burned out, are forced to miss work, often leave work and in severe cases even end up committing acts of retaliatory workplace violence. Not only is the problem of workplace bullying severe, it is pervasive. No organization is immune from workplace bullying and workplace bullying is not simply naturally prevented or eliminated. Millions of working Americans are the targets of workplace bullying on a daily basis.

Workplace bullying is a pervasive problem in the American workplace and it is a problem that has severe impacts. Considering that targets, friends, families, communities, organizations and society all experience the negative impacts of workplace bullying, it is likely that we have all been impacted in some way or another. Consider the rude customer service agent, or the rushed nurse or the forgetful faculty member you might have been frustrated by not too long ago – could they have been the target of workplace bullying? Could it have been the effects of this targeting that led to their inability to serve your needs? Consider the absence of parents in your community organizations – are they busy making up for the lost productivity at their job as a result of workplace bullying, or are they also targets of bullying and too exhausted or depressed to contribute? Workplace bullying is pervasive. It is severe. It can be prevented. However, as I will discuss in the next chapter, too many organizations allow for the preconditions for workplace bullying and too many individuals are willing to engage in bullying behaviors.

Notes

1 (Gardner & Johnson, 2001).
2 (Keashley & Neuman, 2004).
3 (Rayner, et al., 2002, p. 51).
4 (Davenport, et al., 2002, p. 33).
5 (Einarsen, 1999, p. 16).
6 (Nielsen, et al., 2015).

7 For an example *see* Lance Compa, *Blood, Sweat and Fear: Worker's Right in the U.S. Meat and Poultry Industries* (Human Rights Watch 2004).
8 *See* http://hrw.org/children/labor.htm
9 For a discussion of a living wage *see* William P. Quigley, *Ending Poverty as We Know It: Guaranteeing a Right to a Job at a Living Wage* (Temple University Press 2003) and also Barbara Ehrenreich, *Nickel and Dimed* (2001) for a look at the conditions of working in jobs at less than a living wage.
10 (Keashley & Neuman, 2004, pp. 350–351).
11 (Yamada, 2004, p. 481).
12 (Coleman, 2004, p. 265).
13 (Gardner & Johnson, 2001, p. 29).
14 (Korkmaz & Cemalugli, 2010).
15 (Powell, et al., 2015).
16 According to Wilson, 5–6 **billion** dollars is lost annually in the United States alone due to "real or perceived abuse of employees by employers" (Keashley & Neuman, 2004). A 1998 ILO report concluded that stress at work cost the United States $80 billion per year (Gardner & Johnson, 2001). In fact, according to Coleman, 20% of all workplace disease claims in the United States can be linked to stress (Coleman, 2004).
17 (Lieber, 2010).
18 (Emdad, et al., 2013); (Hansen, et al., 2014).
19 (Berry, et al., 2012).
20 (Mikkelson & Einarsen, 2001).
21 (Agervold & Mikkelson, 2004).
22 (Riley, et al., 2011).
23 (Namie & Lutgen-Sandvik, 2010).
24 (Feldblum & Lipnic, 2016).
25 (Riley, et al., 2011).
26 (Carbo & Hughes, 2010).
27 (Feldblum & Lipnic, 2016).
28 (Cortina, 2008).
29 (Herschcovis, 2011); (Raver & Nishii, 2010).

4   Why does bullying occur and endure?

Vanessa explained that the bullying and mobbing she had endured made her feel like she was worthless. She stated that many times she had hoped to leave her situation, to find another job. However, her bullies had made her feel so low about herself that she no longer believed any other employer would want to hire her. She felt ashamed and depressed. She had endured bullying from her co-workers in her department, including from direct reports. She also had experienced bullying from other managers of other departments that she worked with on a daily basis. The bullying had worn her down. She felt defeated. She had been stripped of her right to dignity and esteem and her employer completely ignored the problem.

My experiences and research in workplace bullying have allowed me to develop what I refer to as the life cycle of workplace bullying. This cycle progresses from the preconditions or antecedents to workplace bullying, to the bullying behaviors, the impact of these behaviors, to the reactions by targets and the outcomes of these reactions. Understanding this life cycle affords us an opportunity to identify potential points of intervention that will be critical in the last section of this book as well as moving forward to prevent, detect, remedy and eliminate workplace bullying. This life cycle is built around the common themes, behaviors and occurrences in workplace bullying events. These are developed from the events I have explored as a researcher as well as those I have witnessed as a target, attorney, manager, advocate and activist.

The preconditions or antecedents

In order for bullying to occur and endure, there are a number of preconditions or antecedents that must exist. These occur at three levels – the macro, the mezzo and the micro levels. In other words, there are societal factors (macro), organizational level factors (mezzo) and individual bully level factors (micro) that are antecedents to workplace bullying. At the societal level, we see social acceptance of workplace bullying behavior along with the acceptance of a profit driven, work-intensified system of capitalism as root causes of workplace bullying. At the very least, we must have a society that allows for these systems to thrive, even if there is not direct support or acceptance of these systems. We also often see at the societal level acceptance of the specific bullying behaviors, combined with an expectation of individual machismo that leads to the expectation that targets need to toughen up and simply defend themselves or deal with the bullying. From the organizational level, we see organizations that either allow for workplace bullying or even go further and support or promote workplace bullying. Organizational leaders may look at bullying as a means to control workers, or at the least may look the other way when managers (especially financially successful managers) engage in bullying behaviors. Finally, at the individual level, there must be a bully who either is knowingly willing to engage in the bullying behavior or is unknowingly willing to engage in the bullying behaviors. The bully may actually have the desire to engage in bullying, knowing the effects of his/her behaviors or preferring this behavior as a style of supervision or interaction with co-workers. However, others may create this micro level antecedent simply by accepting the behaviors they are engaged in as proper management or even modeling their behaviors after other bullying leaders or co-workers, without realizing the very devastating outcomes of their behaviors.

The desire for and the acceptance of control, in particular control by employers over employees helps to create these preconditions. The idea of employers looking to exert control over workers is nothing new, in fact it is perhaps the hallmark of the history of the American working relationship. We cannot simply brush aside that the first vestiges of the employment relationship in the United States entailed masters of indentured servants and slaves. These slave owners used force and violence, the literal whip to control their workers. They also used state laws, and the U.S. Constitution to maintain control over their "employees." Slave owners formed militias to prevent slaves from escaping and to capture escaped slaves. The "necessity" of these militias at least in part led to the passage of the Second Amendment to the U.S. Constitution.

While slavery was abolished nearly 100 years later, this desire for control by employers hardly disappeared. Consider that the first treatise discussing the employment relationship was entitled "Master and Servant."[1] This seems to suggest a strong relationship of control. Further, this treatise erroneously or fallaciously provided a legal basis for employers to have control over their employees under a system of employment at will.[2] A system that was immediately and widely adopted in the United States and of course still exists today.[3] This system in essence allows the employer to terminate the employment of any employee at any time for any reason. Consider how this threat of loss of employment can be and indeed is used to control employees.

This desire for control has always been evident when we look at the history of labor relations in the United States. Unions and concerted activity that provide voice, bargaining power and some form of control for workers have been opposed by employers throughout the history of employment in the United States. Employers have fired workers, sued workers and even resorted to state-sanctioned and organization-implemented violence to break up unions. After workers were given the legal power to form unions, employers made it clear they would readily concede some finances in order to retain power: A power that in the labor relations language became known as management rights.

While the slave owners used whips, laws, militias and even crafted the Second Amendment to assure control over the workers in their fields, early industrialists used company towns, fear and even violence to control their workers. In the more modern workplace in the United States, Burawoy describes the use of game playing and manufacturing consent as a way that employers controlled their workers in a more modern setting.[4] Barker has described employer's concerted control through self-directed work teams, and others have looked at the employers' use of surveillance to control their workers' movements down to the second.[5] Workplace bullying is often simply a new method in a long line of methods to maintain control.

Employers resist giving up this control, both within their organizations by refusing to implement policies that would eliminate workplace bullying and outside by opposing legislation. Employers have a great deal of influence over the employment laws. We see attempts to pass anti-workplace bullying legislation in the United States run up against opposition from employers and employer groups.[6] Employers often suggest that this type of legislation would lead to an avalanche of frivolous lawsuits with little or no evidence to support such claims. Of course, this ignores the myriad of evidence that suggests that most cases of bullying still would not be brought forward – just as we see with instances of workplace harassment. Despite this, the employer claim leads to activists scrambling for ways to address an unfounded fear – an exercise in futility which will at best water down any solution and leave targets without protection even if the law were to be passed.

The employer desire to maintain control and the influence they have over legislation and the public acceptance of working conditions explains two of the preconditions that must exist for bullying to occur – a society that allows or even promotes workplace bullying and an organization that does the same. From the organizational standpoint, this command and control culture is one possible antecedent to workplace bullying. However, general poor management and negative workplace cultures of various sorts have been found to lead to workplace bullying. For instance, a better organizational climate and "healthy" working environment has been linked to less workplace bullying.[7] Absent leadership and leadership that supports bullying also are linked to workplace bullying.[8] However, in order for bullying to occur, there still must be a willing and able bully.

From a societal standpoint, there is also something more than this ability of employers to control and influence public policy. There is often a societal acceptance of this advanced system of capitalism that places profit before human rights. As a society, we often buy into myths that all human beings are economically minded, and are only in pursuit of economic interests, that businesses only exist to create wealth for owners and shareholders, that organizations must be lean and mean to be successful and that if the system is successful in terms of the financial measures (GDP, profit, wealth creation) then this will be good for everyone.[9] As a result of this, we simply accept the system that has turned businesses into wealth-creating machines that exploit and abuse the workers within these organizations. Too often we ignore the social and human development role of the corporation that is readily recognized in the Catholic Social Tradition.[10] We forget that part of the ethical responsibility of the businesses is to look out for the well-being of the employees.[11] As a result, not only do we see that businesses have an influence over public policy (a form of the fox guarding the hen house when we are talking about workplace bullying), but we have a society that accepts this cruel form of capitalism and thus allows these bullying behaviors to be accepted. Too often we see workplace bullies glorified in the popular press and media (on TV shows like *Hell's Kitchen*, but also in reports of bullying leaders like Bill Gates and Steve Jobs). Too often society accepts bullying working conditions as "part of the job" and puts the burden on the target to "toughen up." We even see this early on as children are too often taught that bullying is a part of life and being bullied will only make them stronger as they overcome it and endure. We engage in this misconception rather than calling out bullying for what it is – abuse of a human being, and taking the steps that we should as a society not to wait for things to get better, but instead to make things better by putting a stop to this abuse.

There are also a number of preconditions or antecedents at the bully level. In order to be able to bully, the bully must have some source of power over his/her target. In my research and experience, the source of power varies from bully to bully, from formal organizational or position power to physical power and to information power. While many bullies in my study possessed formal power over their targets, many others did not. Participants shared experiences with bullies who were supervisors, co-workers and even subordinates in the formal organizational structure. However, in every case, the bully was able to exert some form of power over his/her targets. In many cases, the power was formal. In one case, the power difference was in physical power, in others it was information power and in some it was relationship power. While power was always a theme of the workplace bullying experiences that were shared, power in this case must be viewed broadly. It is the power that enables the bully.

However, possession of a power source alone is not the only necessary precondition to workplace bullying. There are many instances of individuals having power (formal or informal) over another. In fact, in every hierarchical structure, those in higher positions of authority possess formal power over subordinates. However, every situation of an imbalance of power does not lead to workplace bullying. Instead, the bully must be willing to engage in bullying or, in other words, be willing to abuse his/her source of power, and the organization must in some manner allow for this bullying to occur. From the experiences of targets, bullies engage in their destructive behaviors for a variety of reasons. In some cases, organizations not only allow for bullying, but they also encourage bullying by promoting these behaviors. A bullying supervisor once explained to me that the organization he grew up in viewed management by intimidation as the best way to supervise (even promoting one person to supervisor because he won a fight in the parking lot). He explained if you wanted to get promoted or wanted to get a raise, you had to show you were tough on your employees. For other bullies, they might just naturally look to bully others. Vanessa described her bullying co-worker as a generally mean person. Other bullies might be looking to maintain their own control or engage in bullying out of fear of others. Others may become bullies due to the pressure they are feeling in the workplace. Increasing workloads and pressure to cut costs have been linked to workplace bullying.[12] Consider, Suzanne and her bullying of her friend and direct report, Greg. Suzanne explained that her bully, the university President continued to lump more and more work on her. He continued to raise the bar on what he expected if her department were to be recognized as a college. She in turn did the same to Greg, offloading some of the impact of her bullying onto her friend and direct report. Other bullies may simply bully because they see this as their way of dealing with the pressures in the workplace. For instance, Kelly suggested that, at least in part, the owner of her office tended to bully as a result of the pressures of running an office of his/her own and the resulting financial pressures. When times were tough or hectic, the bullying would increase. During the normal, yet profitable months, Kelly suggested that the office would be much friendlier and it was these months that led to her staying for so long. Finally, there is evidence that at least some harassers engage in harassment because they do not know better or do not know that their behavior is harassing. The same possibility exists in workplace bullying. It is only once these antecedents are present that bullying can occur and endure.[13]

The bullying behaviors

While the bullying behaviors are described in Chapter 3 of this volume, there are still some common themes to be discussed about these behaviors. When interviewing targets of workplace bullying, control by the bully was both a common cause of workplace bullying as well as a common form of workplace bullying. Bullies would use control to bully, and would use bullying to gain greater control. Bullies would also use their behaviors to quash and strip the voice of targets. Kelly believed that the bully in her office used his bullying as a way to quickly manage the workers in his office, to control their behaviors and to limit their questions. Kevin explained how the support staff bully in the financial company used information to maintain control over the financial agents in the office. Several faculty members at one university agreed that the bullying President engaged in his bullying (direct, via proxies and by policies) to control the faculty in "his" university and to quiet these same faculty. In another university setting, the bully's tactic was one to often times exert control – control over classroom decisions including grades, control over search committees that were led by faculty and control over research funding and rewards that were critical for faculty member job success. The former soldier Jim's voice was squelched through the use of leave policies. The silencing of worker voice seems to either be a very common form of bullying, or the goal of other forms of bullying. Aside from the actions by the optometrist and the one university president, this form of bullying most often was handled through less overt behaviors. It took place in the university through the elimination of committee assignments, the assigning of additional work, the implementation of policies with little or no discussion, by not providing opportunity for training or even by simply ignoring the attempts at having a voice. These same covert methods seemed to be used by the commanding officer of the former soldier.

This theme of control existed across all of the different types of jobs, workplaces, and bullies. In the restaurant, the owner wanted to exert complete control over the wait staff in terms of their dress, grooming, demeanor, make-up, etc. to create what she deemed the "Poky-Perfect" waiter or wait staff. The bully who used physical intimidation was trying to control the food service co-worker, and, according to the research participant, this bully even stated that she would "tell her how to do her job." In one university setting, peer bullies used a post-tenure review process to control how a senior faculty member managed her classroom. In this same university, an administrator controlled a faculty member by changing her grades and even coming into her classroom unannounced. In almost every case, the target reported that they felt they were being controlled, that his/her voice and his/her ability to choose his/her own behaviors were being limited by his/her bully.

Outcomes for targets

An important point in the flowchart of the bullying life cycle in Figure 4.1 is the understanding that the impact of workplace bullying often occurs even before the target identifies himself/herself as having been bullied or develops any level of class consciousness. For instance, Kevin never even thought about the fact that he was being bullied, but each day he left work, he talked about how defeated and depressed and often angry he felt. Kevin was not alone; Julie, Suzanne and many other participants in my research experienced the effects of bullying before they understood that they were even the targets of unfair and aggressive, negative workplace behaviors. All of the impacts of workplace bullying discussed in Chapter 3 of this volume occur whether the target recognizes the bullying or not. Targets will react in different ways to these negative outcomes depending on their level of awareness of the bullying behavior and whether they perceive their rights as being violated. However, no matter the level of awareness or consciousness, there will be responses from the targets.

Target reactions

Targets will react to bullying in different ways depending on their own level of consciousness about bullying. Targets oftentimes completely lack a consciousness that they are being bullied or that they are the target of bullying. Despite this lack of realization, targets still experience the negative outcomes of workplace bullying described in Chapter 3 of this volume and they respond to these negative effects. Targets gain a consciousness about being bullied at different times and levels. However, once targets understand they are being bullied, their reactions tend to be different. They will in this case rather than just dealing with the symptoms look to address the bullying. However, they do so at an individual level because they see themselves as being alone in their experiences. Finally, targets of bullying may gain a form of class consciousness and realization that they are not alone as targets. At this level of consciousness, targets are more likely to be willing to engage in concerted actions to address the bullying.

Target reactions without consciousness of being bulled

Again, targets feel the effects of being bullied even before they identify the behaviors as bullying. Kevin, Julie and Vanessa specifically stated that they never thought of themselves as being targets of bullying, yet they knew there was something that was not right and that work was the source of their concerns. Kevin explained he would get in his car and blast his music after work to let off steam. Vanessa explained she wanted to look for work elsewhere, but felt like nobody would ever want to hire her. Julie explained that she felt like she must be doing something wrong to have upset her department. They all felt these effects before identifying as targets of bullying. When targets feel these effects, they will take steps to address the problem. These steps usually involve self-help coping type of mechanisms. These could include problematic types of steps such as self-medication, or turning to doctors for prescription medications. In my time in the industry as an HR manager, I witnessed many workers get hooked on self-medication or prescription drugs and many who spoke with me pointed to pressures at work, many of which were related to bullying supervisors. I also have seen clients who have been targeted for harassment visit my office months after going to their physicians for prescription drugs. Several of my research participants also shared that they found themselves drinking more, arguing with their family more and in one case throwing themselves into exercise in what she described as an "obsessive level."

Despite this suffering, one of the most interesting things I discovered during my research is the silence and perhaps even denial under which targets of bullying will suffer. The effects of the bullying are oftentimes experienced by targets well before they gain a conscious realization that they have become targets of bullying. When targets of bullying and harassment have come to my law office, they are often there because the effects of the bullying are no longer bearable. Even as an HR Manager, most targets of bullying or harassment within my organizations who took the step to report, only did so after enduring a great amount of suffering over sometimes extremely long periods of time – measured in months and even years. However, in all of the cases I have seen of workplace bullying, no target took any formal steps until they recognized that their rights had been violated in some manner.

Individual consciousness and corresponding reactions

In my research on workplace bullying, on numerous occasions I have witnessed a "gaining-of-consciousness experience" for targets of bullying who have taken part in my research. In other words, during the course of the research, the targets realize that they have been targets of a bully or bullies. They gain an understanding of why they were feeling the negative experiences at work and at home. On the individual level, this is most clearly exemplified by a university staff member, Julie, who stated that she felt guilty for even complaining about her working environment during the research interview. It was not until she read the survey and began to think about her situation that she even considered her experiences to meet any definition of workplace bullying. By this point in time, Julie had experienced personal bullying that included sexual harassment, ostracizing and brow-bearing and organizational bullying that included ignoring her ideas and assigning menial tasks in place of meaningful work. Still it was really only during the interview process and the focus groups that she gained a greater consciousness that she was a target of bullying and not to blame. Kevin described a similar experience when taking the intro survey on workplace bullying. He explained that he knew something was wrong and he knew it was his work. As a result, when he saw the call to participate in the survey he thought he would see if it led to making some sense of his situation. He stated that as he took the survey, he saw how everything he was experiencing was directly listed in the survey and that he felt compelled to continue to provide insights to the ongoing research. As employees become aware of the extent of bullying and have the opportunity to step back and to reflect on their own working environment, there will be an increase in the number of reports of bullying as these employees gain a consciousness about their own situations.

At this stage, self-help is still a common response by targets. However, the self-help tends to be more directed towards the bullying behavior and bringing an end to that behavior (or at least escaping the behavior). Several targets engaged in self-help methods. For instance, Julie stated that after realizing she was not to blame she began to call her mother and discuss her work. Kevin continued to take out his frustration on his long drive home, but also decided to switch career fields. Like Kevin, other targets often responded by separating from work in one way or another. Greg stopped devoting as much time to service activities for the university, focused on his own office outside of the university and eventually retired early. Vanessa and Julie both began to look for and eventually secured other employment. A telemarketing worker, John quit his work, as did Mary, a land services worker, and Bryan, an employee in a big box company. Even Kelly left her office after managing it for ten years. Suzanne simply attempted to avoid her bully but also eventually left her employment.

Two participants responded to their bullying through interpersonal communication with their bully. One participant, Kelly, the office manager, confronted her bully, or "bullied back," on numerous occasions. The office manager's response tended to stop the bullying for a short time, but others in the workplace would still bear the brunt of the optometrist's bullying. Another target, Jim, the soldier, dealt with his bullying through ingratiation. When his bullying commanding officer's grandmother died, this soldier made sure to send flowers to her funeral. This seemed to alleviate the bullying. However, none of the respondents were truly satisfied with their individual methods of responding to their workplace bullies. They stated as much during the interviews and focus groups. This and the fact that every one of the respondents I know of today, just a few years since the initial interviews, has left their employment indicates these individual methods were not effective. The possibility of self-help or even co-worker interventions will be explored further in Chapter 8 of this volume.

Of the 16 formal research participants in my initial research, 10 at one time or another filed some sort of formal complaint to their managers. However, at the time of the interviews, only one still felt confident in reporting a complaint to a manager or a formal employer complaint system. Of the remaining nine, eight had no confidence in reporting a complaint to an employer because of their specific experiences with their initial complaint. The hotel workers' general manager simply pushed the complaint back down to the assistant manager who was bullying the employees in the first place. One university staff member felt that complaining worsened the bullying, and another believed that filing a formal grievance would be "career suicide." Several faculty members did indeed feel pressure to and did leave their university AFTER reporting a claim. Two faculty members who filed a formal complaint are still working in their Universities, but both have had to take leave as a result of the experiences they suffered after filing a complaint. The lack of success of these formal complaint systems will be addressed in Chapter 9 of this volume as I present a model for successful employer interventions or anti-bullying policies.

The majority of targets of workplace bullying that I have met in my research and throughout my career never advance beyond this individual level of consciousness. The vast majority of targets I have spoken with have viewed themselves as alone in their struggles. As a result, even once they have decided to address the workplace bullying, they have selected individual responses – from bullying back, to ingratiation, to filing complaints, to quitting their employment. The targets who believes they are alone will seek out individual solutions.

Class consciousness

Targets of bullying also gain a class consciousness when they come together. I have experienced this in the workplace as an advocate for targets and also experienced this in focus groups in my research on workplace bullying. Julie was also a good example of the "gaining of consciousness" at the collective level. Even after understanding she had been bullied, she continued to believe she was an exception rather than a norm and that she in some way brought about the bullying that was in turn unique to her working environment. It was only during the interview and then the focus groups that Julie began to view the problem with bullying was not her own, isolated experience, but was a collective problem for much of the working class. Beyond just recognizing that they are not alone as victims, targets also gain an even truer consciousness when they share their experiences. When targets began to share their experiences during focus groups, they began to develop into a support group. Group members lent support and also began to recognize themselves as having been targets. Targets would often become extremely upset that co-participants were subjected to the behaviors they experienced. This led to a type of class consciousness and a desire to do something to address workplace bullying in a collective, concerted activity. This might also explain some of the findings in the nursing profession of nurse bystanders taking on bullies that they witness, such as the research conducted by Gafney and colleagues. Nursing has a high rate of workplace bullying, so it is quite possible that these bystander intervenors are not just witnesses, but they themselves have been targets. Much like the targets in the research focus groups, they are upset to see others targeted in similar ways and desire to take action. Unfortunately, as will be discussed later, both bystanders and targets have a limited ability to address workplace bullying.

In addition to the potential for bystander intervention as a result of the collective consciousness, the possibility of more formal, concerted activity or collective action also emerged. Several members in the focus groups discussed their willingness to participate in the group protests to protect the rights of other targets. This led to a discussion about the possibility of unionization and formal concerted activity. Further, this led to a focus group that explored in detail an example of such an effort from a local union. Since that time, I have witnessed several unions who have taken effective steps to help members who have become targets of workplace bullies. I have also seen unions who have failed to address the issue and even made the bullying worse in organizations. The possibility of concerted activity as a solution will be discussed in more detail in Chapter 10 of this volume.

What is clearly missing from this flowchart (see Figure 4.1) is a legal path for recovery and remediation for targets of workplace bullying. There simply is no effective remedy in the United States to address the majority of workplace bullying. For the most extreme cases of workplace bullying, there may indeed be a tort remedy and for bullying that is clearly based on a protected status targets may have a claim to file with the EEOC (although even this protection is limited). This lack of a legal remedy in the United States will be discussed in detail in the next chapter.

Outcomes of the target reactions

Target reactions to workplace bullying have the potential to disrupt or to accelerate the bullying life cycle. A target's reaction to workplace bullying could indicate to a willing bully that the bullying is "working." This would lead to the bully engaging in even more bullying. The reactions could also potentially break the cycle of bullying. They could impact the antecedents or disrupt the behaviors.

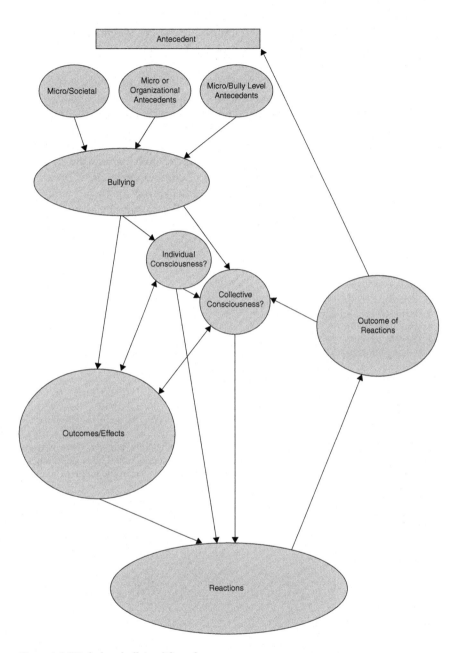

Figure 4.1 Workplace bullying life cycle

The reactions also have the potential to moderate or ameliorate the negative effects on the targets, organizations, families and society. Potential reactions to workplace bullying and the outcomes of these reactions will be explored in detail in Section 3 of this book.

Workplace bullying has a life cycle of its own. In order for bullying to occur, there are preconditions. These conditions come from society, organizations and the bullies themselves. It is only when these conditions exist that bullying occurs. For the targets of bullying, as soon as the bullying occurs, they begin to experience the negative effects, and these effects spread to the organizations, family, friends and society. Targets will react to the bullying and the negative impacts based upon their level of awareness of consciousness about their bullying. These reactions have the potential to either disrupt or to accelerate the workplace bullying life. The reactions may ameliorate the negative effects of bullying or they may worsen these effects.

Notes

1 (Wood, 1877).
2 (Frieman, 1976).
3 (Rothstein & Liebman, 2011).
4 (Burawoy, 1979).
5 (Barker, 1993).
6 (Cheng Chu, 2014).
7 (Cabrera, 2012); (Powell, et al., 2015).
8 (Dussault & Frenett, 2015); (Namie & Lutgen-Sandvik, 2010).
9 (Mintzberg, et al., 2002).
10 (Kennedy, 2006); (Naughton, 2006).
11 (Carroll, 1991).
12 (Yamada, 2000).
13 There may be more antecedents to bullying than these four. Further, there may be numerous moderators or mediators of bullying at this stage as well. This is definitely an interesting and needed area of study. However, this was not within the scope or focus of this chapter.

Section 2

Workplace bullying can be addressed but is not in the United States

In this section, I will explore the shortcomings in the U.S. legal system in addressing workplace bullying. I will explore the laws in the United States that most closely relate to workplace bullying. From a statutory standpoint, this will entail an analysis of the U.S. Equal Employment Opportunity laws and how these are interpreted to prohibit status-based harassment in the workplace. I will also explore the potential but lacking coverage in the U.S. common law through the tort of intentional infliction of emotional distress. I will also explore the problems and potential for administrative remedies in the United States. This analysis will paint a clear picture that many targets of workplace bullying are left without an effective legal remedy in the United States.

In addition to exploring the laws in the United States, I will explore the laws in other countries that address workplace bullying. This analysis will include an exploration of statutory, common law and administrative remedies that address workplace bullying around the globe. This analysis will demonstrate that workplace bullying can be addressed. The contrast between the actions taken in these other countries and the lack of action in the United States will be clear. The actions from abroad will also provide the beginning steps to exploring solutions that can and should be implemented in the United States to prevent, detect, remedy and eliminate workplace bullying.

5   Gaps in the U.S. employment law

Workplace bullying can be, but is not being, addressed

John just wanted the bullying at his job to stop. He knew the job was not the best in the world and the work was boring, but he just wanted something to get him through while he finished up his degree. Still he could no longer stand the constant negative comments from his supervisors, the fact that he was constantly being watched, that every tenth of one second of his day was being tracked and that every time he made a mistake he was berated in front of all of his co-workers. Even as a college student, John believed that if his employer would not address the bullying he must have some legal recourse. John was shocked when he first found out there was nothing he could do to end the bullying. He had approached the organization and they would not do anything and then he had even contacted an attorney and been informed he had no claim.

John is not alone in his belief that general workplace harassment or bullying must be unlawful, nor in his shock when he found out there are no protections for targets of these behaviors. Each year I teach undergraduate students a course in employment law and each year the majority of these students believe the legal protections for targets of workplace bullying are much broader than what they are. As an attorney, many potential clients have come through my doors with the same type of story that John experienced and much like the attorney John visited, I have often had to turn the individual away with the explanation that our legal system simply does not protect targets of generalized harassment or workplace bullying.

The reality is that workplace bullying is a phenomenon that can be eliminated and at the very least detected and remedied. Workers' right to dignity in the workplace can indeed be protected. There are clear examples of addressing workplace bullying across the globe, from Sweden who has led the way to France, Australia, Canada and many other places. There are also examples of positive employers eliminating workplace bullying. We also know from harassment studies that there are, at a minimum, steps that employers can take to limit the amount of workplace bullying. However, as of today, employees in the U.S. for the most part have no real, meaningful avenue to address workplace bullying. John along with millions of other targets of workplace bullying are left with no meaningful recourse. The rates of bullying and the rates of ongoing levels of unlawful harassment indicate that American employers are not effectively addressing the issue of workplace harassment let alone the broader issue of workplace bullying. Further, even employers who espouse to having anti-bullying policies most often do not.[1] Employers often fail to even meet the minimal requirements for policies addressing unlawful forms of workplace harassment or bullying.

The vast majority of workplace bullying does not violate any law, and even the protections that targets have from harassment based on a protected status have major gaps in coverage. Targets of workplace bullying have no adequate avenue of recourse available in the U.S. employment system. Only a strong law, strongly enforced will eliminate workplace bullying, or in fact provide a remedy for most acts of workplace bullying. The current legal system in the United States falls well short of addressing workplace bullying, but there is no reason that workplace bullying cannot be addressed.

The gaps in current U.S. laws

The current U.S. employment law system clearly fails to present an effective solution to the epidemic of workplace bullying in the United States. There is no effective statutory, common law or administrative remedy for targets of workplace bullying in the United States. While Title VII of the Civil Rights Act, the Americans with Disabilities Act, and the Age Discrimination in Employment Act (as well as related state laws) make it unlawful to engage in discriminatory harassment (harassment based on race, color, gender, national origin, religion, age status over 40 or a disability), they fail to address bullying as a behavior. These EEO laws at best only protect targets from bullying that is based on a protected status (and even in those cases there are other wide gaps in coverage). The possibilities of tort claims of outrage or intentional infliction of emotional distress are even less promising and only address the most severe and intentional acts of bullying (if any acts of bullying are covered) and only where they lead to severe emotional distress. Finally, administrative remedies such as worker's compensation, unemployment compensation and OSHA protections fall short of protecting targets of workplace harassment due to limited remedies and an inability to address bullying before the target is irreparably harmed.

Insight into protection from workplace harassment under EEO laws

Workplace bullying has often been compared to the U.S. standard for unlawful workplace harassment under Title VII, and expansions of Title VII coverage have been offered as potential solutions to the problem of workplace bullying. Researchers including Yamada, Chow and Lehman have all suggested that some form of expansion of workplace harassment law could the path to addressing workplace bullying.[2,3,4] Several of the anti-bullying laws and directives in other countries use the terminology of harassment (i.e. general harassment, psychological harassment or moral harassment) to define workplace bullying.

I have also focused on a harassment based definition of workplace bullying (as will be discussed later). There are strong similarities between the definition of workplace bullying I have developed and the legal definition of workplace harassment. It seems to make sense to have at least some hope that the U.S. laws addressing workplace harassment would address workplace bullying. That is until we take a closer look at the laws and interpretations of the laws that address workplace harassment.

To begin to understand the shortcomings of harassment jurisprudence, we can look at the definition of sexual harassment in the federal register:

> Harassment on the *basis of sex* is a violation of section 703 of title VII. \1\ Unwelcome sexual advances, requests for sexual favors, and other verbal or physical conduct of a sexual nature constitute sexual harassment when (1) submission to such conduct is made either explicitly or implicitly a term or condition of an individual's employment, (2) submission to or rejection of such conduct by an individual is used as the basis for employment decisions affecting such individual, or (3) *such conduct has the purpose or effect of unreasonably interfering with an individual's work performance or creating an intimidating, hostile, or offensive working environment.*
>
> (emphasis added)[5]

Harassment on the basis of other protected statuses, such as race, color, national origin, religion, age and disability, can be defined in a similar manner.[6] There are many holes in this definition of harassment that will allow the vast majority of workplace bullying in the United States to go unaddressed. The status-based requirement is perhaps the most obvious of these. However, the focus on the working environment, the focus on work-related outcomes, and the standard for defining hostile and offensive all leave major gaps in coverage of some of the most common forms of workplace bullying.

The need to show protected status – The focus on discrimination versus dignity

The focus on discrimination in the U.S. harassment laws leaves the majority of targets of workplace bullying unprotected. According to Namie and Namie, less than 25% of workplace bullying targets are targeted based on a legally protected status, leaving 75% of bullying cases outside of the coverage of the EEO laws before the behaviors of the bully or the harm to the target are even analyzed.[7] The Supreme Court's 1993 concurring opinion in *Harris v. Forklift* states that "The critical issue, Title VII's text indicates, is whether members of one sex are exposed to disadvantageous terms or conditions of employment to which members of the other sex are not opposed."[8] This standard is so well accepted by the Supreme Court that it was cited in their Oncale Ruling in 1999.[9] There is a clear requirement that the harassing behavior be based on a protected status for a plaintiff to sustain a claim under any of the EEO laws.

Not only are many instances of bullying eliminated from coverage because they are not based on a protected status, but in some cases, courts make it extremely difficult to prove that the harassment was based on a protected status. For instance, in *Riske v. King Soopers*, the 10th Circuit Court of Appeals dismissed the plaintiff's Title VII claim because according to this court, the unpleasantness of the environment was not due to the plaintiff's gender.[10] In this case, the plaintiff was subjected to an ongoing pattern of increasingly unusual gifts of flowers and rather unusual cards, including a notes saying "Being manager is hard, but I hope I look as nice as you when I'm bitching" and "I am going to miss you in your tight-ass jeans."[11] Yet the court determined that this was not enough to show the harassment was based on gender. In another case, the court decided that a male target could not show that being hit repeatedly in the scrotum was harassment based on his gender.[12]

Based on my research, many victims of bullying will be left without a remedy due to this protected-status-based standard. In my discussions with the research participants, it was rare to find a clear-cut example of harassment based on a protected status. For one participant, Maria, it did appear that her manager was picking on her due to her religion. As a Seventh-Day Adventist, this participant's religion prohibited her working on Saturdays. At one point, the manager, in response to the employee needing Saturdays off due to her religious beliefs, stated, "Well I do not get to miss work every Sunday." Further, a fellow employee, also a Seventh-Day Adventist, was reportedly suing this employer for religious discrimination. Even here, the participant stated she was not sure the actions were due to her religion. She herself suggested she may have been targeted due to her immigrant status or for some other unknown reason. Whereas Katherine suggested that her employer's requirement to be "Poky-Perfect" might have a greater impact on female wait staff, she did not feel the policy was really discriminatory based on sex. Other participants including Julie and Adrienne shared examples of sexual harassment along with other forms of workplace bullying. In other circumstances, the research participants pointed out that their bullies were "equal opportunity" bullies. Several research participants specifically said that the bully in their workplace treated everyone the same way. For example, Kelly explained that the optometrist in her office bullied everyone. Vanessa's screaming bully also bullied anyone who got in her way. She explained that she picked on people who were weak and susceptible to bullying. The bullying university Presidents and deans had as many complaints from male faculty as from female. In other circumstances, the bullies seemed to pick their targets based upon a non-protected status. For instance, Jennifer, the research participant who worked in food services at a rest home was referred to as a "little girl" by her bully. In this case the bully seemed to feel superior due to her older age and seniority level. The target's young age status is not a protected status under federal law,[13] nor is it protected in the home state of this individual. Another university employee felt that non-tenured faculty, staff and employees with lower levels of seniority were most likely to be bullied. In any case, for all of these targets of workplace bullying, it would be difficult to show that the bullying was based on a protected status.

The sexualized nature of the gender status-based requirement

Even when targets are protected as a result of status-based bullying, the focus on discrimination versus the focus on dignity can lead to less than desirable results. According to Vicki Shultz, one of the problems with the law of sexual harassment is that

> much of what is harmful to women in the workplace is difficult to construe as sexual in design.... By emphasizing protection of women's sexual selves and sensibilities over and above empowerment as workers, the paradigm permits or even encourages companies to construe the law to prohibit some forms of sexual expression that do not promote gender hierarchy at work.[14]

According to Anne Marie Marshall, the manner in which the court rulings are implemented in practice by employers tends to limit the rights of the female (or presumably other minority victims) rather than protect them from the discrimination, and therefore the laws may not even adequately protect the 25% of bullying victims who are victimized based on a protected status. As Ehrenreich has stated:"[W]orkplace harassment whether sexual or non-sexual against both women and men is fundamentally a 'dignity harm' against victims' 'dignity and personality interests.'"[15] The reality that Title VII and the other EEO laws fall short of protecting targets of workplace harassment is not lost on the EEOC. In fact, this is the major reason why the EEOC Commissioners called a Special Task Force to look at the coverage and protections against unlawful discrimination.

Even if the EEO laws would protect against all forms of sexualized harassment, a standard should not focus on the sexual nature of the harassment, but rather on the damage to the targets' dignity. Sexual banter may not damage a target's dignity under certain circumstances, while non-sexual banter or bullying may indeed damage the same target's dignity. However, courts at times continue to require the showing of not only a link to one's gender, but a form of sexually tinged behavior in order to show a status-based claim. In other cases, courts simply interpret the wording of sexual harassment claims as requiring a showing of a sexual nature of the acts or motives going beyond the requirement of showing harassment based on the protected status of gender.[16] In each of these cases, the targets had strong arguments that the bullying they endured was based on a protected status, yet they were still denied the protections under Title VII of the Civil Rights Act as the courts required them to show that the harassment was sexual in nature in order to make a protected status-based claim.

Sexual banter can indeed be damaging and harmful. Two of the research participants, Katherine and Jennifer, were deeply offended by sexual banter at a restaurant. In fact, as a result of this behavior, they quit their jobs. However, they were also equally offended by non-sexual bullying behavior at their current employers. It makes little sense that they would have an easier time proving legal liability for the sexual banter when both forms of bullying had the same effect. Of the remaining research participants, only one other participant discussed an issue of harassment of a sexual nature, yet all of these participants suffered unacceptable, unnecessary negative outcomes as a result of being targeted by bullies. A conversation with one research participant also supported the positions of legal scholars Vicki Shultz and Ann Marie Marshall. This research participant had been the target of bullying and sexual harassment at work. However, toward the end of our conversation, she stated that in her opinion, women were more often the victims of bullying, but that the bullying did not take the form one would normally expect. She stated that the bullying was not necessarily sexual in nature or even clearly based on gender, but that the bullying might be more subtle. I suggested that perhaps part of the bullying of female employees was forcing them to adopt the typical white male patterns of workplace practices, and she readily agreed.[17] This type of bullying is not addressed under any current U.S. employment law, yet it indeed had a profound negative effect on this individual, her dignity, and eventually the organization. This participant stated that the bullying environment affected her at work and at home. She found herself taking her frustrations home with her. Finally, the bullying led to her leaving her employer. She was a valued employee, and this was also a clear detriment to the organization as well.

The focus on discrimination and status-based harassment under the EEO laws creates another problem for targets of workplace bullying. Because the law around workplace harassment is so focused on discrimination rather than dignity, it would appear that employers could avoid liability for workplace harassment by assuring that any harassers in their employ make sure to harass all employees. In fact, the 8th Circuit upheld a ruling that made this fairly explicit, accepting as a defense the fact that the abusive behavior was directed at both male and female employees.[18] This equal opportunity offender defense might actually promote more pervasive bullying rather than helping to eliminate bullying in any manner. This class or status-based requirement for a cognizable harassment claim is not the only gap in the harassment jurisprudence.

The severe or pervasive standard

The legal interpretations of harassment in the United States set an unusually high standard for proving that actions are "severe or pervasive" enough to constitute a legal violation. While 75% of the targets of workplace bullying already excluded from the purview of protection under the EEO laws due to a lack of behavior based on a protected status (and others will be excluded because they cannot meet the heightened standard in some courts to prove status-based harassment), many others are left without protection because of this heightened standard of the types of behaviors that constitute harassment. A review of recent circuit court decisions in the area of unlawful harassment demonstrates that even when the harassing conduct is clearly based upon a protected status, the legal hurdle is still too high. Many courts in the United States make it very clear that the protection against unlawful harassment is not a protection of civility in the workplace; in fact, in many cases it seems to be no protection at all.

Perhaps two paragraphs in Justice Souter's majority opinion in *Faragher v. Boca Raton* best sum up the Supreme Court's view of unlawful harassment:

> [I]n Harris, we explained that in order to be actionable under the statute, a sexually objectionable environment must be *both objectively and subjectively offensive,* one that a reasonable person would find hostile or abusive and one that the victim in fact did perceive to be so. We directed courts to determine whether an environment is sufficiently hostile or abusive by *"looking at all the circumstance,"* including *"the frequency of the discriminatory conduct; its severity; whether it is physically threatening or humiliating, or a mere offensive utterance; and whether it unreasonably interferes with an employee's work performance."* . . . we explained that Title VII does not prohibit "genuine but innocuous differences in the way men and women routinely interact with members of the same sex and of the opposite sex." . . . A recurring point in these opinions is that "simple teasing," offhand comments, and isolated incidents (unless *extremely* serious) will not amount to discriminatory changes in the "terms and conditions of employment."
>
> These standards for judging hostility are sufficiently demanding to ensure that Title VII *does not become a "general civility code."* Properly applied, they will filter out complaints attacking *"the ordinary tribulations of the workplace, such as the sporadic use of abusive language, gender-related jokes and occasional teasing."*
>
> (Emphasis added)[19]

Justice Souter suggests that the Supreme Court's definitions of hostile-environment harassment will lead to assurances that innocent, innocuous work behaviors will not be actionable, that the standard the court has set will "filter out the ordinary tribulations of the workplace." The argument could be made that the SCOTUS has established a fairly reasonable standard. However, the SCOTUS does not hear and decide every harassment case, and the lower court interpretations of this standard are often quite disturbing.

One of the worst examples of a court supporting behavior that clearly violated the target's human right to dignity was the *Baskerville v. Culligan International Co.* case. In this case, Judge Posner held that

> only a woman of Victorian delicacy – a woman mysteriously aloof from contemporary American popular culture in all its sex-saturated vulgarity – would find . . . a gesture intended to simulate masturbation, grunting

sounds as she walked by her alleged harasser, and a statement that one public address announcement really meant that all pretty girls run around naked . . . more distressing than the heat and cigarette smoke of which the plaintiff did not complain.[20]

While a jury found that these actions could indeed create a hostile working environment, Judge Posner intervened and overturned this decision. In order to do so, not only did this mean that Judge Posner disagreed that these actions created a hostile working environment, it meant that in his opinion looking at the facts in the light most favorable to the target, there was no way that these behaviors could have been unlawful harassment. However, these actions were clearly bullying, harassing behaviors that stripped or at least could have stripped the target of her esteem and right to a safe working environment. Posner's condescending and degrading language from the bench further exacerbated this harm. However, this case may not even be the most damning for claimants of sexual or other unlawful forms of harassment.

In *Hartsell v. Duplex Products*, the 4th Circuit agreed with the Western District Court of North Carolina that an environment in which supervisors had informed an employee that they had made every female in the office cry and would also make her cry, called a female sales assistant his slave, pointed out a "buxom" catalog model and asked why they did not have sales assistants like that, referred to the plaintiff's husband as a "stay at home wife," and asked the plaintiff, "Why don't you go home and fetch your husband's slippers like a good little wife, that's exactly what my wife is going to do for me," was not an actionably hostile working environment. The defendants were granted a summary judgment at the lower court level, and the appellate court upheld this decision. In other words, these judges decided not only that this was not actionable harassment, but also again that no reasonable jury could find that this was severe and/or pervasive enough to create a hostile working environment.[21] The courts in this case clearly went beyond the protection of innocent, innocuous working behaviors. It is difficult to see what place these behaviors and statements had in a working environment. The statements by these supervisors clearly were degrading to the target and did not afford her a reasonable level of esteem or dignity.

Hartsell and *Baskerville* have both been cited favorably dozens of times by other courts as recently as 2010 and 2014 respectively. In one such case, *Lenihan v. Boeing Co.*, the U.S. District Court for the Southern District of Texas cites *Hartsell* and *Baskerville* to find that the allegations by the plaintiff in this case did not constitute enough of the "hellish" environment and did not meet the standard for severe or pervasive as set out in the *Baskerville* and *Hartsell* cases.[22] The court here has gone well beyond the protection of innocent behaviors and has established the standard of a "hellish" environment. If the standard was to protect one's dignity, then of course one would be afforded the right to something more than a just-better-than-"hellish" working environment.

The 7th Circuit Court of Appeals cited *Baskerville* and this "hellish" standard to conclude that no unlawful harassment could have occurred when a female police officer was told by a commanding officer that he would like to be the policy book in her back pocket and that her breasts looked nice in that red turtleneck as she exited the locker room, or was asked if she had a boyfriend or needed one. The CO also made a regular habit of interfering with the officer's duties, including making threatening remarks, showing up to her service calls even when he was not her CO and directly interfering with her handling ser-vice calls.

For these judges, unless a plaintiff can show that his/her working environ-ment is "hellish," they will be unable to prove an actionable hostile environ-ment. The standard for legally objectionable behavior in these jurisdictions is an extremely high standard. There are many behaviors that violate workers' human rights to dignity, esteem, voice and other human rights that the judges in these cases have cast aside as trivial or meaningless. These judges clearly have not con-sidered the right to dignity of these plaintiff employees. Instead, their only focus continues to be on the economics of the organizations involved or perhaps, even further, a completely hands-off approach to regulating employers, as so many of these behaviors would have no economic benefit. Employees may not only be stripped of their dignity in a workplace that falls below a "hellish" level, but they may be suffering serious physical, psychological and emotional con-sequences. Further, in some cases, the judges themselves readily admit to this high standard. "Under Title VII, the standard for establishing that the offending behavior constituted sexual harassment is rather high."[23]

When the legal standard for a hostile environment is set so high, as one sees in these cases, it is hard to imagine that Title VII could ever really provide any type of protection for many victims of workplace bullying. While judicial interpretations of the hostile-environment standard seem to brush aside "minor incidents," it is important to understand that as researchers McCarthy and May-hew have concluded, "even seemingly minor behaviors can have significant negative effects when they occur frequently and over extended time periods."[24] Further, while judges seem to focus on only severe and direct actions, "research indicates that most hostile behavior at work is indirect, passive and verbal in nature."[25] In other words, judges, in deciding whether harassment is severe and/ or pervasive enough to rise to the level of an actionable claim, are often look-ing for behaviors that are much different from many of the types of workplace bullying that can be so damaging to the targets of these behaviors. Even if one is concerned only with discrimination in the workplace and not dignity, work-place incivility and low-level harassment may indeed be the "new" form of dis-crimination in today's workplace.[26] To eliminate these behaviors from coverage may render Title VII and other EEO laws useless in the battle against workplace harassment and bullying.

One research participant, Julie, shared a very interesting thought on the level of severity of her bullying. She related to me that she felt guilty in even complaining about the bullying behavior, due to what outsiders might think. In particular, she stated that her co-worker leaning over the conference table, pointing his finger and talking to her in a mean voice, might not seem like much or might seem "minor" to someone else looking in from the outside, but to her it is not minor. The same could probably be said for every one of the plaintiffs' complaints that were so easily minimized by these judges, in many cases in complete opposition to the determinations made by a jury of the plaintiffs' peers. The reality is that this standard (although not applied in all jurisdictions) creates a large gap in coverage for targets of workplace bullying.

Gap created by the required outcome of job effect

The gaps in the EEO laws as solutions to workplace bullying do not stop with this heightened standard. We also see gaps in terms of the harm that must be shown. In *Meritor Savings Bank v. Vinson*, the Supreme Court ruled that unwelcome sexual advances and other forms of hostile environments may create an abusive working environment and thus create actionable discrimination under Title VII of the Civil Rights Act.[27] While this same standard was applied by the Supreme Court in *Harris*,[28] both Justice O'Connor's majority opinion and Ginsburg's concurrence began to place more focus on the showing of additional work-related outcomes separate from the hostile environment itself. O'Connor explicitly pointed to the fact that an abusive environment may "detract from an employee's job performance, discourage employees from remaining on the job, or keep them from advancing in their careers."[29] Ginsburg concurred that

> [T]he adjudicator's inquiry should center, dominantly, on whether the discriminatory conduct has *unreasonably interfered* with the *plaintiff's work performance*. To show such interference, "the plaintiff need *not prove* that his or her tangible productivity has declined as a result of the harassment." It suffices to prove that a reasonable person subjected to the discriminatory conduct would find, as the plaintiff did, that the harassment so altered working conditions as to "make it more difficult to do the job."[30]

While the language of the Supreme Court could reasonably be interpreted to mean that the abusive environment created by the bullying or harassment alters the working conditions and thus fulfills the required showing of harm, other courts seem to place much more emphasis on the job performance language.

In *Hockman*, the Fifth Circuit's applied an extremely stringent requirement of showing not only a job effect but that the harassment "*destroy[s]* a protected class member's *opportunity to succeed* in the work" in order to survive summary judgment.[31] This language was cited again by the 5th Circuit in 2005 in *Williams v. the U.S. Dept. of the Navy* and in 2007 in *Jordan v. Memorial Hermann Southeast Hospital*, in both cases to support a summary judgment against a plaintiff. In total, the language from this one headnote from the *Hockman* case has been cited by courts over three dozen times.

This standard would eliminate a great deal of targets of workplace bullying from protections under the EEO laws. The reality is that targets of bullying are able to succeed. Many of targets overcome the obstacles put in place by their bullies in order to succeed. In my research, most of the targets who shared their experiences were extremely successful in their careers. Targets were successful teachers, researchers, managers, leaders, administrators, even soldiers. The fact that these targets mitigated the harm created by their bullies would actually eliminate them from potential protection according to the courts that follow this *Hockman* standard.

Further, the focus on job-related outcomes is misplaced. The effects of workplace bullying may be seen in the job. However, the effects are also seen outside of work. In a study by Mikkelson and Einarsen, 73.6% of targets reported bullying led to diminished relationships with friends and family and diminished leisure, household and sexual activities. However, unless these targets could also show a job effect, they most likely would not have a claim under the U.S. EEO laws.

For all of the participants in my research, the bullying did make their jobs tougher, thus meeting the standard as set out by the earliest Supreme Court decisions. However, the higher standards and the more direct job measures of later federal court decisions were not always met. Many of the research participants have been very successful in their positions, despite the bullying. Kelly managed her office for 10 years under these bullying conditions. When Jennifer left her employment due to the bullying, her supervisor called and pled with her to return to work. Katherine seemed to be pretty "Poky-Perfect" as she had the longest tenure of any employee at her restaurant. The university administrator and the faculty members all had received recognition and rewards at various times for their service to the university. If these employees were working in the 5th Circuit, even if they could show that the bullying was due to a protected status, their work success would defeat any chance for their claim to be successful. As discussed in Chapter 3 in this volume, the tangible outcomes of workplace bullying vary from target to target. This specific requirement that the opportunity to succeed be destroyed prevents many targets of workplace bullying from being protected at all and in fact, the more successful the target, the less their chance is to be protected.

Gap created by a heightened reporting requirement for targets

A final gap that I will explore in the EEO laws is created by the requirement for the plaintiff to show that he/she has taken specific steps to report the harassing behavior. In the *Faragher* and *Ellerth* rulings, the Supreme Court laid out a two-pronged employer affirmative defense for unlawful supervisory harassment that did not lead to a tangible adverse job effect.[32] Under this standard, an employer can defend against liability if they could show that "the employer exercised reasonable care to prevent and correct promptly any sexually harassing behavior, and that the plaintiff employee unreasonably failed to take advantage of any preventive or corrective opportunities provided by the employer or to avoid harm otherwise."[33] The SCOTUS and the EEOC both seem to be in agreement on a reasonableness standard for reporting. However, as is the case in the gaps discussed earlier, the interpretations of these standards by lower courts creates large gaps in coverage.

Many lower courts have interpreted this standard as placing a high burden on targets of workplace harassment to follow their employer's reporting guidelines. First, some courts have set out a strict standard that targets must follow their employer's reporting avenue. In the 11th Circuit, "it is incumbent upon the employees to utilize the procedural mechanisms established by the company specifically to address the problems and grievances."[34] In that case it was not enough that the target brought her concerns to a member of management. By failing to follow the specific reporting requirements, the court decided the target destroyed her right to a claim for workplace harassment.

A target of bullying is often reluctant to report the behavior at all and the reality is that they have very good reason not to report. The decision to report harassment and bullying in the workplace under the best of circumstances is a difficult decision. According to Dr. Bergman's testimony to the EEOC Select Task Force for the Study of Workplace Harassment, given the likelihood of rather severe negative consequences, versus the possibility of often very minor positive results, those who are reporting harassment to their employers are making the "unreasonable decision." Despite this, courts continue to place greater and greater reporting requirements on targets in order to preserve any rights to recovery.

For many targets, it may take time to build up the courage to report incidents. However, even when targets find the courage to report, even a seemingly short delay in reporting the harassment might be considered an unreasonable delay according to the standard of the 11th Circuit Court. In *Walton v. Johnson*, a delay of five days after the last behavior was enough for the court to dismiss the plaintiff's arguments that she had effectively notified her employer that she was harassed.[35]

Many targets justifiably fear that they might be fired if they report harassment. Despite recognizing the validity of this fear, courts have held that the plaintiff bears the burden of taking this risk.[36] While recognizing the intimidating nature of being harassed, the court still places the responsibility for bringing the harassment to an end back on the victim.

> Reporting sexually offensive conduct by a supervisor would for many or most employees be uncomfortable, scary or both. But because this will often or ordinarily be true, as the Supreme Court certainly knew, its regime necessarily requires the employee in normal circumstances to make this painful effort if the employee wants to impose vicarious liability on the employer and collect damages under Title VII.[37]

Workplace bullying can be traumatizing and paralyzing. Targets are often left with no idea of where to turn or what to do to address their situation. However, some courts have put a direct burden on the target of harassment to take steps to avoid the harm or end the harm.

> If the victim could have avoided harm, no liability should be found against the employer who had taken reasonable care, and if damages could reasonably have been mitigated no award against a liable employer should reward a plaintiff for what her own efforts could have avoided.[38]

For the research participants, Greg was bullied by being taken off committees when he brought up issues of concern about the finances of the university. This seems to have been an example of bullying to get the employee to "shut up." My own experiences as a target of workplace bullying were also clearly in response to lodging legitimate complaints to the leadership at this university. Jim, the former soldier, was denied privileges as a way to force him to stop lodging legitimate complaints. However, once again, it appears that a few judges isolated from the normal working environment have failed to consider the realities of bullying and harassment. These judges suggest targets will be able to freely complain about the attempts by bullies that may very well be targeted to silence their targets. Retaliation, and not any form of help, is the most common response that those who report receive from management.[39]

In my conversations with the targets of workplace bullying, the failure to report the bullying was a common theme: 13 out of the 16 research participants in my dissertation research suggested that at least in some of their experiences there was no reason to report the bullying because nothing would be done. In two of the situations, the bully was the owner of the business. In six of the situations, the target pointed to examples where other incidents had been reported to their employer and nothing had been done. One of the participants suggested that filing a grievance with her employer would be "career suicide." Fear of reprisal for reporting (either direct or indirect reprisal) was mentioned by 12 of the research participants. Several of the participants pointed to very specific past incidents that led to these conclusions. Two of the participants had reported incidents in the past and nothing positive came from these reports. Three others had suggested that they saw specific incidents reported by others and either the outcome was nothing, or the situation became worse after incidents were reported. Two faculty members suggested that their complaints on any subject often led to unfavorable committee assignments. Incidents also went unreported as targets felt they should not complain. One participant felt that she did not deserve to file a complaint. In fact, she claimed that she felt ashamed to be complaining at all, even during our conversations. She felt that perhaps this behavior was just part of work and that others were much worse off. Two participants felt that they should not complain about the sexually tinged discussions in a restaurant because that was just the way things were and the other employees did not mind. However, all of these targets felt that something should have been done about the bullying they endured. They all wanted to have some avenue of redress that they felt was otherwise unavailable. In addition to these research participants, Patrick, Sara and Susan all reported the harassment they endured to management and to their union leadership. In all three cases, management and the union made the situations worse and sent a message that the harassment would be supported or at least allowed. For Lindsey, reporting harassment to her HR department led to her being bullied by her HR manager and eventually forced out of work. At one employer, I worked with a female employee who had discovered that male co-workers had been spying on her while she showered in the company locker room. She discovered this by finding a Polaroid picture of herself at a male co-worker's work station. When she reported this to HR, the HR manager ended up sharing the picture with his buddies in management. As will be discussed later, reporting HR policies and HR practitioners rarely assist the target of bullying or harassment and they have the potential to create a great deal of harm for the target. Because of this, the reporting requirements under the *Faragher* ruling really put targets of harassment in a bind.

The standard set by at least some of the federal courts seems to ignore the reality of the difficulty targets will have in reporting harassment and bullying. Further, these standards ignore the reality that an employer may receive notice of harassing behavior in ways other than a report through a formal system. The fact that so many victims fail to report harassing behavior through employer systems should suggest to the courts that these systems have failed. These employer systems would seem to have unreasonably failed to detect and thus remedy the workplace harassment that exists and therefore are unreasonable and should fail the first prong of the *Faragher* defense. However, the fact that at least in the cases referred to earlier, judges have made the determination that the targets have failed to self-remedy this workplace harassment creates another gap between the U.S. law around workplace harassment and the necessary legal protections to address workplace bullying.

U.S. EEO laws are not an effective remedy for workplace bullying

Despite the fact that workplace bullying is often compared to or even equated with harassment or general harassment, the U.S. EEO laws that address unlawful forms of harassment are clearly an ineffective remedy for dealing with workplace bullying or general harassment. The very basic requirement of showing that the harassment is based on a protected status eliminates most incidents of workplace bullying (or general harassment) from protection. There are many other problems with these laws that make coverage for targets of bullying even lower. First, even if the bullying is based on a protected status, many courts apply a high standard for the target to prove this connection. For the targets who can show that the bullying is based on a protected status, the heightened standard of showing that the bullying conduct created a "hellish" environment in many jurisdictions to showing that the harassment completely destroyed any chance for the target to be successful on the job will eliminate remedies for many targets. Targets must often show that they are failing at work as a result of the bullying and that they were extremely clear about the behavior being unwanted. The targets are often expected to follow onerous or even ridiculous reporting requirements put in place by employers. Courts have given control to employers to require employees to jump through very specific hoops to report the behavior. These barriers leave very few of the millions of targets of workplace bullying and harassment with a remedy under the EEO laws.

Gaps in the U.S. common law

While the interpretation of workplace harassment under U.S. EEO laws does not provide an adequate remedy to workplace bullying, the protections under U.S. common law likewise offer little hope for the targets of workplace abuse. The tort most commonly associated with workplace bullying is the tort of intentional infliction of emotional distress (IIED) or outrage. A base review of this personal injury claim demonstrates that it is not an effective tool to address workplace bullying.

Intentional infliction of emotional distress

According to the Restatement of Torts 2nd § 46, "One who by extreme and outrageous conduct intentionally or recklessly causes severe emotional distress to another is subject to liability for such emotional distress, and if bodily harm to the other results from it, for such bodily harm."[40] A simple review of the elements in this definition of the claim of outrage, or intentional infliction of emotional distress (IIED) claims, indicates a clear gap in the abuse that is covered under this standard and the typical abuse of workplace bullying. Many types of devastating bullying and abusive work behaviors are not prohibited under this common law standard, and in fact only the most extreme and obvious cases of workplace bullying would be covered.

The first problem with this tort as a potential solution to workplace bullying is the high standard required for behavior to rise to the level of actionable behavior. This standard of "outrageous conduct" is even higher than the highest standards courts have applied in the instances of harassment discussed earlier. The WV Supreme Court in defining this standard, ruled that

> the first element of the cause of action is a showing by the plaintiff that the defendant's actions towards the plaintiff were atrocious, intolerable, and **so** *extreme and outrageous as to exceed the bounds of decency.* The defendant's conduct must be more than unreasonable, unkind or unfair; it must *truly offend community notions of acceptable conduct.*[41]

The Third Circuit Court of Appeals, a neighboring jurisdiction, suggested in *Cox v. Keystone Carbon Co.*: "[I]t is *extremely rare to find conduct in the employment context that will rise to the level of outrageousness* necessary to provide a basis for recovery for the tort of intentional infliction of emotional distress."[42] Clearly, this tort even by its first element is meant for conduct that is much rarer and harsher than the vast majority of workplace bullying incidents. In contrast to these shocking and outrageous acts, bullying in the workplace is not rare. What would be rare would be finding a successful claim of IIED by a target of workplace bullying.

As indicated by many of the research participants in this study, workplace bullying often takes the form of managerial decisions and employment practices. However, at least in the 9th Circuit, managerial practices would not ever rise to this required showing of extreme and outrageous conduct. Under California law, "[a] simple pleading of personnel management activity is insufficient to support a claim of *intentional infliction of emotional distress, even if improper motivation is alleged*."[43] The removal of the faculty members from committees, the failure to provide training opportunities, the seat checks, the dress codes, the performance review systems, the promotion policies and the monitoring of policies all would be personnel management activity and would thus not support a claim for IIED. Bullying in general, as discussed earlier, may itself be a management technique used to limit dissent.

The conduct a plaintiff must prove for an IIED claim is much more severe than the conduct required in a sexual harassment claim.[44] Given the fact that the standard in many unlawful harassment cases has gone well beyond the realm of behavior that violates the employee's right to dignity and thus fits within my definition of workplace bullying, the standard for IIED claims is even further astray and thus does not adequately protect the targets of workplace bullying.

Because bullying has become so common, it is conceivable that judges would never consider bullying to be "outrageous" or conduct that would "shock the conscience." As several of the research participants stated, the behavior they described as mistreatment or even bullying in the workplace, they also described as just being "part of work." In two cases, research participants working in the food industry simply accepted that even sexually harassing behavior was just "part of the job." They simply left one restaurant where the atmosphere was particularly hostile. They stated there was "nothing they could do" and that was "just the way things were" and it was "easier to just leave." In neither case were they shocked or outraged by the yelling in the kitchen or the sexual banter and harassment. In so many of the examples given by the research participants, their bullies seemed to use managerial practices. For the university professor, the "changing" of committee assignments could be viewed as a managerial decision; for the university administrator, much of the bullying could be interpreted as managerial decision-making style. Another university employee stated that, from the outside, her colleagues' finger-pointing and leaning over the table might not seem like much, but to her it was. Would someone from the outside look at this as meeting that standard of outrageous conduct?

Second, an IIED claim by its very definition requires a showing of intent. As I will discuss later, intent should not be an element of the definition of workplace bullying. Determining intent places an unfair burden on the target to prove what only the bully can ever truly know. Even the alternative requirement of showing recklessness focuses on the behavior rather than the outcomes of such behavior and would not address a great deal of the bullying that occurs in the workplace. Again, this is a very high standard. Many of the research participants mentioned they believed a negative intent on the part of their bully. For instance, the office manager stated the optometrist liked to be mean. Several of the participants from the university stated the university president intended to bully to force his agenda. However, rarely did they state that the employer or bully intended to harm them. The targets tended to assume there was an intent to intimidate or control. This seems very reasonable considering that the dictionary definition of bullying mentioned earlier does indeed include "to intimidate." For another, there seemed to be the intent to force them out of the workplace. Some did mention that "they wanted to humiliate me," or "make me feel bad," but never did the words "they wanted to cause severe emotional distress" cross the lips of any of the research participants. Further, nowhere in the written narratives did a research participant include as an element of their definition of workplace bullying the intent to cause severe emotional distress.

The third element of severe emotional distress also is likely to exclude even more targets of workplace bullying. Again, turning to the analysis of the law around workplace harassment discussed earlier, even where there is not a requirement to show any type of severe emotional distress, many courts have required plaintiffs to show an extremely high level of harm, thus leaving many targets of bullying uncompensated. While the effects of workplace bullying may indeed be devastating to the targets, these effects may not always rise to the level of severe, emotional distress and may seldom meet this requirement under the legal definitions of IIED. As can be seen under Davenport's analysis, bullying, if it persists, goes through an escalation of effect.[45] However, to sustain a claim under the tort of outrage or IIED, a plaintiff must show a third element of an IIED claim – severe emotional distress. In *Love v. Georgia Pacific Corporation*, the Supreme Court of West Virginia mentioned that emotional distress may not be enough to sustain a claim even when there is expert testimony and the plaintiff is receiving treatment.

The evidence offered by Appellant regarding the emotional stress that she suffered as a result of the retaliatory conduct of her former employer was minimal. Her treating physician, Dr. Thomas, testified that the symptoms with which Appellant presented to him "were not the symptoms of severe emotional distress" and that he prescribed for her "the lowest dose ... [he] could use" of an antidepressant. When questioned as to the dosage amount of the antidepressant, e.g. one tablet per day, Appellant was unable to recall the amount of medication she had taken.[46]

It is difficult to find one of my research participants, clients or any of the employees I worked with throughout my career who experienced the level of emotional distress that would meet this high standard. None of the research participants were seeing a therapist as a result of being bullied, and none were on anti-depressants as result, not even at the lowest dose. The university administrator talked about losing hair, and sleeplessness. Several talked about taking work home with them. One research participant said it stayed with her for a long time because she did not have someone at home to vent to, as her mother had been able to vent over dinner when she was growing up. One participant said he took a lot of anger home with him for a short time until he decided to fight back against his bully. One research participant related his experiences of being bullied in school to workplace bullying. For him, the bullying in school led him to be unsure of himself, lowered his esteem and made him timid. However, once he grew to well over six feet tall, he was able to turn the table on his school-place tormentors and stood up for himself. For a while, the bullying in his workplace made him feel like the little boy who had been bullied before his growth spurt. For the other research participants, nobody specifically pointed to any greater level of emotional distress. However, employees are morally entitled to more than a working environment that does not lead to a debilitating level of emotional distress. All of the research participants had some effect from the bullying behavior or the mistreatment at work. Most of the participants felt that the behaviors did not afford them their dignity and that the behaviors either impacted their own esteem or likely would have negatively affected the esteem of other employees who were less self-confident.

It is possible that many of the targets in my research were in the early stages of Davenport's progression and may have indeed suffered more intense emotional distress as time passed. These participants may have sought medical assistance at some point. However, other participants who had been exposed to their bullying for long periods of time often found solace in taking self-help steps. For instance, one university employee became active in two union movements, and also directly confronted his harasser. The optical office manager likewise confronted her bullying boss, as did the university administrator. Another university faculty member's coping mechanism was, in essence, to brush off the importance of work and spend as much time as possible at his own company. However, other participants did not really see a way to address their workplace bullying. Perhaps they were simply lucky enough to move on before they suffered from the severe emotional distress they would be required to show in order to gain any type of relief under an IIED claim. An employee should not have to endure what could be irreversible harm before these acts should be addressed. In order to have an actionable IIED claim, the target will have to suffer a severe level of distress. This is simply an unacceptable standard and expectation.

Finally, an additional problem with IIED complaints is the available remedy. Even if the target of bullying is able to show that such bullying is outrageous conduct, that the conduct was intentional or reckless and that it led to severe emotional distress, the employer may not be found vicariously liable for the actions. The goal is to eliminate bullying from the American workplace. However, the reality is that in order to deter workplace bullying, employers must experience consequences for allowing these behaviors to occur. Employers must play a role in eliminating and preventing these behaviors (whether they do so voluntarily or via a mandate). If the employer is able to avoid liability, they are not likely to take effective steps to prevent and eliminate these negative behaviors. When targets are harmed by workplace bullying, they should be, at the least, made whole. The typical legal remedy to effectuate a deterrent and to make a plaintiff whole is cash compensation. Unfortunately, even if the target has been able to show that the behavior in question "shocks the conscience," that the actor intended to cause harm or recklessly caused harm, and the harm was a severe level of emotional distress, they still may not be able to collect any form of compensation because employers will not be held liable for these acts. The employer may be only vicariously liable where the actions are done in the furtherance of the employer's interest[47] or, under a second standard, the employer will be liable only if the actions are done within the scope of their employment.[48] Further, in many circumstances, employers will be liable only under the state workers' compensation laws. In West Virginia, claims outside of workers' compensation for negligent infliction of emotional distress are barred by Code Section 23–2–6 of the West Virginia Worker's Compensation Act. Likewise, in California, most claims of emotional distress in the employment context are also barred by the exclusive remedy provision of the state workers' compensation act.[49]

Administrative remedies – another dead end

Workers' compensation indeed raises another possibility for coverage of workplace bullying – administrative remedies. Unfortunately, even a basic analysis shows that workers' compensation is an ineffective method of dealing with workplace bullying. First, even if the target of workplace bullying is successful in obtaining worker's compensation, the remedy is very limited. State workers' compensation laws also exist to deal with work-related injuries and illnesses. Even for successful claims, the nature of a worker's compensation claim makes this a rather ineffective remedy. Worker's compensation claims are most often limited to a portion of lost wages (2/3 is the most common standard).[50] According to Coleman, this is not enough to have any real deterrent or punitive effect for the bully or for the organization that allows the bullying to occur.[51]

Unemployment compensation is an equally inadequate remedy for targets of workplace bullying. First, even this limited remedy is often unavailable to the target of bullying who quits his/her job to avoid the bullying behavior. To receive unemployment compensation, the target must prove that the quitting was a constructive discharge. I have had several clients who have been in such a situation, and even with the very limited remedy of unemployment, proving a constructive discharge is not easy. In one case, a client felt compelled to quit because she was fearful of a physical attack by her supervisor. This client had been yelled and screamed at by her supervisor, who was 30 years her junior, more than a foot taller than she and more than twice her weight. His defense was that this was common practice in the restaurant industry, and the administrative law judge agreed. One of the research participants also addressed unemployment compensation. She stated that many employees would quit due to the owner's bullying behavior and would then file for unemployment compensation benefits. The employer, an optometrist, would contest every claim. In this employee's 10 years of service with the employer, the employer never lost an unemployment hearing. Even if the target wins this claim, the remedy is weak. The compensation is a partial replacement of one's wages and is limited to 26 weeks.

OSHA presents yet another potential remedy and many researchers have called for workplace bullying to be addressed under OSHA. We also see safety laws in Australia used at least in part to combat workplace bullying. However, the OSH Act as it stands today provides no real possible remedy for targets of workplace bullying. Under OSHA, the employer's duty is to guard against physical harm. While bullying may indeed lead to physical harm, by this point, the damage to a target may indeed be irreparable. Second, as pointed out by Harthill, it is extremely unlikely that OSHA inspections would lead to the uncovering of workplace bullying.[52] Treating bullying as a harm to workplace safety has merit. Targets clearly suffer harm. However, to address this under the OSH Act, there would need to be major amendments to the law. Even after these amendments, the law would not be an ideal solution.

Conclusion on legal remedies

There is little legal protection for the victims of workplace bullying in the United States. Even for the victim of bullying that is based on a protected status, cases such as *Hartsell* and *Baskerville* show that the alleged harassing behaviors will have to be quite severe to be actionable. For other targets, the situation is even less hopeful. While there are potential victories under IIED claims, this standard is extremely difficult to meet and clearly, taken as a whole, will do little to eliminate workplace bullying. In my time as a manager, attorney, researcher and advocate, I have seen dozens of targets of workplace bullying suffer with no meaningful legal recourse. I have seen many leave their careers, and/or jobs prematurely, take the bullying home with them and turn to medication or even self-medication. The damage is severe and the problem is extremely pervasive. In every case I have witnessed, the targets' human right to be treated with dignity was clearly violated. In fact, the right to be free from bullying in the workplace is indeed a human right. There is no excuse for workplace bullying. Even in an economic system singularly focused on profit, workplace bullying does not produce profit; instead it costs our economy billions of dollars in direct and indirect costs. Despite this, the U.S. legal system offers no meaningful hope. Further, as will be discussed later, there is little hope for bullying legislation in the near future at the state or federal level, and the legislation that is commonly proposed is watered down to meet the concerns of employers who seem to be suggesting that bullying should be at least available as a management tool. The reality is that we can do better. We can learn from the myriad of other countries who have done better, we can learn from our own mistakes, we can learn from the targets of bullying so that we can address this plague on the American workplace. These steps will be discussed in detail in Section 3.

Notes

1 (Cowan, 2011).
2 (Yamada, 2000).
3 (Lehman, 2000).
4 (Chow, 1999).
5 Sexual Harassment 29 C.F.R. § 1604.11 (1999).
6 From the EEOC web site *at* http://www.eeoc.gov/types/harassment.html. Harassment is unwelcome conduct that is based on race, color, sex, religion, national origin, disability and/or age. Harassment becomes unlawful where 1) enduring the offensive conduct becomes a condition of continued employment, or 2) the conduct is severe or pervasive enough to create a work environment that a reasonable person would consider intimidating, hostile or abusive. Anti-discrimination laws also prohibit harassment against individuals in retaliation for filing a discrimination charge, testifying or participating in any way in an investigation, proceeding or lawsuit under these laws; or opposing employment practices that they reasonably believe discriminate against individuals, in violation of these laws.

   Petty slights, annoyances and isolated incidents (unless extremely serious) will not rise to the level of illegality. To be unlawful, the conduct must create a work environment that would be intimidating, hostile or offensive to reasonable people.

7 (Namie & Namie, 2009).
8 (Harris v. Forklift, 1993, p. 25).
9 (Oncale v. Sundowner, 1998, p. 85).
10 (Riske v. King Soopers, 10th Cir. 2004, p. 1093).
11 (Riske v. King Soopers, 10th Cir. 2004, p. 1088).
12 (Linville v. Sears and Roebuck, 8th Cir. 2003).
13 The Age Discrimination in Employment Act only protects employees from discrimination based on an age status of 40+ years.
14 As cited by Coleman, B. (2004) in Coleman, B., 2004. Pragmatism's Insult: The Growing Interdisciplinary Challenge to American Harassment Jurisprudence. Emp. Rts. & Emp. Pol'y J., 8, p. 239.
15 (Ehrenreich, 1999, p. 2; 2004).
16 (Pedroza v. Cintas, 8th Cir. 2005); (McCown v. St. John's Health, 8th Cir. 2003).
17 This statement is perhaps most interesting in contrast to the facts of the *Price Waterhouse v. Hopkins* case 490 U.S. 228 (1998). In this case, the employer seemed to make the decision to turn down the plaintiff for a partnership based on her being aggressive. The employer allegedly made this decision based on the stereotype that women should not be aggressive, that this aggression was meant for men. I am not sure if this research participant was forced to work in male environment while meeting these same female stereotypes or whether she was expected to adopt male stereotypes in order to succeed.
18 *See* Hesse v. Avis Rental Car Systems, 344 F.3d 624, 630 (8th Cir. 2005): "The record shows, however, that Johnson's loud behavior was directed at both male and female employees. Hesse has acknowledged that everyone in the office was subjected to Johnson's deliberate shoe squeaking and that he clapped his hands loudly to get the attention of male garage technicians. Hesse relies on the incident in which Johnson banged on a window to get Sheila Sexauer's attention, but that incident does not establish that Johnson's conduct was based on sex since he engaged in similar behavior to get the attention of male employees"; and also *see* Holman v. State of Indiana, 24 F. Supp2d 909 (N.D. Ind. 1998) in which an employer who harassed both husband and wife could not have committed sexual harassment.
19 (Faragher v. Boca Raton, 1998, p. 788).
20 (Baskerville v. Culligan Int'l. Co., 7th Cir. 1995, p. 431).

21 (Hartsell v. Duplex Products, 4th Cir. 1997).
22 (Lenihan v. Boeing Co., S.D. Tex. 1998).
23 Singleton v. Department of Correctional Education; Commonwealth of Virginia, 115 Fed. Appx. 119 (4th Cir. 2004, 122). In this case, the 4th Circuit affirmed the district court's decision that the plaintiff had not met this high standard under the following circumstances – "[A]lmost immediately after she began employment . . . Shinault began sexually harassing her. The offending conduct . . . occurred approximately four times a week from July 2000 to October 2001." The conduct included Shinault telling the plaintiff's supervisor that he should spank plaintiff every day, Shinault staring at plaintiff's breasts whenever he spoke to her, measuring the length of her skirt for compliance with the prison dress code and then stating the skirt "looked real good," talking about what good shape Shinault himself was in for his age, Shinault asking the plaintiff if he made her nervous, being named her supervisor even though he worked under a different government agency and installing a security camera to watch her at her desk "for safety" reasons even though the only place she had contact with prisoners was in the library and there were no security cameras in that location.
24 (McCarthy & Mayhew, 2004, p. 83).
25 (Grubb, 2004, p. 410).
26 (Cortina, 2008).
27 (Meritor Savings Bank v. Vinson, 1986).
28 (Harris v. Forklift, 1993); (Harris v. Forklift. 510 U.S. 17 1993).
29 (Harris v. Forklift, 1993, p. 20).
30 (Harris v. Forklift, 1993, p. 25).
31 (Hockman v. Westward Communication, 5th Cir. 2004, p. 325).
32 (Faragher v. Boca Raton, 1998); (Burlington Industries, Inc. v. Ellerth, 1998).
33 (Faragher v. Boca Raton, 1998, p. 807).
34 (Madray v. Publix Supermarkets, Inc., 11th Cir. 2000, pp. 1298–1299).
35 (Walton v. Johnson and Johnson Services, Inc., 11th Cir. 2003, pp. 1289–1291).
36 (Baldwin v. Blue Cross/Blue Shield, 11th Cir. 2007).
37 (Reed v. MBNA Mktg. Sys., Inc., 1st Cir. 2003, p. 35).
38 (Walton v. Johnson and Johnson Services, Inc. 347 F.3d 1272, 11th Cir. 2003, p. 1290).
39 (Feldblum & Lipnic, 2016).
40 Restatement (Second) of Torts § 46 (1965).
41 Restatement (Second) of Torts § 46 (1965) 369, 375 (emphasis mine).
42 Cox v. Keystone Carbon Co., 861 F.2d 390 (3d. Cir. 1988, p. 395) (emphasis mine).
43 (248 Fed. Appx. 832, p. 835) (emphasis mine).
44 For a discussion of this *see Glover v. Oppleman* at 642: claims of intentional infliction for emotional distress have survived motions for summary judgment in sexual harassment cases. *See*, e.g. Speight v. Albano Cleaners, Inc., 21 F. Supp. 2d 560 (E.D.Va. 1998) (putting hand under employee's skirt and attempting to grab her buttocks, and separate attempt to grab her breast was sufficient outrageous conduct). However, all other precedents cited by the parties have involved denials of relief in these kinds of cases. Dwyer v. Smith, 867 F.2d 184, 194–195 (4th Cir. 1989) (sexual comments, accusations of sexual relations with employees and placing of pornography in plaintiff's mailbox not sufficiently outrageous); Paroline v. Unisys Corp., 879 F.2d 100, 112 (4th Cir. 1989) (supervisor's course of sexually suggestive remarks and touching, and one instance of groping in an automobile not sufficiently outrageous); aff'd in part, rev'd in non-relevant part, 900 F.2d 27 (4th Cir. 1990); Webb v. Baxter Healthcare Corp., 57 F.3d 1067 (4th Cir. 1995) (unpublished), opinion at 1995 U.S. App. LEXIS 14534, 1995 WL 352485 (4th Cir. 1995) (gender- and ethnic-based ridicule of a sale representative concerning the weakness and unfitness of women in the workplace, unfair criticism and defamation concerning dress, tardiness, behavior with clients and the plaintiff's sanity, as well as a comment that "You Jews are all alike" was not considered "utterly intolerable in a civilized society"); Burke v. AT&T

Technical Services Co., Inc., 55 F. Supp. 2d 432, 441 (E.D.Va. 1999) (stating that the "great majority of discrimination cases . . . will not meet this demanding standard").

45 See Chapter 1 of this volume.

46 (Love v. Georgia Pacific Corp, 2001).

47 (Liadis v. Sears, Roebuck & Co., 6th Cir. 2002).

48 This is the standard applied in West Virginia and has been interpreted rather broadly: "Generally, the course and scope of employment includes any conduct by an officer, agent or employee in the furtherance of the employer's business. We have generally accepted the proposition that an employer may be liable for the conduct of an employee, even if the specific conduct is unauthorized or contrary to express orders, so long as the employee is acting within his general authority and for the benefit of the employer. For example, in Nees v. Julian Goldman Stores, Inc., 106 W.Va. 502, 146 S.E. 61 (1928) . . . 'We stated that a master may not limit his liability to such of the conduct of his servant as is discreet and within the bounds of propriety, and avoid liability as to such conduct as is indiscreet and improper. Where a master sends forth an agent he is responsible for the acts of his agent within the apparent scope of his authority, though the agent oversteps the strict line of his duty.' Travis v. Alcon, 30–31."

49 (Shoemaker v. Myers, Cal. 1990). *See also* (Bracke v. County of L.A., 9th Cir. 2003) (summary judgment appropriate in emotional distress action where the parties were not plaintiff's employers and his exclusive remedy was the workers' compensation act).

50 (Walsh, 2007, p. 461).

51 (Coleman, 2004).

52 (Harthill, 2008).

6 Evidence from abroad

Steps can be taken to eliminate workplace bullying

The entire flight back from her friend's wedding, Maria could feel the pain in her stomach. Just thinking about returning to work made her feel sick. She wondered what her boss, Mark, would have in store for her tomorrow. He had been giving her a hard time since he was hired six months ago and Maria could not understand why. She was a hard worker, never missed a day of work and for the first time in two years of working, she had asked for a day off to attend her friend's wedding. On her way home from the airport, she decided to stop into the hotel to check her schedule. She was shocked to see posted on the schedule for all of her co-workers to see "Maria – SUSPENDED TWO WEEKS WITHOUT PAY." She felt humiliated and wanted to run out of the building but she was frozen, staring at the words. She could not help but think back to the kids who had bullied her on the playground when she was growing up.

While the laws in the United States clearly come up short in addressing workplace bullying and general harassment, this does not mean that the law cannot provide a path to solving workplace bullying. In fact, during my conversations with Maria, she informed me that she had legal training in her home country and could not understand how employers were able to get away with so much in the United States. Maria came from a Latin American country that did not have a specific anti-bullying law, but did provide workers much more say and protections in the workplace, including the presence of a just cause standard for discipline and termination. Maria's home country was far from an exception, instead it is the U.S. system that is the exception when it comes to protecting (or failing to protect) the rights of workers. A review and analysis of laws throughout the globe suggests that statutory laws as well as common law systems can indeed provide a path to preventing, detecting, eliminating and remedying workplace bullying. In countries such as the United Kingdom and Germany, workplace bullying is addressed either through the common law or through already existing statutes. Others countries, such as Sweden, France, Australia and Canada have taken much more direct steps to address workplace bullying. In Sweden, France and the Province of Quebec, specific anti-bullying statutes have been passed. Australia has turned to administrative and common law remedies or the application of related statutes to address workplace bullying. The steps taken internationally do indeed point to potential legal solutions to address workplace bullying and confirm that steps can be taken to prevent, detect, remedy and eliminate workplace bullying. The question becomes whether the political will exists to do so.

Sweden

Much of the initial research on workplace bullying was undertaken in Sweden, so it makes sense that Sweden would also be the first country to pass a law to protect targets of workplace bullying. In 1993, the Swedish National Board of Occupational Safety and Health adopted an Ordinance Concerning Victimisation at Work. The ordinance contains provisions and measures against victimization at work and a general recommendation on the implementation of the provisions. Like many of the laws I will review, the Swedish law does not focus on the term *bullying*. Instead, the law defines victimization as "recurrent and reprehensible or distinctly negative actions which are directed against individual employees in an offensive manner and can result in those employees being placed outside the workplace community."[1] The ordinance characterizes victimization as forms of behavior such as "adult bullying, mental violence, social rejection and harassment – including sexual harassment." The behaviors covered under the law are wide and varied and contain a number of different constructs that all tend to have the same impact on the targets of such behavior. Swedish employers are obligated to institute measures to prevent victimization and to act responsively if "signs of victimization become apparent, including providing prompt assistance to targets of abusive behavior."[2] Preventative measures are an important piece of this law.

The Swedish law is very comprehensive. The law addresses potential reasons for workplace bullying, with an emphasis on working conditions and what many in the United States might refer to as managerial practices:

> The background to victimization can, for example, be shortcomings in the organization of work, the internal information system or the direction of work, excessive or insufficient workload or level of demands, shortcomings of the employer's personnel policy or in the employer's attitude or response to the employees.
>
> Unsolved, persistent organizational problems cause powerful and negative mental strain in working groups. The group's stress tolerance diminishes and this can cause a "scapegoat mentality" and trigger acts of rejection against individual employees.[3]

It becomes clear that the law in Sweden focuses on the culture of organizations and holds employers responsible for the climate and culture of their workplaces. The Swedish law is very explicit in placing the burden on eliminating bullying with the employer. This responsibility includes not only addressing specific unwanted behaviors, but assuring that work is organized in such a way as to prevent the behaviors in the first place.

Section 2

The employer should plan and organize work so as to prevent victimization as far as possible.

Section 3

The employer shall make clear that victimization cannot be accepted in the activities.

Routines

Section 4

In the activities there shall be routines for the early detection of signs of, and the rectification of such unsatisfactory working conditions, problems of work organization or deficiencies of co-operation as can provide a basis for victimization.

Section 5

If signs of Victimization become apparent, counter-measures shall without delay be taken and followed up. In doing so, a special investigation shall be made to ascertain whether the causes of shortcomings of co-operation are to be found in the way in which work is organized.

Section 6

Employees who are subjected to victimization shall quickly be given help or support. The employer shall have special routines for this.[4]
The act, in addition to defining victimization, gives examples that include personal forms of bullying as well as organizational forms.

The following are some instances of victimization:
Slandering or maligning an employee and his/her family.
Deliberately withholding work-related information or supplying incorrect information of this kind.
Deliberately sabotaging or impeding the performance of work.
Obviously insulting ostracism, boycott or disregard of the employee.
Persecution in various forms, threats and the inspiration of fear, degradation, e.g. sexual harassment.
Deliberate insults, hypercritical or negative response or attitudes (ridicule, unfriendliness etc.).
Supervision of the employee without his/her knowledge and with harmful intent.

Offensive "administrative penal sanctions" which are suddenly directed against an individual employee without any objective cause, explanations or efforts at jointly solving any underlying problems. The sanctions may, for example, take the form of groundless withdrawal of an office or duties, unexplained transfers or overtime requirements, manifest obstruction in the processing of applications for training, leave of absence and suchlike.

Offensive administrative sanctions are, by definition, deliberately carried out in such a way that they can be taken as a profound personal insult or as an abusive power and are liable to cause high, prolonged stress or other abnormal and hazardous mental strains on the individual.[5]

Swedish law has gone much further to protect targets of bullying than any American law. First, the Swedish law is status-neutral. There is no concern with whether the bullying is based on a protected status. Instead, all forms of bullying, no matter the reason, are unlawful. Further, many of the actions prohibited under the Swedish ordinance would seem to be accepted managerial practices in the United States. Specifically, many of the systems of monitoring employees may fall under the provision of "supervision of the employee without his/her knowledge." It is becoming more and more common for American employers to use electronic monitoring of employee workstations, and self-managed work teams (SMWTs) may be utilized as examples of stealth monitoring of employees. The law also addresses many of the factors that have been found to lead to bullying in prior research and that have been identified as bullying in the narratives and interviews from research participants in this study. The Swedish law also places the burden on the employers to eliminate this hazard to employees in the workplace both by preventing the specific bullying behaviors, but also by assuring the workplace is organized in such a way as to prevent bullying. The employer is held accountable for their workplace climate – a theme that is common in many of the bullying laws and interpretations of these laws in the European Union.

However, Swedish law is not perfect. There are some problems in the language of this law in terms of defining workplace bullying. For example, in defining victimization, the law reads that the behavior must be "recurrent." There are many examples of behavior that may be bullying and may strip the target of his/her dignity that do not have to be recurrent. Even in the U.S. definition of unlawful harassment there is a weighing of the combination of severity and pervasiveness. While the Swedish law does cover isolated incidents, the fact that the recurrent requirement is used in the definition of the law is of concern and may lead to skepticism of single incidents. In a review of the Swedish law, Hoel and Einarsen found that the law did not go far enough in requiring preventative measures by employers.[6] They also pointed to problems with the lack of individual bully responsibility. However, the most important insight provided by this Swedish law is that workplace bullying can indeed be addressed through employment laws. Even if this law is flawed, it is a much stronger protection for targets of workplace bullying than anything in the U.S. legal system.

The majority of targets' experiences in my studies of workplace bullying would be covered by the Swedish law. The removal of the faculty members from the committees and the suspension of the hotel worker would seem to fit squarely under the excessive administrative sanctions. The CSA's (Kevin's bully) behavior would have been defined as excessive monitoring under the Swedish law. Many of the research participants' responses would fit under the intentional insulting behavior and the hypercritical or negative responses and the inspiration of fear prohibited under this act. Further, the targets of workplace bullying in my study as well as all potential targets would be protected by the requirement of a much more aggressive response by employers to eliminate and prevent workplace bullying.

France

France has also responded to workplace bullying through a statutory response. However, even before the passage of a specific statute, the concept of moral harassment has been mentioned in French court decisions since the 1960s.[7] In the late 1990s, French psychologist Hirgioyen published a book on "moral harassment," which helped to provide the terminology of the phenomena, which the French courts adopted.[8] The French labor movement also played an important role in establishing the French response to workplace bullying. In March 2000, employees at Eclatec went on strike to demand that the president of the board of directors leave. The employees of Eclatec had accused the president of moral harassment.[9] The combined forces of the French courts and the public awareness led to strong French legislation addressing bullying. On January 17, 2002, France's Social Modernization Law (*loi de modernisation sociale*) accomplished this task with the introduction of Articles L. 122–49 through L. 122–54 to the Labor Code and Article 222–33–2 to the Penal Code.[10] As a result, "moral harassment" is a violation of both the nation's labor and criminal codes. "The Labor Code now provides that no employee shall suffer repeated actions which have the purpose of causing a deterioration in working conditions by impairing the employee's rights and dignity, affecting employee's physical or mental health, or compromising the employee's professional future."[11] Offending parties can face fines and imprisonment under these codes.[12]

The implementation of the French law has clearly provided a path to protect many targets of workplace bullying. Unlike the American law of IIED, the French courts have found no need for malicious intent to be shown, and employers have been found to be strictly liable where such moral harassment occurs in their workplaces.[13] While the letter of the law again looks at the repetitive nature of the bullying acts, the clear emphasis in both the statute and the interpretation has been the protection of workers' positive rights to dignity in the workplace. Similarly, the language of the law does point to work outcomes as evidence of moral harassment, but the focus again has been on protecting the integrity of workers and there has not been a strict requirement of showing a work detriment as is seen in many cases interpreting U.S.

harassment law.[14] The French law also avoids the problems we see with the Faragher defense by requiring employers to take "all necessary steps" to prevent moral harassment.[15] The French law also defines moral harassment very clearly. Again, this law would most likely cover many of the actions described by the research participants.

The United Kingdom

The legal system in the United Kingdom addresses workplace bullying in a different manner than Sweden and France. Workplace bullying in the UK has been addressed through the common law and through collective bargaining. While the current remedies for bullying in the UK are common law responses and collective bargaining, the UK has also come close to adopting legislation to directly address workplace bullying.

Like the French labor unions, unions in the UK have also played an active role in pushing for a legal response to workplace bullying. UNISON, the largest union in the UK, has taken an active approach to dealing with workplace bullying by commissioning a number of studies on the issue.[16] MSF, another UK union, was instrumental in the push for the introduction of the "Dignity at Work Bill." This bill was not introduced, but did raise awareness of the problem of workplace bullying and is credited as leading employers to implement "dignity at work" and "anti-harassment" policies.[17]

In addition to the work done by labor unions, the UK is an example of how general unjust dismissal laws in a legal system can provide a remedy for targets of workplace bullying where the American doctrine of employment at will does not. According to Yamada, "there is a line of employment tribunal and court decisions" under the unjust dismissal provisions of the Employment Rights Act of 1996, "where employees have claimed that they were constructively dismissed at least in part by being subjected to severe bullying."[18] Yamada cites to two cases as evidence of the efficacy of this law. In *Ezekial v. The Court Service*, dismissal of an employee who engaged in bullying was found to be a fair dismissal.[19] In *Stone v. Lancaster Chamber of Commerce*, the plaintiff prevailed on a claim that she had been bullied out of her job and that this was thus an unjust dismissal. Constructive dismissal has been found in other, similar cases of bullying in the UK.[20] The unjust dismissal rulings protect targets of workplace bullying by affording employers the legal right to terminate an employee for bullying another and also by affording the target a claim for unjust dismissal if they are forced to quit as a result of their bully's behavior.

Employers may also be liable for the psychological injuries to targets of workplace bullying in the UK. In *Hatton v. Sutherland*, the court determined that employers are indeed liable for psychological injuries that occur at work under the same standard as any other injury.[21] In *Pakenham-Walsh v. Connell Residential and another*, Judge Geddes dismissed a claim for damages by an employee against her employer for psychological injuries. However, even in this case, the judge agreed that *Hatton v. Sutherland* was the applicable legal standard, but did not feel that the injury to the plaintiff in this case was reasonably foreseeable.[22] An employer would be liable for the outcomes of workplace bullying in a situation where such risk was found to be reasonably foreseeable.

Further, the UK's Protection from Harassment Act of 1997 provides yet another avenue of protection for the targets of workplace bullying. While this act was not initially passed to protect targets from workplace bullying, the language of the act suggests that harassment of any form, including workplace bullying, would be unlawful. Under this act, any person is prohibited from engaging in conduct that amounts to harassment of another.[23] In 2005, the law was successfully used to litigate a claim on behalf of an employee who had been bullied at work, and it was held that an employer could indeed be vicariously liable under this act.[24]

Harthill (2008) emphasizes that the UK legal system took a shift away from a negative rights focus on discrimination to a position of protecting worker dignity in order to address bullying or harassment in the workplace. This same type of shift would need to occur in the United States in order for our laws to effectively address workplace bullying. Much like the passage of the moral harassment law in France, this shift in the UK depended on involvement from the labor movement, in conjunction with advocates addressing the specific issue of harassment in the workplace.[25] This shift has also led to a large percentage of UK employers self-policing and adopting policies against bullying or generalized harassment.[26] The UK provides a clear lesson about how the United States could also forge such a change.

Common law rulings in the UK have proven to provide much greater protection to targets of workplace bullying than the laws in the United States. Other countries analyzed in this section aside from the United States also have similar unjust dismissal laws regarding termination of employment. So perhaps the interpretations by the British courts will provide direction for those countries that have not directly addressed workplace bullying under their termination of employment laws.

The protections for targets of workplace bullying in the UK, like those provided in Sweden and France, are much more effective than those in the United States. The legal response in the United Kingdom also presents an additional method to address workplace bullying. By providing protection from unjust dismissal, the UK legal system has provided targeted employees a potential remedy through a claim of constructive discharge. Such a claim would have provided protection to many of the research participants in my study who felt they needed to leave their jobs as a result of the bullying.

Canada

The employment law of Canada provides an example of combining statutory and common law to remedy workplace bullying. Employment law in Canada is mostly a provincial matter.[27] However, employment is not at-will in Canada. Rather, the common law of employment in Canada starts with the presumption, that absent just cause (which is interpreted restrictively in favor of employees), an employment contract can only be terminated upon reasonable notice or pay in lieu of reasonable notice.[28]

This provides the possibility that workplace bullying could be addressed as a form of constructive discharge and thus unjust dismissal. Much like the UK, the presumption of employment for term or cause in Canada makes constructive discharge a relevant tort in the battle against workplace bullying. In both *Shah v. Xerox Canada* and *Whitting v. Winnipeg River Brokenhead Community Futures Development Corp.*, plaintiff employees were successful in proving constructive dismissal based on workplace bullying.[29] Of course it is important to note that under this type of action, the prevailing plaintiff is then entitled to the same damages as for any type of unjust dismissal.[30] Canadian plaintiffs have also experienced some success in tort suits for intentional or negligent infliction of nervous shock and have directly recovered for the damages from bullying.[31]

Canadian discrimination law is also more expansive than U.S. law in that sexual orientation is a protected status in the laws in every province. Family status, marital status, criminal conviction and political belief are protected in the legislation in some provinces.[32] Therefore, more claims of bullying would be considered unlawful harassment under the Canadian laws.

The biggest difference between the Canadian and U.S. laws on workplace bullying exists in Quebec. In Quebec, the protection against workplace bullying goes beyond the common law. Quebec has adopted the first North American law banning workplace bullying. Under Section 81.19 of the Revised Statutes of Quebec, "Every employee has a right to a work environment free from psychological *harassment, and every employer* must take reasonable action to prevent psychological *harassment* and, whenever they become aware of such behaviour, to put a stop to it."[33] Under this statute, psychological harassment is defined as

> any vexatious behaviour in the form of repeated and hostile or unwanted conduct, verbal comments, actions or gestures that affects an employee's dignity or psychological or physical integrity and that results in a harmful work environment for the employee. A single serious incidence of such behaviour that has a lasting harmful effect on an employee may also constitute psychological *harassment*.[34]

While the language of the statute would seem to perhaps place too much emphasis on the repetitive nature of the bullying, in practice this does not seem to be the case. In fact, Cox's (2010) analysis of cases brought under the Quebec law demonstrates the importance of avoiding only addressing repetitive acts. Cox found that 13% of all psychological harassment decisions were based on a single incident and that these incidents had a 50% acceptance rate versus an overall acceptance rate of only 30% for claims under the law.[35]

For employees in the Province of Quebec who are covered by a collective bargaining agreement, this statute is automatically considered part of such agreement and would be addressed under the terms of the CBA. Other employees have the right to file a complaint with the Commission de la fonction publique within 90 days of the last event of psychological harassment. This commission will attempt to mediate the claim. If no agreement is reached through mediation, the case will then be referred to the Commission des relations du travail. At this stage, several remedies are available, including reinstatement, back pay and punitive and moral damages. Employers may also be ordered to take measures to assure that the workplace is free of psychological harassment.[36]

Clearly, the laws of Canada do much more to address workplace bullying than those of the United States. Even under the common law of Canada, an employee who is forced out of his/her employment due to bullying in the workplace would have a claim for unjust dismissal. For residents and workers in the Province of Quebec, the avenue for relief is even clearer. These employees are covered by a fairly comprehensive statute that directly addresses workplace bullying. Targets of workplace bullying in Quebec have avenues to redress bullying in front of the provinces labor commission, and plaintiffs are provided a labor attorney at this commission.

Both the common law tort of unjust dismissal and the Quebec statute on psychological harassment would provide a much better opportunity to remedy workplace bullying than any of the legal protections in the United States. Again, many of my research participants would have a potential claim for constructive discharge under the Canadian laws, as several have either already been forced out of their profession or are contemplating changing employers due to their bullying experiences. Further, while some of the experiences of the research participants may fall out of the bounds of this statute due to the requirement of repetitive nature or heightened severity of a single incident, the statute would at least provide all of the participants an opportunity to have their concerns addressed and would also provide an opportunity for the participants to approach their employers for relief. Again, while this law may not be perfect, it does suggest that workplace bullying can indeed at least partially be addressed through statute. The analysis by Cox demonstrates that a bullying statute does not necessarily mean there will be an overburdening of the judicial system. The Quebec statute is extremely well known, yet the courts have not been overburdened with claims. However, those who have been targeted have been afforded a legal remedy and employers have engaged in steps to prevent bullying in the workplace.

Belgium

Belgium also has passed a specific anti-bullying/general harassment law. Like other European laws, the focus of the enforcement of this law is on the protection of worker dignity. Like Quebec, we see that Belgian courts have not been overburdened with litigation. Instead, the law has led to employers addressing bullying and harassment in meaningful ways before damages occur. Not only are Belgian employers required to implement necessary measures to promote workers' well-being, but they also must have a prevention adviser on board. Employees are free to utilize internal measures or to turn to civil service tribunals to bring claims of workplace harassment. Like the rest of Europe, these wide protections are simply accepted as necessary to protect workers' human right to dignity in the workplace. They have been adopted as a common part of the workplace cultures across the continent. Again, targets are afforded legal remedies and employers as a result of these remedies take seriously their obligation to take all possible measures to prevent, detect, remedy and eliminate workplace bullying.

Australia

Australia is an example of how the common law and other non-bullying or general harassment statutes can help to address workplace bullying, but also the shortcomings of this approach. In South Australia, the OSHA law addresses workplace bullying.[37] In Queensland and Western Australia, provincial codes of conduct are often used to address workplace bullying or general harassment.[38] The government of Queensland has been active in investigating workplace bullying for well over a decade. In 2001, the Queensland government formed a task force to study workplace bullying. This task force recommended adding workplace harassment as an actionable claim under the Australian Industrial Relations Act. Further, Queensland's government has addressed workplace bullying under health and safety laws by issuing pamphlets explaining legal recourse for bullying victims, and the Supreme Court of Queensland found an employer liable for workplace bullying under common law and health and safety laws in 1998. Further, at least three court rulings suggest that workplace bullying is addressed under the Australian common law. There have been fines levied against employers under the OSH laws as well as the codes of conduct on safety and of course the common law tort awards. However, one thing that has become clear in Australia is that unlike the jurisdictions that have specific anti-harassment laws, the government can do very little to step in before damages occur. There is no requirement to prevent such actions or to have anti-bullying policies in the Australian workplace.

Other responses to workplace bullying

In Germany, the prohibition of workplace bullying has been found to fit into their general jurisprudence system.[39] This code again places an emphasis on dignity:

> [T]he German Federal Labor Court defines "mobbing" in conformity with section 3, paragraph (3) General Treatment Act that stipulates: Harassment

shall be deemed to be a form of discrimination, when unwanted conduct related to any of the grounds referred to in section 1 takes place with the purpose or effect of violating the dignity of a person and of creating an intimidating, hostile, degrading, humiliating or offensive environment.[40]

German law recognizes what is referred to as the right of personality – this is the right to live as a dignified human being in the way one chooses.[41] By protecting this right, the German law clearly provides a wider avenue for recourse for targets of workplace bullying than we see in the United States.

In Spain, a criminal case was heard in 2002 for humiliation at work, and debate has been ongoing to implement legislation prohibiting bullying or mobbing.[42] The Spanish Constitution also protects the right to dignity and, based on this right, the courts have applied protections from psychological harm in the workplace.[43]

While the application of U.S. laws might leave us with the feeling that addressing workplace bullying via legislation is a hopeless measure, the global laws paint a much different picture and present meaningful lessons about how we can address workplace bullying via the legal system. The first lesson is that the view of workers' rights must dramatically change in the United States. These international laws are successful in places where the right to dignity in the workplace is readily recognized. If we are ever really going to address workplace bullying, we must shift our focus to this positive right, the same way the focus shifted in the UK. This is a meaningful shift away from the narrow U.S. focus on discrimination. However, there is no reason that this shift cannot occur. As Harthill (2008) points out, the United Kingdom went through a very similar shift before they began to effectively address workplace bullying. However, this shift did indeed take a movement – a movement led through a partnership of specific anti-bullying advocates along with worker organizations – the labor movement. The UK was at a similar level of union density as the United States currently sees, yet the power of the labor movement was still meaningful and enough to help to push this movement for worker dignity. No such alliance exists in the United States and this will need to be the first step in achieving meaningful legislation.

The second lesson is that we do not need to be overly worried about overburdening the judicial system. In every case, the reader can see that there is no discussion of the great burden placed on employers or unbearable levels of litigation – arguments that opponents of workplace bullying legislation in the United States often use and arguments that are too readily accepted by advocates of bullying legislation. The focus remains on the target and there is no reason we cannot do the same. Protecting workers from bullying is not some onerous task for employers. There is no reason we cannot have legislation protecting workers' right to dignity, requiring employers to address bullying and general harassment without having the plethora of frivolous lawsuits opponents of such legislation suggest. In fact, we know from the experiences with workplace harassment in the United States that the vast majority of targets never file a complaint internally or externally.

A third lesson is to recognize the common features of these laws. The specific findings in Quebec, along with the language in other laws show the importance of allowing claims for single incidents. We also see the need for the protections to be broad, rather than limiting the acts that would be considered bullying or harassment. These laws also show that there is no need to include intent of the bully within the analysis and that requiring such a showing (as we see with the U.S. IIED tort) would be detrimental to the goal of protecting worker dignity. The fourth and most important lesson is that steps can indeed be taken to prevent, detect, remedy and eliminate workplace bullying and to protect workers' right to dignity. There is much to learn from these international laws addressing workplace bullying and in the final chapter of this volume I will return to these lessons.

Notes

1 (Davenport, et al., 2002, p. 26).
2 (Yamada, 2004, p. 512).
3 Ordinance of the Swedish National Board of Occupational Safety and Health containing provisions against Victimisation at work AFS 1993, p. 17.
4 Ordinance of the Swedish National Board of Occupational Safety and Health containing provisions against Victimisation at work AFS 1993, p. 17.
5 Ordinance of the Swedish National Board of Occupational Safety and Health containing provisions against Victimisation at work AFS 1993, p. 17.
6 (Hoel & Einarsen, 2010).
7 (Guerrero, 2004).
8 (Guerrero, 2004, p. 488).
9 (Guerrero, 2004, pp. 490–491).
10 (Guerrero, 2004, p. 492).
11 (Yamada, 2004, p. 512).
12 (Yamada, 2004).
13 (Lerouge, 2010).
14 (Lerouge, 2010).
15 (Lerouge, 2010).
16 (Sheehan, et al., 1999).
17 (Sheehan, et al., 1999).
18 (Yamada, 2004, p. 513).
19 (Yamada, 2004).
20 (Yamada, 2004).
21 (Hatton v. Sutherland, Court of Appeal Civil Division, Feb. 2002).
22 (Pakenham-Walsh v. Connell Residential (Private unlimited company) and another, Court of Appeal – Civil Division, 21 Feb. 2006).
23 UK Protection from Harassment Act of 1997 [21 March 1997]. Protection from Harassment Act 1997, Ch. 40, s. 1 (Eng.). Available at http://www.legislation.gov.uk/ukpga/1997/40/contents
24 (Majrowski v. Guy's and St Thomas's NHS Trust, House of Lords, 12 July 2006); (Dyer, 2005).
25 (Harthill, 2008).

26 (Harthill, 2008).
27 (Parkes, 2004, p. 428).
28 (Parkes, 2004).
29 (Parkes, 2004, p. 430).
30 (Parkes, 2004).
31 (Parkes, 2004).
32 (Parkes, 2004, p. 429).
33 Revised Statutes of Quebec Section 81.19. (Emphasis mine).
34 Revised Statutes of Quebec Section 81.19. (Emphasis mine).
35 (Cox, 2010).
36 (Cox, 2010).
37 (Squelch & Guthrie, 2010).
38 (Squelch & Guthrie, 2010).
39 (Fischinger, 2010).
40 (Fischinger, 2010, p. 155).
41 (Fischinger, 2010).
42 (Coleman, 2004, p. 262).
43 (Velazquez, 2010).

Section 3

Ending workplace bullying

It is highly unlikely that we will ever be able to eliminate all workplace bullying, harassment or general harassment from the global workplace. However, from a national standpoint, it is clear there is much more that can be done to prevent, detect, remedy and eliminate workplace bullying. There are indeed paths to solving workplace bullying. Employers could conceivably take it on themselves to eliminate bullying from their workplaces. However, they would have to truly adopt meaningful anti-bullying policies. I will discuss why this is unlikely on a large scale in Chapter 9. There are also some partial solutions including creative plaintiff's attorneys, concerted activity and bystander and even target responses. However, these will not entirely solve the problems for targets and will leave many targets with no protection. Any true solution to workplace bullying must address all of the precipitating factors – societal, organizational and individual. To have this type of reach, any true solution must come at the public policy level. As we have seen in countries such as Sweden, the United Kingdom, Belgium, France, Canada and Australia, public policy, statutes and common law and court interpretation of statutes play a critical role in providing targets avenues of recovery as well as providing the incentive to employers to prevent and quickly remedy workplace bullying and harassment. These public policies are also the only route to provide employee advocates such as attorneys and union reps the tools to effectively protect targets of harassing behaviors in the workplace.

In the final section of this book, I will discuss the steps needed to fully address workplace bullying, to eliminate all forms of harassment from the American workplace. This process will start with defining the phenomena we are dealing with in a comprehensive manner to assure that we are providing paths to protect the dignity of all workers. This definition will be developed in Chapter 7. There are many parties that can play a role to partially address this issue under our current circumstances. There are steps that employee advocates can take to help to address workplace bullying. There are steps that can be taken by bystanders, there are steps that employers can take and there are steps that unions can take. These currently available measures will be discussed in Chapters 8, 9 and 10 respectively, as will the shortcomings of these measures. In order to prevent workplace bullying, employers, advocates, targets and union leaders will all need to play a critical role. However, they each respectively must be provided with the incentive and the tools to address workplace bullying. This incentive and tool will come through public policy. It is also only through this shift in public policy that we can truly provide targets a remedy to protect their dignity and to make them whole. In Chapter 11, I will discuss the path forward to achieve this meaningful public policy change as well as describe the elements of a statute to effectively eliminate workplace bullying and generalized harassment in the American workplace.

7 Defining the problem

A transformative definition of workplace bullying

Julie thought back to how excited she was when she first joined the staff of the university. She had so many projects she wanted to work on and loved the fact that the staff in her department had weekly meetings to discuss ideas. She could not believe that just a year later she dreaded those meetings more than anything. She knew she would be ignored, just as she was each morning as she arrived to work and each afternoon as she left. Her ideas would either be ridiculed or stolen by her colleagues and she was sure her boss and her male colleagues would lean over her and berate her at least once each meeting. Still she could not help thinking that this was her fault. Maybe she was just a whiner, maybe she brought this behavior on, and perhaps she should just grin and bear it. After all, she had the job she had spent the last six years of her academic career working towards, she was living where she wanted to and she was making more money than she expected. Who was she to complain when so many others struggled just to put food on the table?

Workplace bullying is an epidemic in the American workplace and really throughout the globe. The reality is that bullying is a part of the current system of workplace relations. Perhaps because bullying is so common, targets like Julie have begun to accept the behaviors as part of the workplace. To end such a system, we must develop a transformative definition. Before we can ever truly, effectively address workplace bullying we must have a clear, consistent, complete definition of the phenomenon. We have not adequately defined workplace bullying in the research, nor in the majority of bills that have been proposed in the United States to address workplace bullying. Instead, much of the attention of the research on workplace bullying and related (if not the same) phenomena focuses on defining and tweaking definitions of the phenomenon. Much of this research seems to start from a blank slate and ignores research in other areas. When we look at legislative proposals, rather than addressing targets' experiences, the proposals seem to focus on what would be acceptable for employers and defense counsel. We must break free from both of these boundaries.

Further, the concept of developing a legal definition of bullying around employer concerns ignores the vast research and jurisprudence on workplace harassment and in essence sets any bill that has been passed for failure. In order to define workplace bullying, we should not ignore the research dealing with the same types of behaviors. Instead we should look to combine and build from these definitions. We also cannot ignore targets, but instead should focus our definitions around targets experiences – ensuring that we capture all of the potential behaviors that can violate their human rights. In the United States, we should also look at both our own systems of jurisprudence in related areas such as harassment and intentional infliction of emotional distress and develop our definitions around the successes of these actions and to overcome the gaps in these actions. Finally, we should also take lessons from the international laws and actions that have directly and effectively addressed workplace bullying.

While the pervasiveness of bullying is shocking based on the studies of bullying, the reality is that we are still undercounting this pervasiveness. This undercount occurs because of definitions of workplace bullying that are simply too restrictive. The bullying definitions used in the self-report method and much of the workplace bullying research clearly lead to an underreporting, but elements of these definitions are also often built into the operational method with acts often only considered bullying if they have occurred over a period of time, or there have been multiple acts of bullying. Further, the proposed legal definition of workplace bullying is often adopted from this research and, as a result, creates the same potential problems of underreporting and under coverage. Even more, these definitions would memorialize into law many of the problems that have been addressed in the area of workplace harassment law as well as leaving many of the same gaps that we currently see in this jurisprudence today.

The current definitions (or at least elements of these definitions) of workplace bullying and other related constructs – incivility, abusive supervision, workplace aggression – provide a starting point for our analysis. As Herchcovis has explained, ignoring the commonalities of different constructs (bullying, harassment, incivility) to develop a single definition of this phenomenon is a barrier to furthering the research and solving the problem.[1] Raver and Nishii find that, despite the variety of labels given to a generalized form of bullying, they all have very similar constructs and impacts.[2] As a result, they use a broader and inclusive term of general harassment.

In order to effectively define workplace bullying, we can no longer afford to ignore various constructs and should do away with the myth that we are working from a blank slate which has never been explored. To define workplace bullying in a transformative, meaningful, complete and effective way, I propose that we look to various sources to guide our way. First, we can indeed use the current definition of workplace bullying and proposed workplace bullying legislation in the United States as a starting point. While there is no clearly agreed-upon definition of workplace bullying (much less a collective definition of related constructs), there are consistent or at least common elements of these definitions that can be explored and analyzed. We should look at the related constructs and the lessons from each. The goal of workplace bullying research and proposed legislation is to protect worker dignity. It would make little sense to ignore other constructs that have been shown to negatively impact or violate this basic human right. Second, from a legal standpoint we must look to the experiences in U.S. law on the related behaviors of harassment and intentional infliction of emotional distress. We must look at both the areas that have led to successful elimination of unwanted behaviors and protections of dignity as well as the gaps in these current laws. We do not want to repeat the same mistakes we see in the way we address harassment in the workplace under EEO laws or tort litigation. We should also look to the international laws to explore the lessons of what works and what is problematic. The United States clearly lags behind other countries in addressing workplace bullying. The benefit of this lagging position is we can learn from the mistakes and successes in other countries, but only if we actually engage in such an analysis. We should also look to the experiences of targets to assure the definition is inclusive and addresses the potential harm to workers' human rights. The exact definition and parameters of workplace bullying has proven to be elusive. Part of this elusiveness is due to the creativity and the diversity of the workplace bully or aggressor. We should take steps to assure we are not overlooking behaviors and leaving the door open for further abuse.

The focus on the experiences of targets is perhaps the most crucial part of this analysis. The purpose of this definition is to truly transform the American workplace. To transform the way we look at the working relationship and to assure the right of dignity for all workers. This definition will need to take a positive rights approach – focusing on the types of rights employees should be guaranteed in the workplace, rather than the traditional negative rights approach to statutory development in the United States. These rights include not just legal rights, but the positive human rights that exist both inside and outside of the workplace. The idea behind this definition and the subsequent models to prevent, detect, remedy and eliminate workplace bullying is to prevent the harm that targets (as well as their family, friends, organizations and communities) suffer. The definition must be broad enough to include the various acts and behaviors that harm these human rights, such as the rights to dignity, esteem and self-worth. The definition must allow us to address bullying in such a way as to protect the specifically enumerated human rights under the UDHR and other human rights documents as well as other broadly recognized human rights. The definition of workplace bullying must assure the foundations of human rights for workers, the right to dignity, whether the actions are discriminatory or not, whether they impact the targets' abilities to work or not. The definition must assure these rights for all workers and provide relief and avenues of recourse for all targets of workplace bullying.

To come to such a definition, I have analyzed the common elements of workplace bullying under a four-part analysis:

1   Analysis from lessons from U.S. harassment and IIED jurisprudence
2   Analysis from lessons from international workplace bullying and related laws

3   Analysis from related constructs in the workplace aggressions research
4   Analysis from the experiences of targets

Current definitions of workplace bullying

When looking at the workplace bullying literature, we continue to see a lack of agreement over the definition of workplace bullying. This disagreement is a great hindrance to our ability to prevent, detect, remedy and eliminate workplace bullying. While Randall explains that an "agreed definition of bullying do[es] not exist,"[3] Farrington suggests that "there is widespread agreement that bullying includes several key elements: physical, verbal or psychological attack or intimidation that is intended to cause fear, distress or harm to the victim; an imbalance of power . . . absence of provocation . . . repeated incidents."[4] The most commonly cited proposed anti-bullying law in the United States is the Healthy Workplace Bill. While there are various iterations of this proposed bill, the current bill as proposed in Massachusetts refers to the problems created by workplace bullying but does not defined the term. Instead, the bill defines "abusive conduct" as:

> Acts, omissions or both, that a reasonable person would find abusive based on the severity, nature and frequency of the conduct, including, but is not limited to: repeated verbal abuse such as the use of derogatory remarks, insults or epithets, verbal, non-verbal, or physical conduct of a threatening, intimidating, or humiliating nature, or the sabotage of undermining of an employee's work performance. . . . A single act normally shall not constitute abusive conduct, but an especially severe and egregious act may meet this standard.[5]

However, it is not necessarily abusive conduct employees are protected from under the bill, it is an abusive work environment, which is defined as:

> An employment condition when an employer or one of its employees, acting with intent to cause pain or distress to an employee, subjects that employee to abusive conduct that causes physical harm, psychological harm, or both.[6]

While these elements from the various definitions are not necessarily agreed upon, they do provide a starting place for analyzing and developing a definition for workplace bullying. For each of these elements – repeated incidents, intent, the level of behavior (i.e. severity and pervasiveness), the type of harm and power differential – I have conducted the four-part analysis mentioned earlier. As will be demonstrated, many of these elements are problematic and if we were to include these elements in a definition of workplace bullying, the definition would fail to adequately address the problem.

Analyzing the elements of current definitions and exploring the content of research participants' experiences

Repeated incidents versus one incident

Many researchers of workplace bullying focus only on repeated, recurring acts in determining whether actions constitute workplace bullying. This is perhaps the biggest error in the debate on defining bullying. Randall states that "[t]he main similarity between the definitions [of bullying] is the implication that bullying is likely to be repeated or systemic."[7] According to Einarsen, "bullying is not normally about a single and isolated event."[8] Both the Quebec law prohibiting psychological harassment at work and the Swedish Victimisation at Work Ordinance include repetitive nature as part of the definition of prohibited acts. Proposed bills in the United States that model the Healthy Workplace Act also include a requirement of repetition.

The use of *repetitive* or *repeated* in the definition of workplace bullying, even when coupled with an aside that bullying may be a single event, has the potential to create a large gap in coverage. Workers' human rights can be violated by a single incident, a series of behaviors, a pattern of behavior or a pattern of escalating behavior. While the pervasiveness of the incidents may indeed make them more likely to damage the target's psyche, morale and dignity, making a determination as to whether the incidents have been systemic or even repeated will not be relevant to the human–rights–based definition of workplace bullying.

When we look at the U.S. laws around similar constructs to workplace bullying, we see that there is an absence of a requirement that actions be repetitive. Under the U.S. harassment jurisprudence, there is a balancing of severity and pervasiveness. The focus is on how harmful the behavior is rather than the number of times a behavior has occurred. The Code of Federal Regulations defining harassment makes no mention of the conduct needing to be repetitive. This is particularly important because even where repetition is not an element of the claim, we know that the harassment laws leave gaps due to the heightened requirement of severity as discussed in Chapter 5 in this volume. Adding a requirement of repetitiveness would simply widen this gap.

Even in the tort of outrage or intentional infliction of emotional distress discussed at the end of Chapter 5 in this volume, there is no requirement of repetitiveness. The fact that a behavior is committed time after time might make it more outrageous and more damaging, but this does not mean that a single incident could not also be damaging.

The laws in Quebec and Sweden leave the door open for single incidents. Further, Cox points out that 13% of the claims of psychological harassment under the Quebec law in its first 10 years stemmed from a single incident and of these, 50% were accepted.[9] Not only were the single incident claims common, but they also had a higher success rate than repetitive incidents. The

French law on moral harassment has been implemented with a focus on protecting the dignity of the worker and placing the burden of such protection on the employer, without concern as to whether the dignity was harmed by a single incident or multiple or repetitive incidents.[10] Common law rulings in the UK likewise focus on the harm rather than the number of incidents.[11]

As Herschovis points out, workplace bullying often differs from other constructs of abusive behaviors in the workplace based on the repetitive nature or "frequent and persistent" nature of workplace bullying.[12] However, other than to differentiate bullying as a social, research based construct there seems to be little reason for this differentiation. As Herschovis and Raver and Nishii conclude, this limited construct of bullying has the same impact on targets of other constructs including unlawful and general harassment and social undermining which do not have repetitiveness as part of the construct.[13]

When I asked research respondents to define workplace bullying in a written narrative format, the definitions referred to repetitive acts as well as single incidents. One written narrative participant labeled bullying as "any attempt," another as "any incident." However, other respondents were more focused on the repetitive nature of bullying – "persistent, offensive . . . behavior," "if this is done continuously." So while it seems clear that bullying may be repetitive in many instances, even a single isolated act may indeed constitute bullying and should not be eliminated from inclusion within the definition of workplace bullying. Perhaps an appropriate stance is to balance the element of pervasiveness with the severity of the action as we see in the EEO laws in the United States. In other words, what may seem like a fairly benign action if done continuously may indeed become bullying (low severity, high pervasiveness), while on the other hand a very serious event, even if it occurred only once, can be equally as damaging (high severity, low pervasiveness).

While the majority of targets I have spoken with and interviewed shared ongoing patterns of workplace abuse in their stories, there were also clear indications that many of the incidents they experienced, when taken alone, had an impact on their dignity, were humiliating, or caused damage to their self-esteem, belongingness, or growth – these single incidents were examples of workplace bullying. For instance, consider the vignette from the beginning of Chapter 6. When Maria came back to see the note left in the employee room for all of her co-workers to see, she felt humiliated. Many of her co-workers told her that they would never have returned to work if that had happened to them. She described this incident as part of a pattern of "mistreatment" directed toward her by the assistant manager. There was no need for the incident to be repeated in order for this to have been perceived as bullying; clearly, this single incident was enough to create a hostile working environment for Maria.

For Vanessa, a mid-level manager at a university, a single encounter with a co-worker/manager from another department was enough to amount to workplace bullying. In this case, Vanessa asked to borrow a file from the assistant in this other department. The manager/bully overheard this and proceeded to "flip out," yelling at this individual. She continued to walk out of the department with the file, yelling at her target as she walked. She continued past co-workers, customers, and the general public, all the while yelling at this other individual. This research participant said she had never felt so angry and humiliated – stating that not even a schoolyard bully had ever made her feel that way. Again, this single incident was severe enough to rise to the level of workplace bullying from this target's perception.

Another research participant, Greg, an associate dean in a university, shared an experience of being forced to work on accreditation requirements for a small college. He tried to explain to the assistant provost that he needed more information to complete the work. His concerns were simply brushed aside by the college administration, and he was told to do the work. While these types of unreasonable expectations and the refusal to listen to the employees of this organization seemed to have become standard operating procedure at this institution according to this target, this single act was enough that Greg considered it to be workplace bullying. He stated that it made him feel like he was not respected.

Of course, this is not to suggest that workplace bullying may never be a repetitive or ongoing phenomenon. In fact, for Maria, Vanessa and Greg, their bullying experiences continued and became a pattern. However, each one of these experiences alone stripped these individuals of their dignity and their esteem and violated their human rights in the workplace. There should be no need for them to show that there was additional bullying behavior in order to be able to show that they had been targets of workplace bullying.

In a university setting, I witnessed numerous single incidents that were clearly examples of workplace bullying of faculty members at both senior and junior levels. When Greg was removed from the budget committee for raising legitimate concerns, this had a serious impact on his well-being. When speaking with Greg, he indicated that the action was demeaning and left him frustrated and considering early retirement. The same President who removed Greg from the budget committee also threatened the entire faculty senate with a lawsuit as they were undertaking their legislative responsibility to evaluate the university President. The president threatened that if the evaluation was negative he would sue the faculty. While most faculty members I spoke with about this incident told me that that they understood how hollow this threat was, others indicated that they felt extremely threatened and intimidated. Finally, in another incident at this same university, the President used his power to disband a committee to bully the members. This committee was tasked with developing an evaluation system for faculty members. The committee hired an outside consultant and utilized internal experts. The committee external expert and internal experts all disagreed with the administration and President's wishes for the evaluation system. As a result, the President completely disbanded the committee. I spoke with a junior non-tenured faculty member about this committee, and it was clear the experience had been demeaning to her and that she felt intimidated and was now fearful about her chances to be awarded tenure. She expressed that she could not believe that simply doing the right thing could, in the end, cost her tenure. This single event caused her a great deal of distress, led to her being extremely nervous about joining other committees and led to at least a partial loss of self-esteem.

While this university President was clearly a serial bully, and perhaps those who knew of these various incidents would identify these as a pattern, for each target, these events were singular events that clearly violated their rights to dignity, esteem and voice in the workplace. Workplace bullying can indeed occur as a single event in addition to ongoing patterns of events, and both forms of bullying have devastating effects for the targets and their organizations. For Maria, many of her co-workers felt this one incident of bullying in the workplace was so severe that they would have left the job. Likewise, Vanessa described the outburst over the file as one of the most shocking experiences of her life and her career. The committee members and faculty Senators who were attacked by the university President all discussed their desire to look for an exit from the university, even if it meant leaving academia or retiring early.

While incidents of workplace bullying may be repetitive and ongoing, others may occur only once or last for a brief time. Both the ongoing and the one-time events may have serious effects on the targets. Both may indeed violate an employee's rights to voice, participation, esteem and dignity in the workplace. It is important that any definition of workplace bullying accommodates both repetitive events as well as single events. Second, these single events do not necessarily have to take on a dramatic form to amount to workplace bullying. The misuse of power, the misuse of policy or the ignoring of employee concerns may be enough to amount to workplace bullying. While the determination of whether workplace bullying has occurred, even from the subjective perspective of the target, will most likely be influenced by the repetitive nature of the event or events and the severity of such events, to require that the events be repetitive to be defined as bullying would be too limiting to truly protect worker dignity and would leave too many targets of bullying with no recourse. The focus must be on the outcome of the actions – (both intended and actual) – and whether the target's rights have been violated.

Ignoring bullying because it has only occurred in a single event can also be devastating to both the target and the employer. I have witnessed employers and union leaders ignore single incidents, brushing them aside as not enough to constitute bullying or harassment in the workplace. When an employer brushes aside a report of bullying, the target is not likely to come back to report continued incidents, and the bullying is likely to continue. The target is left with the belief that the employer does not want to address the issue and the bully is left with the belief that his/her behavior is acceptable. The EEOC has long recognized a reasonable belief that a process is ineffective as a reason that employees would not bring claims forward.[14] Having one's claim ignored would indeed lead to such a perception of ineffectiveness.

In my work with targets, they have all been very unlikely to go back to their employer or even to their union if their initial complaint was brushed aside. A unionized faculty member, Sara, was clear that she would never report anything to her union leaders again when they decided to ignore her initial complaint to them. In fact, she cut ties with the union, stopped participating in union activities and eventually left the university all together when the behaviors continued. Before leaving, she suffered emotionally, psychologically and even physically. Likewise, another faculty member, Sally, at this same university had a similar experience with the union and ended up becoming ill and taking leave because the behavior continued. At one of my employers, the prior HR team had ignored one-off incidents from a supervisor to the point where his one-off behaviors had risen the level of a potential strike issue when I was hired as the HR Manager. For the target of workplace bullying who feels he/she has no avenue to report his/her suffering (and unfortunately rightly so), the bullying can be devastating, leading to emotional, psychological and physical suffering, leaving their employment (as it did for the majority of my research participants and clients) and, even worse, death due to illness and even suicide. Unfortunately, a definition of workplace bullying that focuses on the requirement (even if it provides exceptions) of repetitive behaviors provides the support for these types of outcomes. There is no place for a requirement or suggestion of the need for actions to be repetitive or ongoing to rise to the level of workplace bullying.

Type of attack/severity of the attack

A second issue with defining bullying is setting the standard for how severe an action must be before it rises to the level of bullying. In many studies, the definition used to define bullying sets a fairly restrictive requirement for severity of the conduct. For instance, Tracy and colleagues exclude from the definition of bullying low-grade incivility.[15] However, if this low-grade incivility has the effect of violating employee rights to dignity at work, then this low-grade incivility should also fit within the definition of workplace bullying.

The Supreme Court has directly addressed the level of behavior needed to rise to unlawful harassment. In the *Faragher* case, the Court confirmed that harassment must be "objectively and subjectively offensive that a reasonable person would find to be hostile or abusive" and that the "ordinary tribulations of the workplace" would not be considered harassment. The Court made it clear that Title VII would not create a "civility code" in the workplace. Of course, the Court did not really explain why workers should not expect a certain level of civility. The language from the Court as discussed in Chapter 5 of this volume has allowed lower courts wide discretion and led to many setting a standard of only behaviors that create a "hellish" environment as rising to the level of unlawful behavior. This standard is nearly as bad as the standard for IIED in the American system of jurisprudence – of behavior that "shocks the conscience." The reality is that the American system of coverage of unlawful harassment and intentional infliction of emotional distress leaves us with strong lessons about not setting the bar too high for behaviors that should be covered. As concluded in Chapter 5 of this volume, the standards for both unlawful harassment and IIED clearly leave dignity damaging behaviors unaddressed.

Many of the international laws provide much broader coverage in terms of the behaviors that could be considered bullying. The Swedish law includes organizational practices, personnel policies and even workload issues as potentially bullying behaviors and practices. The Swedish law puts much more focus on the harm to the target than it does on limiting the types of behaviors.[16] Similarly, the French law on Moral Harassment also leaves the door open for a wide array of behaviors being covered and, like the Swedish system, focuses on the potential harm to the target's dignity.[17] As Harthill points out, in the UK, the focus on the positive right of workers to dignity rather than a negative rights approach of making specific behaviors unlawful has been a critical component to effectively addressing workplace bullying.[18]

As Lilia M. Cortina suggests, workplace incivility leads to lower job satisfaction, lower creativity, greater stress and even higher levels of substance use. In this case, workplace incivility is described as "low intensity deviant behavior with ambiguous intent to harm the target, in violation of workplace norms for mutual respect. Uncivil behaviors are characteristically rude and discourteous, displaying a lack of regard for others."[19] This low-grade incivility clearly is injurious to the targets and seems to have no legitimate place at work.

While researchers such as Tracy and the current position of the U.S. Supreme Court is to eliminate incivility from definitions of bullying and harassment respectively, there is no indication from either Tracy or the SCOTUS that these behaviors are acceptable and if they are acceptable what makes them acceptable. In fact, there seems to be a realization that these behaviors are wrong, but they do not cross some imaginary line of unacceptability as to fit into these definitions. Further, as demonstrated by Hershcovis, incivility has a similarly damaging impact to targets to the traditional definitions of workplace bullying, abusive supervision and other forms of workplace aggression.[20]

By making a bright line that low-grade incivility is not bullying, a determination must be made on a case-by-case basis of what behavior crosses the line into bullying. The idea that eliminating low-grade incivility from coverage might protect employers, will instead actually create more confusion and frustration. Workplace incivility can indeed strip targets of their dignity and violate targets' human rights, so it makes no sense to have a seemingly bright-line (if we know where that line lies) exception for workplace incivility from coverage in the definition of workplace bullying. Rather than focusing on these behaviors, a definition of bullying should be built around the outcomes – those that harm the rights of the targets.

The example of low-grade incivility perhaps gives us our best example of why we do not want to be quick to eliminate any specific behaviors from the definition of workplace bullying. If we turn to schoolyard bullying to help us to define bullying, we see that what would perhaps fit into the definition of low-grade incivility – "low intensity deviant behaviors with ambiguous intent to harm the target, in violation of workplace norms for mutual respect"[21] – can indeed also fit into any reasonable definition of bullying. According to Rachel Simmons, due to societal and cultural reasons, "girls use backbiting, exclusion, rumors, name-calling, and manipulation to inflict psychological pain," rather than the prototypical schoolyard style of bullying of boys.[22] These behaviors by girls would be more likely to fit under incivility than the typical definition of bullying. However, according to Simmons this typical "incivility" many girls suffer at the hands of their "friends" from school has lifelong negative effects at work and home for the targets, including a lack of confidence, anxiety, and a fear of messing up. These same types of "chronic, low-key stressors can 'wear down' an individual, both psychologically and physically" whether they take place at home, at school or at work.[23] Further, Cortina hypothesizes that workplace incivility may indeed be a new form of covert discrimination in the workplace.[24] If incivility can be used as a form of discrimination, it most assuredly can be a form of inappropriate behavior that strips the target of his/her esteem, dignity, voice or other human rights.

Returning to Vanessa, the university administrator, in addition to her run-in with the manager of a different department, she told me that her colleagues ignored her and left her out of training sessions as the pattern of bullying emerged in her workplace. Her co-workers behaved in the same way as the school bullies described by Rachel Simmons, and their behavior would seem to fit Cortina's definition of low-grade incivility. However, these behaviors still had a huge impact on Vanessa's self-esteem and dignity. She explained that she had begun to feel "worthless and small." She explained that she found herself in a constant bad mood both inside and outside of work. Vanessa later stated that she never got over this until she finally made the move to leave her employer.

Another target of bullying, Katherine, worked as a waitress at a local restaurant while going to school full-time. At this place of employment, the waitress was required to be what the owner defined as "Poky-Perfect." This meant her hair, her attire, her jewelry, her shoes, and her make-up all had to live up to the owner's expectation. If she was not found to be "Poky-Perfect" on any given day, whether at the beginning, middle, or end of her shift, her boss might ignore her or compliment others, intentionally leaving her out of any recognition. This individual indicated that she felt degraded, belittled and insulted by the owner's behavior.

For a university faculty member, the failure to recognize work that he had accomplished, and the failure to show appreciation when he had been forced to do additional work beyond the scope of his duties, was a definite source of unhappiness at work that eventually led to an early retirement. A professional staff member, Julie, at same the university described how continued incivility, such as her supervisor ignoring the staff member's attempts to say good morning or good-bye, led to a hostile environment. While other actions also contributed to the bullying working environment, this incivility from the participant's supervisor was enough to make her working life miserable and to affect her at work and even at home. Both of these targets left their employer specifically to get away from the bullying, bullying that would fit within the definition of low-grade incivility.

While all of these examples may indeed be defined as incivility at work, and an outsider might hesitate to include these as workplace bullying, the reality is the effects of these behaviors can be very severe, and my focus is again on the outcomes of the behaviors. While these behaviors may sound minor by being called incivility or low grade, these behaviors are unnecessary and have no place at work. There really is no excuse to eliminate these behaviors from the definition of workplace bullying. These types of behaviors have the potential to violate targets human right to dignity in the workplace and the targets I have described experienced such harm.

Much like the requirement of repetitiveness, the exclusion of workplace incivility can lead to devastating outcomes for the target, the organization and society. Several research participants I interviewed expressed feelings of lost esteem and even depression over pervasive acts of low-grade incivility. Many of these research participants left their organizations by quitting their jobs and even retiring early. However, one of the most disturbing experiences I handled with bullying that could be considered low-grade incivility dealt with a client who was constantly berated by small, degrading or disrespectful acts first from her manager, then co-workers and then even individuals that she was in charge of training. This low-grade mobbing incivility became so bad that she began to become paranoid, began experiencing nervous tics and got to the point where she was completely unable to work and was forced to leave her job. Adding insult to injury, her employer denied her unemployment (luckily, she was awarded her UE benefits at an administrative hearing). Low-grade incivility has led to even more disastrous outcomes for other targets and has even led to a number of different fields of research on related topics including the emerging research on microaggressions.

While low-grade incivility should not be excluded from the definition of workplace bullying, there is an argument to balance the severity of an act against its pervasiveness. In my discussions with research participants, none of them pointed to any single low-grade incident as bullying. Instead, the participants perceived these behaviors as rising to the level of bullying as they became persistent. For Julie, her supervisor engaged in a pattern of ignoring her greetings each morning and her attempts to say good evening to the point that this research participant decided to no longer attempt to be polite. Vanessa's co-workers did not simply exclude her once; this was a pattern and perhaps even escalating pattern of behavior. The restaurant owner's derisive remarks towards Katherine and other wait staff occurred on a daily basis and were part of a regular pattern of abuse. In these cases, the pattern and persistence of these behaviors led to an insulting and degrading working environment. Further, employees are simply unlikely to report a single act of incivility to their union rep or to HR. Reporting claims of harassment and bullying take a great deal of courage. We know that the vast majority of reports of even unlawful workplace bullying (harassment in the United States) go unreported. We do not have any type of macro level issues of overreporting. Instead, the behaviors must rise to a certain level of unacceptability for the target to overcome his/her hesitance to report. This simply is very unlikely to happen with a single incident of incivility.

However, as we balance this severity with pervasiveness, we must be careful not to confuse pervasiveness with strict repetitiveness. While the bullying and incivility experienced was pervasive in these examples, it is important to note that the behaviors themselves did not always take the same form. For instance, Vanessa's co-workers would ignore her on one day, exclude her from training the next and give her the least-preferred work assignment the next. These were still patterns of abuse, but the specific behavior was not repeated, and this might mask the pervasiveness of the abuse. Even as the need for severity is balanced with the level of pervasiveness, it is important to assure that the target is not required to show that the same acts are repeated. Based on these examples, it is clear that while bullying may indeed include a pattern of abuse, bullies may use a number of different behaviors within this pattern.

Level and type of harm

We also must consider what type of harm targets would need to show in order for behaviors to be considered bullying. In many cases, workplace bullying researchers and advocates are simply too quick to require a heightened standard of harm to targets. The Healthy Workplace Bill requires a showing of some level of physical, psychological or economic harm. This requirement goes beyond even the requirement of harm under the U.S. EEO laws. As discussed in Chapter 5 of this volume, the Supreme Court of the United States was clear in their Ruling in the *Harris v. Forklift* case that a plaintiff did not need to show psychological or physical harm in order to prove unlawful harassment. Instead, the Court focused on the potential harm to the target's ability to work, but even here the Court was clear (as mentioned in Chapter 5 of this volume) that the plaintiff would merely need to show that the behaviors in question made it more difficult to do the job.[25] However, as discussed in Chapter 5 of this volume, even this focus on job outcomes is problematic as many targets of bullying endure and continue to be successful in their jobs in spite of their bully. As demonstrated in Chapter 3 of this volume, bullying leads to a variety of harms. These harms will vary from one target to the next. Many targets will indeed suffer psychological and even physical harm. However, others may not. Some targets of workplace bullying may suffer adverse job effects, others may not.

When we look at laws throughout the globe, the focus is clearly on a broader type of harm – the harm to the target's dignity. The right to dignity in the workplace and the steps to eliminate behaviors that violate this dignity have been the focus of the laws in France, Sweden, Quebec, Belgium, the UK and really in every jurisdiction where workplace bullying has been effectively addressed. This harm to dignity would include the types of psychological and physical harm described in the Healthy Workplace Bill, but it would also include harms that would seem to fall outside of these – harm to one's esteem, belongingness or other human needs and rights would be included in a harm to dignity.

In my conversations with targets of workplace bullying, the harms they experienced were many and varied, and many if not most would have fallen outside of the requirements of showing psychological or physical harm that courts may require if the language of the Healthy Workplace Bill were to be adopted. Most of the targets I have had the chance to interview have continued to be successful at their jobs. For instance, Sara was a prolific publisher and received numerous teaching awards even while being subjected to bullying; Greg likewise was winning teaching awards and had been promoted to assistant dean. It would be hard for most of the targets I spoke with to show psychological or physical damages. Except for a few, none were seeing a counselor or taking medications as a result of being bullied. However, as mentioned in Chapter 2 of this volume, they all still suffered adverse effects as a result of the unacceptable behaviors of their bullies. For some like Vanessa, there was clear damage to their self-esteem, for others like Kevin, the bullying led to increased stress. In all cases, the target's right to dignity in the workplace had been infringed.

Necessity of intent

Whether or not intent of the perpetrator should be a required element in defining bullying is a hotly debated issue. As Einarsen has stated, it is usually impossible to "verify the presence of intent."[26] The difficulty in determining the existence of intent may be one reason why, according to Randall, "many behavioral psychologists are . . . opposed to the infusion of intent in definitions of this sort."[27] From a legal standpoint, while intent is not an explicit element of the definition of unlawful harassment, we see the problems caused when targets are forced to prove that harassers' behaviors were "based on" a protected status. Even worse, we see the problems targets of IIED have with being able to show intent. The French Court of Cassation recognizes this problem with intent in the French moral harassment law, and in essence has a strong presumption of intent by both the perpetrator and the organization when bullying has occurred.[28] This is a much different standard than what is applied in the American legal system and any U.S. law addressing bullying must be careful not to include intent.

If preserving employees' dignity is a concern, then whether an action was intended to threaten, coerce, etc. is not nearly as relevant as the outcome of the behavior. Perhaps a better place for the discussion of intent would be in the remedy phase. For instance, if a perpetrator of an act had no intent to commit an act, then it may not make sense to hold him/her responsible in the same way as if he/she intended the act or intended the resultant harm. While punishing the bully who truly acted in an unintentional manner may do no good, one still wants to make sure the action has stopped. As will be discussed later, any effective employer system to eliminate workplace bullying will have an investigation stage and a remedial stage. At the investigation stage, the focus should be on whether harm was or could have been caused. However, at the remedial stage, intent will be an important factor in determining the correct remedy to stop the bullying. Further, the innocent victim who has suffered some loss should be compensated accordingly.

Kelly, an optometrist's office manager, who was bullied by the optometrist in her office, described her boss as just being mean. The optometrist would come into the office in the morning and sometimes huff and puff and slam doors. She would be belligerent to her employees, and they would often try to hide from her. The office manager clearly stated that this was an example of workplace bullying. However, at least in part, she credited this to a lack of managerial skills that "exists with all optometrists." While there may have been some intent to harm involved, the office manager stated that all optometrists lack the people side of management, but she still considered it bullying, the actual intent or specific intent did not matter.

Katherine, the "Poky-Perfect" waitress, and Jennifer, a food service worker at a rest home, both happened to share the same former employer and both experienced a sexually harassing environment while working at this restaurant for a very short time. In this case, the environment was hostile enough that both quit, but in both cases, they stated that this sexually hostile environment was just the way "the industry was." Neither of these research participants thought there was an intent to create a hostile environment, yet the environment in essence controlled these two separate workers to the extent of forcing them to quit. In this case, even though the targets themselves did not feel there was bullying, these inappropriate, unnecessary behaviors forced them to leave their employment.

For other targets of bullying, the bully's intent may not be so clear and may not come into focus until the target is close to leaving the organization. For Vanessa, the intent of her bullies dawned on her as a method to hold her down, to make her feel she was not worthy and thus could go nowhere else. She described the intent as retention by "making you feel worthless." She stated that the bullying made her feel as if no other employer would possibly want to hire her. However, this was not immediately apparent to her and, in fact, she stated that the bullying had lowered her self-esteem to the point that she began to think she had no value as an employee. These effects occurred well before Vanessa had any conception of her tormentors' intent. It was not until she spoke with a friend who asked her to do some consulting work that she realized that the culture of bullying was meant to destroy her esteem.

Some targets of workplace bullying do mention intent as an element. However, the reality is that many targets are unable to identify the intent of the bully. Intent might be assumed, but proving intent can be impossible. Even in the public berating of Vanessa described earlier, the bullying department manager ended up denying the events even occurred, much less that she intended to bully her co-worker. In these types of circumstances, just proving that the behavior occurred may be a big enough hurdle for the target; to then prove intent might very well be impossible. Intent should not be a factor in defining bullying, but may be a mitigating or aggravating circumstance in finding that bullying occurred and in remedying the bullying.

Power differential

Einarsen et al. conclude that conflict that is between two parties of close to equal value cannot be considered bullying.[29] While it makes sense that two individuals with a true equality of power are engaging in conflict rather than bullying, care must be taken to not define power too narrowly. There are many different sources of power. For instance, in organizational leadership studies, it is common to define sources of power as either personal or position power. As far back as 1959, French and Raven defined different bases of power ranging from reward, coercive and legitimate power to referent and expert power.[30] Position power, or the power from one's rank, is easily identified, and according to various studies, a differential in position power does exist in the majority of workplace bullying incidents. However, bullies can indeed have equal or even less position power than their targets. Less formal sources of power such as personal power also must be recognized within this element of power. Simply being able to take away another person's dignity is an example of the use of power. Einarsen and colleagues also note that this power source need not be a formal source of power.[31] In order to capture all of the different incidents of workplace bullying, if power is a piece of the definition of bullying, the term "power" will have to be used in a very broad manner. Focusing only on the conflicts that take place between supervisors and subordinates or looking to supervisor/managerial behaviors will not eliminate all forms of workplace bullying.

In many cases of bullying I studied, the bully was indeed in a formal position of power higher than that of his/her target. In some cases, the bully was the owner of the organization. This formal power position did create many obstacles in the minds of the targets. For instance, when asked if there was a way to remedy the workplace bullying, one target stated, "No, it was her [the bully's] business so she could do whatever she wanted." The manager of the optometrist's office stated that the owner/operator of a vision store was the bully, and thus had the right to do whatever the bully chose. Jim, a member of the U.S. armed services, experienced bullying from a commanding officer in the military and felt that due to the chain of command in the military, there was not much he could do other than to come up with ways to convince the bully to change his behavior. Greg, the university faculty member had been bullied by his dean and the associate provost. Another faculty member at the same university, Robert, had been bullied by past and present university presidents. Sara and Patrick, faculty members at a different university, were both bullied by their dean. Further, most of the clients who have passed through my office or have simply asked my advice have indeed described their bully as their supervisor or boss. Bullying from those in formal power positions was a very common theme of the research participants and in each instance created a perception by the targets that the bullying was accepted by the organization and there was no internal recourse.

However, I have also studied numerous incidents where formal power was irrelevant to the bullying. For instance, Jennifer, the rest home kitchen worker mentioned earlier, was bullied by another worker from a different department in a very similar position to her own. However, this other worker was much older and more experienced than the target of her actions. The bully also relied on what she perceived to be a physical power difference and threatened physical harm to this research participant. In the workplace, some may not consider the potential for use of physical power over another, but instead would limit their definition of power to the typical formal supervisory type of power that provides the ability to make decisions that would directly impact tangible working conditions of the target. The threats by this co-worker violated Jennifer's rights at work. By all measures, this co-worker did not have any type of additional formal power at work, but relied on physical intimidation as her source of power.

Again returning to Vanessa's experiences, she was targeted by a peer as well as individuals who ranked lower than her in terms of formal power. In addition to being publicly berated by the manager of the other department, Vanessa became the target of an administrative assistant in her own department. This bully took deceitful steps to make this Vanessa's life difficult. She would often tell visitors that Vanessa was not in her office when she was indeed in her office (and later state that she thought Vanessa had left). She would also go as far as stealing memos from Vanessa's desk, and engaged other members of the department to ostracize Vanessa and to engage in mobbing types of behaviors. This target relied on information power as well as collective or relationship power to bully Vanessa. Despite the lack of positional or formal power, Vanessa stated that this bullying was perhaps even more harmful to her esteem and more than the bullying manager made her want to leave her job.

Robert, a faculty member mentioned earlier, told me that he had been bullied by younger junior faculty. These faculty members, with the support of the administration, told senior, experienced faculty how to teach and how to develop their courses. This would happen at faculty-wide meetings with junior faculty first sharing ideas, then would trickle down to department meetings with junior faculty setting the direction for course development during meetings, and for senior faculty who did not comply they would eventually have one-on-one meetings with these junior faculty, the purpose of which was to bring the senior faculty into compliance. The senior faculty members' experiences were not considered, and they were not afforded the opportunity to express their concerns at any time during this process. At this same university, a former dean, Susan, told me that she felt a faculty member who reported directly to her had been allowed to bully her. She stated that the administration's lack of support for her decisions had led to and even supported this bullying by this faculty member. A senior faculty member at another university, Sally shared being ostracized by her colleagues, many of whom were junior colleagues, and how these same colleagues were able to use a departmental post-tenure review process to continue to bully her. Sara, a tenured faculty member at this same university, stated that her colleagues' bullying – or perhaps mobbing – led her to leaving a tenured position for a less secure job.

Finally, Kevin, an intern at a financial services company sought me out because he knew I was conducting interviews of targets of workplace bullying. He told me he felt obligated because his experiences were such prototypical examples of bullying. He explained that the customer service associate (CSA) in his office was bullying him as well as bullying all of the financial advisors. Interestingly, in the formal structure of the office, the CSA really reported to the financial advisors and at one point had even attempted to move up to be a financial advisor. However, this research participant suggested the CSA was able to bully for two reasons. First, she was the only CSA in the office, so the financial advisors were very dependent upon her services. Second, the industry was highly regulated and the financial advisors operated in a constant fear of violating a regulation. The CSA often used threats that an auditor could be coming any day to keep the financial advisors in line. Again, this is an example of a use of power outside of the formal hierarchy of an organization that was still a very effective enabler for this workplace bully. In fact, she was so effective at bullying that this intern decided that financial services would not be a part of his future career.

The element of power should be a piece of the definition of workplace bullying; but power must be carefully defined. I am not suggesting that the majority or even a large portion of workplace bullying occurs by individuals with equal levels of formal power. However, my interest is not just in eliminating the majority of workplace bullying, it is my goal to develop a model to eliminate all forms of workplace bullying. There are many different forms of bullying and bullies will use any source of power they can find. In my experiences, bullies used information power, position power, relationship power and even physical power to torment their targets. Bullying does occur from those in formal positions of power; however, bullying also occurs from bullies who rely on informal sources of power. All bullying should be eliminated, not just the supervisory-level workplace bullying.

The potential problems with "unwanted"

The EEOC defines unlawful harassment as "unwelcome conduct that is based on race, color, sex, religion, national origin, disability, and/or age." The Supreme Court in Meritor also made it clear that unwantedness is a key to defining unlawful harassment.[32] While it is clear that it would make little sense to make unlawful conduct that the target of such conduct has requested, the element of "unwelcomeness" in a definition of workplace bullying raises some issues for concern.

First, it is important to recognize that behaviors that may be welcome, wanted and even chosen by some targets may indeed be "unwelcome" bullying conduct for others. Second, it is important to be careful in how a determination is made as to whether behavior is unwanted. In one case, the Western District Court of Arkansas found that behaviors were not unwanted because the plaintiff so easily testified about them.[33] In *Kouri v. Liberian Services, Inc.* the Eastern

District Court of Virginia found that the behaviors were not unwanted because the target was not clear enough in her complaints to the harassing supervisor.[34] In *Gibson v. Potter*, the 5th Circuit suggests that because a target of potential sexual harassment laughed off the comments these may not have really been unwanted.[35] So if targets were too comfortable with reporting harassment, the behaviors were found to be wanted, but if they were too slow to report the behaviors were also found to be wanted. These types of decisions put targets in the awkward position of finding just the right balance between being too confident in reporting and too timid in reporting, creating a ridiculously unfair burden, the type of burden that should be avoided on the front end in defining workplace bullying.

What is clear is that targets of bullying will react in different ways. Targets may turn their anger inward in many ways. Many victims of workplace bullying simply do not report the incidents. As Kleiman has pointed out, even in the cases of sexual harassment, the majority of incidents go unreported.[36] These different reactions should not be used to determine if the behaviors were unwanted.

Targets may not report the bullying behavior for a number of reasons. For instance, as mentioned earlier, two targets in the restaurant industry both claimed that the bullying they experienced was just a natural part of the restaurant business. Other targets I interviewed did not report because they felt they were being weak, and others did not report due to a lack of confidence in the available remedial measures. Some targets mentioned "laughing off the bullying" and even engaging with their bully in hopes of limiting the impact. However, in no way did these targets ever indicate the bullying was not unwanted. However, it is conceivable that courts like those aforementioned could find these actions to be evidence that the bullying was not unwanted. The evidence shows that how a target reacts to workplace bullying is not a sound basis for determining whether the workplace bullying was unwanted.

While it is clear that actions that are wanted should not be considered unlawful bullying, it is important to be careful about how "unwanted" is determined. If the target says the action was unwanted (at any point), then it is unwanted. A defendant could present a defense that the behavior was wanted, but by putting the burden on the plaintiff to prove the negative of "unwantedness" in the case of unlawful harassment, the courts have shown the risks of this requirement. There are still many other pieces of the definition and potential defenses to liability available to the bully and the employer; a jury attempting to get into the mind of a target to determine whether or not they "really did want" the bullying is not a proper avenue. In every case, the research participants said the conduct was unwanted. However, from the outside looking in, it would have been conceivable in many circumstances to believe the behaviors were not truly unwanted.

Only attacks that are unwanted can fit into the definition of workplace bullying. However, it is imperative that the definition not be interpreted to require some heightened showing of "unwantedness" as many courts have required in proving unlawful harassment. There would need to be some type of statement within or explaining the definition of workplace bullying that different targets will react to workplace bullying in different ways and that a target's reaction is not necessarily indicative of whether the behavior is wanted.

Summary of the exploration of the agreed-upon elements

When looking at the majority of agreed-upon elements in the definitions of workplace bullying, many of these elements are problematic. The specific intent required under the proposed healthy workplace bill is not found in any of the international laws addressing workplace bullying. This intent has been shown to create an artificial barrier to recovery for plaintiffs in the United States pursuing IIED claims. The requirement of showing the bully's intent should also not be a part of the definition of workplace bullying. Intent is too difficult to determine to be a required element. There are many instances of targets of bullying having been stripped of their esteem or dignity at work, where they are unable to prove any intent on the part of the bully. These actions should also be prevented in the workplace. However, perhaps showing intent could be one of the optional ways to prove that bullying has occurred. For instance, to again borrow language from the workplace harassment laws, perhaps workplace bullying has the intent or effect of stripping employees of their human right to dignity in the workplace.

The focus on repeated incidents also creates an unnecessary barrier. We see that in the application of international laws single incidents have been common forms of workplace bullying. Research participants and targets of workplace bullying have also shown the repetitive requirement to be unnecessary to rise to workplace bullying. While bullying has traditionally been thought of as an escalating and ongoing event, there is no reason to limit the definition of this term by requiring that events be repetitive. While a definition might make sense that balances the severity and pervasiveness of attacks in deciding whether workplace bullying has occurred, in several cases out of only 16 interview participants, it became clear that singular events could indeed be intimidating, controlling and strip workers of their dignity. To eliminate these single events from the definition of workplace bullying would afford bullies an opportunity to intimidate all employees enough on one occasion to gain the control they are looking for. Further, this would leave many targets of workplace bullying unprotected.

We must also be careful about requiring too high of a showing of severity of the behavior as well as high levels of harm to be shown. While it makes sense to balance the requirement of severity with pervasiveness, there is simply no justification to completely exclude low-grade incivility and other acts from the definition which can indeed violate targets' human rights. We also must be careful to recognize that bullying causes many different kinds of harm to targets. These harms were detailed in Chapter 3 of this volume. We also must be careful to understand the goal of any definition of workplace bullying should be to stop the behavior before harm has occurred.

Finally, two elements that should be included in the definition, but perhaps should be further explained in any definition, are those of unwantedness and power differential. First, in terms of unwantedness, my concern is that this standard becomes an "objective" standard or, more specifically, becomes a standard that a single judge determines whether he/she feels the behavior was truly unwanted. Further, my concern is that too much credence will be placed in the targets' reactions to workplace bullying in how unwantedness is determined. I suggest that steps must be taken to assure that a target's reaction is not the basis for determining whether he/she wanted to be subjected to these bullying behaviors. In terms of using power within the definition of bullying, it is clear that power should be a part of the definition of bullying. However, it should be footnoted that power can come from many different sources. Power may be formal, organizational position power or it may come from personal sources or even physical sources. Therefore, this element of the definition of bullying should be stated as the use of any source of power.

So, analyzing these elements of workplace bullying from the experiences of targets, a review of research on bullying and related behaviors and by exploring the successes and failures in laws in the United States and around the globe, I have developed the following definition of workplace bullying: *workplace bullying is the unwanted abuse of any source of power that has the effect of or intent to intimidate, control or otherwise strip a target of his/her right to esteem, growth, dignity, voice or other human rights in the workplace. Workplace bullying may take the form of harassment, incivility, abusive supervision, violence, aggressions and other types of objectionable behaviors. Further, these behaviors may take the form of interpersonal interactions or organizational practices. The behaviors may come from any level of the organization – supervision, co-workers, customers and even direct reports. The source of power shall not be considered as limited to formal organizational power or authority.*

This definition is meant to capture all of the potential acts of workplace bullying and to provide a broad protection for workers' right to dignity. By using this definition, we will be able to more fully address the very real and devastating problem of workplace bullying. Further, this definition does nothing to trample reasonable behaviors that are needed in workplaces to assure production and the delivery of goods and services. In fact, this definition will help employers to assure they are eliminating unnecessary and destructive behaviors in their workplace.

Notes

1 (Herschcovis, 2011).
2 (Raver & Nishii, 2010).
3 (Randall, 1997, p. 3).
4 (Farrington, 1993, p. 384).
5 Story, E. & Flanagan, J.L., House Docket 2072, No 1771, 2015. *An act addressing workplace bullying, mobbing, and harassment without regard to protected class status*. Massachusetts: The House of the Commonwealth of Massachusetts.
6 (Ibid.).
7 (Randall, 1997, p. 4).

 8 (Einarsen, 1999, p. 7).
 9 (Cox, 2010).
10 (Lerouge, 2010).
11 (Harthill, 2008).
12 (Herschcovis, 2011).
13 (Herschcovis, 2011); (Raver & Nishii, 2010).
14 (Feldblum & Lipnic, 2016).
15 (Tracy, et al., 2006).
16 (Einarsen, 2000).
17 (Lerouge, 2010).
18 (Harthill, 2008).
19 (Cortina, 2008, p. 56).
20 (Herschcovis, 2011).
21 (Cortina, 2008, p. 56).
22 (Simmons, 2002, p. 3).
23 (Simmons, 2002, p. 26).
24 (Cortina, 2008).
25 (Harris v. Forklift, 1993).
26 (Einarsen, 1999, p. 12).
27 (Randall, 1997, p. 5).
28 (Lerouge, 2010).
29 (Einarsen, et al., 2003).
30 (French & Raven, 2006).
31 (Einarsen, et al., 2003).
32 (Meritor Savings Bank v. Vinson, 29 C.F.R. § 1604.11, 1986).
33 (Tindall v. Housing Auth. of the City of Ft. Smith, W.D. Ark. 1991).
34 (Kouri v. Liberian Services, ED Va. 1991).
35 (Gibson v. Potter, 5th. Cir. 2008).
36 (Kleiman, 2003–2004).

8 The potential for micro level solutions

When Anna and Brenda came to my office, I could see how mad Brenda was. In fact, she was so angry that she was shaking. She told me that Anna had dealt with her supervisor, Jon, for long enough. Brenda told me that Anna had tried everything to stop Jon's bullying and that we needed to do something about it. After I got Brenda to calm down, I found out that Jon had been bullying Anna for the past month. He had put her in the worst job on the line, would yell at her in front of everyone, spent his days staring her down and constantly nitpicked her work. Anna had met with Jon to get the bullying to stop. She had tried to tough it out and at one point even screamed back at him on the line. The bullying just got worse. Brenda had also tried to step in by confronting Jon and found herself working right next to Anna in the insulation "hole."

Perhaps the most basic place to start looking for solutions to workplace bullying is to ask what steps individuals can take to address workplace bullying. There are potential solutions to workplace bullying at this micro level. Targets and even bystanders can and do take steps to address workplace bullies. For targets, these potential solutions to workplace bullying often occur even before there is an individual consciousness that he/she has been a target of bullying. At times, target reactions or responses are instinctual reactions to the attacks directed toward him/her. In other cases, the reactions are more calculated. Many of these target-level reactions could be defined as ameliorative measures, while others might even be considered measures to eliminate the bullying behavior or to prevent exposure to the bullying levels. Bystanders or witnesses can also play a role in eliminating workplace bullying behaviors and, in least some cases, bystanders do at least make attempts to do so. Finally, individual advocates can also play a role in responding to workplace bullying. In this chapter, I will review all of the responses I have seen at the individual level as well as other potential theoretical responses. While these steps may indeed supply a band-aid to deal with workplace bullying, in the end, my analysis suggests that any individual-level response will fail to be an effective remedy for workplace bullying.

Target responses

In all of my dealings with targets of workplace bullying (research, management and as an advocate) all targets have some level of reaction. These range from cognitive justification to bullying back to leaving the organization. In my initial research on workplace bullying, I saw all of these different responses. As an attorney and advocate, I have seen the same types of responses from targets who came to my office looking for help. In most cases, these targets did not come to me until well after they had attempted some individual steps to address the workplace bullying. What I have not experienced (although I am sure there are instances) is a target of bullying being able to fully address the pain they are enduring through his/her own efforts. In each of these cases, the results were never fully satisfying for the targets of workplace bullying. Most often, the responses have left the target less than whole – suffering some level of economic, emotional, psychological or even physical damage.

The justification/self-blame response

One of the most common responses to workplace bullying I have seen is for the target to take some type of mental steps to justify the bullying. Most often this entails some level of self-blame. For instance, Amy, a university staff member, stated on several occasions that she felt guilty to even claim she had been bullied, that she so often felt like she should just toughen up and that what she was experiencing was just a part of work. The bullying itself often promotes the idea of justification or rationalization. For Vanessa, another university staffer, she explained the bullying made her feel like she was worthless and eventually this led her to believe she deserved to be mistreated at work. Kevin, new to the workforce, at first rationalized to himself that the bullying was really just a normal part of work, then later he decided perhaps it was just a normal part of the financial industry where he was working at the time. The justification and rationalization was not an adequate remedy for any of these targets. The bullying continued and even though they excused the bullying, it still led to a toll for these targets. All of the targets who took this step as a response to their bullying continued to suffer in one way or another. Vanessa lost her self-esteem and suffered physical manifestations of her stress. Julie ended up exiting her employment, while Kevin decided to completely change his career aspirations. This target response does not end the bullying and often allows the bullying to escalate. As a result, these targets suffer additional negative impacts and most often take some other step to deal with this added stress and pain.

Attempting to stop the bully

Other targets of workplace bullying do make attempts to stop the bully on their own. For instance, one target I interviewed, Kelly, stated that she would bully back at her abusive boss. Her hope was that he would see how the bullying felt or that he would see she could not be intimidated. Unfortunately, this failed to stop the bullying behavior and in fact might have intensified the boss' abuse. Another target was a bit more successful by "sucking up" to his bully. Jim, the soldier I interviewed, explained that he tried to find things out about his bullying CO and then engage in ingratiating behaviors. He gave his CO a card for the CO's mother's birthday, would pick up little gifts for his CO and even bought flowers for the CO's mother on one occasion. Jim claimed that this led to a reduced amount of direct bullying, but his CO still denied leave and other benefits that he granted to others. Kelly did not want to be a bully and Jim did not want to have to "suck-up." Both of these targets explained that engaging in these behaviors took a mental and emotional toll on them, and in neither case did it make them whole or really stop the bullying.

Stress relief in many forms

Ameliorating the effects of workplace bullying through various stress release techniques also is a common individualized response for targets. For instance, Kevin, who also rationalized his bullying, dealt with the stress he felt as a result of being bullied by blasting loud music on his drive home from work. He explained this at least made him feel better by the time he got home, but that the stress would settle back in as he thought about returning to work. Greg, the Associate Dean and faculty member, would escape his bullying by keeping himself busy doing other things. He would throw himself into his work in his own business outside of his day-to-day job. Unfortunately, stress-relieving medication also seems to be a common theme for targets of workplace bullying. Lindsey ended up on anti-anxiety medication to cope with the bullying she suffered at work. Despite this medication, she still shook at the thought of returning to work and eventually could no longer force herself to go to her place of work. A UNISON study in 2000 found that 10% of targets went to their doctors for help in dealing with the bullying. In addition to prescription medications, self-medication is another response to workplace bullying. Numerous targets I have spoken with indicated that they began to drink more, eat more, or even used illicit drugs to deal with the workplace bullying. Again, like other avenues of self-help or individualized responses, the stress relief is also an ineffective or at least incomplete remedy. While these tactics might allow targets to better deal with the stress or the bullying, they do nothing to stop the bullying behavior and they also take a toll on the targets.

Escaping the bullying

Another common method of self-help is to escape the bully. As an HR Manager, one of the first indicators I saw of a bullying supervisor was the bidding out of his area by nearly every direct report. The bullying supervisor was known throughout the plant and not only would his employees bid out of his area as soon as possible, it was difficult to find workers to bid into his area, to work overtime in his area or really to go anywhere near his area. At another facility, workers learned to avoid a bullying supervisor's gaze as they realized eye contact could draw him into a discussion that would inevitably end in some form of bullying. As he would approach the work area, the employees often looked like school students putting their heads down to avoid a teacher calling on them. In two other settings, workers were explicitly told when bullying corporate managers would be in the office and they were given recommendations to keep their doors shut or to work in other areas of the plant to avoid the bullies and their wrath. I have seen faculty members engage in more and more work off-site to avoid bullying deans and department chairs, leaving office areas looking like ghost towns for large parts of the academic year.

While these targets learned methods to avoid their bullies while staying on the job, another common form of escaping or avoiding the bully is job exit. For some targets, the exit may be temporary. For instance, several targets I worked with as an advocate took extended periods of leave to escape a bullying dean in a university setting. Many targets in the course of my research told me that they regularly missed work because they simply could not endure seeing their bully. As an HR manager, I found a consistent theme amongst bullying supervisors of absenteeism problems amongst their workers.

While these short-term and mid-term avoidance tactics are common, perhaps a more common escape is much more long term. The majority of targets I have worked with in my research, advocacy, and even as a manager have at least considered leaving their employment to get away from their bully. In my initial research on workplace bullying in the course of working with targets of workplace bullying and conducting in-depth interviews of 16 targets, all of the targets suggested they were considering leaving their employment. One target, Vanessa, stated she would have left long ago, but the bullying convinced her she was so terrible that no other employer would ever hire her. By the end of the year-long research, 10 of the targets in my research had left their employment or taken formal steps to do so (announced their retirement, interviewed for other positions). At this point in time, I have heard from an additional four targets who have informed me they finally left their bullying employer. Many of these targets have shared stories with me of co-workers leaving to escape the same bully.

Just like the other self-help remedies, this remedy of escape leaves much to be desired. This escape often forces the target to uproot himself/herself and his/her family members, it leads to lost income, lost opportunity costs and often leads to the bully searching out new targets. In one setting, a bullying administrator was so successful at driving targets out of the workplace that it seems that other bullies took notice and have engaged in the same types of practices, driving an entirely new set of targets to leave the organization.

Bystander interventions

There is a great deal of support for the concept of bystander intervention to deal with bullying behaviors. We see this concept emerge in the battle against sexual assault through campaigns such as See Something, Say Something and It's on Us. These campaigns are so powerful in suggesting that bystanders can solve the problem of sexual assault that the EEOC adopted as part of its report on sexual harassment that bystander intervention should be given a strong focus.[1] Unfortunately, in the case of workplace bullying and harassment, there is not a lot of evidence that bystander intervention will work. First, according to Namie and Namie, co-workers are nearly four times more likely to take negative actions towards the target (57%) than to take positive actions (15%).[2] Bystanders often end up joining in on the bullying and engaging in what is often termed mobbing behavior. Vanessa shared stories of how her entire department began to bully her after taking the lead from her bullying supervisor; Julie experienced the same mobbing behavior in her department.

Despite the findings of Namie and Namie and the experiences of Julie, Vanessa and many other targets of bullying who have found themselves the targets of mobbing, there is some hope for bystander intervention. Gaffney and colleagues found that nurses do indeed make attempts to stop bullying of others, especially junior nurses. These bystanders often use deflection (changing the conversation) or even assist the target in filing a report.[3] Nursing has historically been a profession that experiences a high rate of bullying, and these bystanders may indeed be stepping in because they understand the impact of bullying. During the course of focus groups I held with research participants who had been targets of workplace bullying, it was clear that the targets had a deep concern for each other. They established a type of class consciousness amongst each other and often made statements that they wanted to stand up for each other. In one case, this did indeed become a common occurrence. Several of the participants in one focus group worked at the same university. After the focus group, they joined forces to assist each other and other targets of bullying in their workplace by intervening as bystanders and eventually as union advocates. Perhaps this same consciousness exists for many nurses. Unfortunately, bullies and unconcerned management or management that supports the bully often makes even this bystander intervention ineffective. While the nurses in the Gaffney et al. study initially engaged in bystander intervention, their efforts were found to be thwarted by threats and retaliation from management and even the bully.

While there is the potential for bystanders to play a role in addressing bullying, the bystanders themselves must have a path to neutralize the power of the bully or to gain their own power over the bully. The bystanders also have to have the desire to help out the target. There are possibilities for both of these. To achieve the former, we really often see a shift from this individual behavior into some form of concerted activity or collective action. This is discussed further in Chapter 11 of this volume. For the latter, there seems to be the possibility that experiencing bullying (perhaps even as a witness) and being educated about bullying and its impact may indeed lead to this class consciousness and desire to side with the target rather than the bully.

The creative advocate role

While the role of advocates will be discussed in more detail later in Chapter 10 of this volume, which specifically discusses the role of union advocates, and in

Chapter 11 of this volume, which specifically discusses the role of advocates in pushing for legislation, there are some things that advocates can do at a micro level to help to address workplace bullying. These advocates include union advocates, attorneys and activists.

From an attorney standpoint, attorneys can and should look to be creative in the way that they address targets who visit their offices. First, attorneys should look for ways to bring bullying claims within the purview of the current laws. The EEOC recently has presented one such example of how to do this, with their interpretation of gender harassment and how it relates to the sexual orientation. In the Baldwin case, the EEOC ruled that harassment based on sexual orientation is "inherently gender based" and thus falls under the protections of Title VII of the Civil Rights Act.[4] The creative advocate should look to build on this EEOC decision that impacts federal sector workers and apply the arguments from the EEOC to private sector employers. Further, as mentioned in the discussion of intent, only the bully truly knows his/her intent. Attorneys should explore whether there is the potential that the bullying was based on or impacted by a protected status. Attorneys should also look to explore tort claims beyond IIED. For instance, perhaps the bullying was also an assault, or perhaps the bullying interfered with the target's employment relationship. The attorney could also look for a potential breach of contract claims if the bullying violated a clause of an employee handbook or even an offer letter. While each of these potential solutions falls well short of the value of a federal anti-workplace bullying law, they may indeed offer some hope to targets and may also offer some incentive to employers to prevent and eliminate workplace bullying.

Union advocates can also look to creative measures to address workplace bullying. These will be addressed in detail in Chapter 10 of this volume. The creative union advocate could look to engage in shop floor concerted activity to bring attention and headaches to the bullying supervisor. The creative union advocate will look for any clause in a CBA that might address workplace bullying. The creative union advocate will figure out ways to shine the light on the bullying supervisor to make the bullying both a productivity and a CBA issue. There are a number of things that union leaders can do to provide outlets for targets in addition to these, such as assuring the targets' rights to leave (including family medical leave) and assuring them that they at least have ameliorative measures available to them (i.e. access to counseling and physicians and medication).

Finally, creative advocates can also play a role by helping targets to deal with their bullying and to overcome their bullying. Advocates can help targets to find resources to ameliorate the effects of bullying. This might include creating databases of counselors who address the specific issue of workplace bullying and identifying support groups. Advocates can help targets to share their stories to bring attention to the problems of workplace bullying.

While there are many possibilities at a micro level of steps to ameliorate, avoid and possibly even end workplace bullying, none of these provide a meaningful and complete solution to bullying. The vast majority of these steps fail to

fully address the bullying, end the harm to targets or make the targets of bullying whole. Targets can often take steps on their own to ameliorate the effects of
workplace bullying, but these seldom address the myriad of negative outcomes
that targets experience and, in some cases, will make these worse. The steps that
might work, such as bystander intervention, are often thwarted by the bullies or
co-conspirators in management. Further, rather than seeing bystanders stepping
in to help the targets, we see that bystanders are much more likely to join with
the bully and to engage in mobbing of the target. Creative advocates can and
should take measures at the individual level, but, again, there is no real record of
success at this level. So while there may be lessons to help targets of bullying in
this chapter, the real message is we must look for other more meaningful and
effective solutions to address workplace bullying. Bullying is more than just a
micro level issue and solutions must likewise be more than at the micro level.

Notes

1 (Feldblum & Lipnic, 2016).
2 (Namie & Namie, 2009).
3 (Gaffney, et al., 2012).
4 (David Baldwin v. Dep't of Transportation, July 15, 2015).

9   Employer-based solutions

When Gilbert the Chief Steward and Dennis the Business Agent came to my office to complain about Jim, they really did not expect anything to change. In fact, they started the conversation with just that claim. However, at the same time, they said they just wanted to make me aware of what was going on since I was the new employee relations manager. When they told me about Jim bullying his workers, they were a bit surprised that I wanted to dig deeper and that I asked for their help and support. Over the next 18 months, many of us in management, union leadership and informal leadership in the plant worked to change the entire culture of our organization. This included implementing and enforcing stronger policies, but, even more importantly, it meant changing the tone of relationships between management and supervision, changing the reward systems, gaining support from the top of the organization and creating a culture of respect.

Employers can take steps to prevent, detect, remedy and even eliminate workplace bullying. As an employee relations manager, human resources manager and consultant, I have helped companies to eliminate workplace harassment. I have also seen companies that have paid lip service to ending harassment and then wonder why new policies and programs were ineffective. In order to truly take steps to prevent, detect, remedy and eliminate workplace harassment and bullying, employers must have the right mindset. They must have the mindset of truly wanting to create a positive working environment, to truly being committed to protecting worker dignity. When employers look only at how they can benefit from taking these steps – either through limiting legal liability or the business case (i.e. increasing profits) employer policies will fail.

The Supreme Court of the United States has consistently supported the idea of the employers taking steps to address the sub-category of workplace bullying – unlawful harassment. In the *Faragher* and *Ellerth* rulings, the Court delineated employer liability for harassment they knew or should have known of unless the *employer took prompt, remedial measures to address such harassment* – a clear recognition that employers can at least remedy workplace harassment once it occurs.[1] Further, for supervisory harassment, employers would be held liable unless they could show they took reasonable steps to prevent, detect and remedy such harassment and the plaintiff/target unreasonably failed to take advantage of available remedial measures. The Supreme Court went further in

Kolstad, recommending that employers adopt specific anti-harassment policies and train employees on such policies.[2] The 6th Circuit in Clark further delineated the standards for a reasonable sexual harassment policy (and has been the only Circuit Court of Appeals to do so). The Clark Court held that a reasonable policy must have four elements:

1   It must require supervisors to report incidents
2   It must permit formal and informal reports of harassment
3   Must allow a target to bypass a harassing supervisor, and
4   Must provide for training on the policy[3]

The recent report form Commissioners Lipnic and Feldblum addressing workplace harassment also make it clear that there are steps that employers can and should take to eliminate workplace harassment.[4] The American system of jurisprudence has not only suggested employers can address these issues, but has placed the burden on employers to prevent, detect and remedy this specific form of workplace bullying.

While employers can take steps much as we did when confronted by Gilbert and Dennis, there is very little if any empirical evidence to support that employer systems are currently effective in preventing, detecting and remedying workplace harassment at the macro level. While some employers may indeed be effectively addressing the problem, the vast majority are not. Problems with workplace harassment persist despite the fact that it is clearly an employer's responsibility to eliminate unlawful harassment from the workplace.[5] In fact, unlawful harassment continues to be such a problem in the American workplace that the EEOC brought together a task force to study workplace harassment in 2015 and recently released a report to reboot the strategies for eliminating harassment in the workplace.

If employers were handling their responsibilities to eliminate workplace harassment, there would not have been a need for such a task force three decades after the *Meritor* ruling and 16 years after the *Faragher* and *Ellerth* rulings mentioned earlier. In fact, according to Fusilier and Penrod (2015), the majority of Universities are not even meeting their obligations under the fairly lenient Clark Standard. The fact that there are so many successful lawsuits against employers for harassment, discrimination, retaliation and other workplace violations suggests that, left on their own, employers do not even meet the second-level, legal obligations much less the third-level ethical responsibilities of Carroll's pyramid of social responsibility.[6] Further, according to Anna-Marie Marshall, harassment policies or grievance systems as they exist today in many companies may actually be counter-productive to eliminating harassment from the workplace. These systems often times redefine harassment in such a manner that many complaints are not filed and many actually harassing behaviors are never addressed.[7] In other words, even when employers meet their legal responsibility under *Faragher* and *Ellerth*, the policies that are instituted do not meet the ethical responsibility of eliminating employee-damaging harassment from the workplace. Marshall proposes that these policies are not implemented to meet legal standards or to protect employees, but rather they are implemented to protect the employer.[8] U.S. employers are not even fully obligated to eliminate workplace harassment even when they have notice that it is occurring. Instead, courts have held that they must merely take measures reasonably calculated to eliminate the workplace harassment.[9] At the macro level, employer systems are not meeting the goal of our solutions. However, this does not necessarily mean that they cannot meet these goals. Finally, keep in mind that when we see the cases in Chapter 5 of this volume where courts have allowed for equal opportunity bullying, or thrown cases out because an employee did not prove that the behaviors were unwanted or did not create a hellish environment, in every one of these cases, the court's holdings were based on the defenses put forward by employers. Rather than taking steps to eliminate workplace bullying, at the macro level, it could be argued that employers are spending much more time trying to limit their liability and to make the protections for targets of harassment meaningless.

Despite the current positions from employers, there are many reasons why employers should be willing to implement effective policies to prevent, detect, remedy and eliminate workplace bullying. Archie Carroll suggests that moral managers undertake a pyramid of responsibilities; these responsibilities include economic responsibilities, legal responsibilities, ethical responsibilities and even philanthropic responsibilities. Further, they owe these responsibilities to ALL stakeholders.[10] Eliminating workplace bullying would help employers to meet several of these responsibilities. Workplace bullying is economically costly to organizations as discussed in Chapter 3 of this volume. Eliminating bullying would directly eliminate these costs. Unlawful harassment is a subset of workplace bullying, thus a policy that prevents, detects, remedies and eliminates workplace bullying would help employers to meet their legal obligations. Workplace bullying destroys targets' human rights and there is perhaps no stronger ethical responsibility of an employer than to protect the human rights of workers who enter his/her doors of employment. The astute employer would see that protecting employees' dignity at work and in particular ridding the workplace of bullying would be a benefit to each one of these responsibilities. Workplace bullying is damaging to organizations and makes it more difficult for managers to achieve capital goals. Workplace bullying can be devastating to employees. As a stakeholder in corporations, it is thus the ethical responsibility of corporations to eliminate workplace bullying. Targets of workplace bullying are also more likely to sue employers.[11] Therefore, based on Carroll's Pyramid of Corporate Social Responsibility, one would expect moral employers to eliminate workplace bullying as a way of meeting their capital, legal and ethical responsibilities.

There are three potential ways for employers to address workplace bullying. The first is through an internal policy that makes bullying a violation of work rules. Such a policy would have to include a reporting system, investigation system, remedial system and a training system. The second is through a system of alternative dispute resolution. This is similar to the internal policy, but might also provide for third parties such as fact-finders, mediators and arbitrators to help in the remedying of workplace bullying. Finally, the third way is by addressing workplace climate and culture such that bullying is frowned upon by all in the workplace. I will look at each of these three alternatives.

An employer policy

The idea of an employer policy falls in line with the SCOTUS rulings, interpretations of these rulings by the Clark court and standards set out by the EEOC. There is also extensive research to confirm the need for strong policies with strong enforcement. Finally, in my own experiences, a lack of a policy, a weak policy or a weakly enforced policy are clear invitations for a culture of workplace bullying and harassment. The idea is that the employer will establish a policy against workplace bullying and this will prevent workplace bullying from occurring and, when it does occur, it will provide a remedy to the target and will stop the bullying from occurring from that point forward.

If an employer's policy is truly going to prevent, detect and remedy workplace bullying, first and foremost it must clearly address the issue accurately. The reality is that most employers do not have a policy that specifically addresses workplace bullying, even if they believe they have such a policy.[12] While most employers do have anti-harassment policies, these policies are too narrow to address bullying, and they are often even too narrow to address all forms of unlawful harassment.[13] So the first key for an employer policy to be effective is to actually specify that workplace bullying is unacceptable. An adequate definition of workplace bullying, such as that developed in Chapter 7 of this volume, should be included in the policy. Further, the employer could give examples of the workplace bullying, but assure that the list is not exhaustive and that any behaviors that meet the definition will indeed be considered bullying and will be addressed under the policy.

Just like any other proposed solution, the employer's policy must provide access to targets, it must provide an adequate remedy to make targets whole, it must deter acts of bullying and it must be strong enough to meet the goal of prevention. A major issue with employer harassment policies is that the majority of targets of harassment do not bring claims forward. Targets often have very good reasons not to report. First, they may not believe that the organization is serious about addressing workplace bullying. In many cases, employers have been slow to implement any types of employee protections until they have been mandated to do so. There is a stark difference between an employer looking to meet his/her legal obligations and one who truly wants to eliminate bullying. In some cases, the lack of reporting is because the target of the harassing behaviors does not have knowledge of the policy or he/she does not know how to file the claim.[14] In other cases, the target often has a very reasonable fear of retaliation for filing their complaint.[15] In order for a policy to work, targets of workplace bullying must have confidence in the policy and they must be willing to file reports of workplace bullying. This will require a number of measures.

The policy

First, employers cannot merely play lip service to the policy or its goals, or simply implement the policy to cover himself/herself from legal liability. There will need to be an honest commitment to eliminating bullying and protecting worker dignity. It is imperative that there is commitment from the top of the organization.[16] The policy should come from the CEO, President, Plant Manager, etc. of the organization. The commitment should be seen as coming from the top of the organization, but also should be coming from someone who the workers in the organization trust. The employer will need to have a true desire to eliminate the harassment, not to merely cover himself/herself from legal liability. Employers cannot want to protect top performers who might be bullies in the workplace. Employers cannot want to protect profits, revenues or clients at the expense of targets of workplace bullying. Employers cannot want to only deal with bullying when it is apparent and the decisions are obvious. Any anti-bullying policy that is instituted with any of these goals or concepts will be doomed to failure.

Second, the policy will need to be enforced in a consistent manner. When an employer fails to take reasonable steps to address workplace harassment, employees of course will lose faith in the process. If the outcomes of the process are not fair, the policy will be seen as lacking distributive justice and workers will not trust it. If the employer has failed to address bullying in the past, this should be addressed in the policy, along with an explanation that more effective steps will indeed be taken under this policy. Just as the outcomes must be fair, more importantly, the process itself must be viewed as fair. Workers will need to know the processes, from reporting through investigating through the remedial process, and these processes will all have to be viewed as being fair or just in order to maintain trust in the system.

Third, in order for the policy to be viewed as procedurally just and for the policy to lead to fair outcomes, the policy must have a number of different components. These components include the reporting system, the investigation system, the remedial process, an anti-retaliation process and an appeals process. The employer will also need to assure the policy is widely disseminated and clearly understood. This will require that the employer engages in the meaningful training of employees, managers and investigators in the system and their roles in the system. This building of trust in the policy and developing a policy that is indeed procedurally and substantively just will allow the policy to meet the first criteria of accessibility (for the employees of that employer).

Reporting structure

The reporting structure will need to be set up so that targets will utilize the structure. There must be pathways to address concerns and reasons that targets would not report incidents. The structure will need to allow for multiple reporting avenues as a well as formal and informal reporting of bullying incidents, as is required by the Clark standard for harassment policies.[17] Targets should never be faced with the dilemma of either reporting bullying to somebody they do not trust or not reporting the bullying. The reporting avenues should not be overly narrow and should assure that targets do not have to report to the alleged bully.[18] This reporting structure is critical to meeting the goals of accessibility. If employers are truly committed to detecting, remedying and eliminating all forms of workplace bullying and harassment, the reporting structure should be as wide as possible and provide as many avenues for reporting as possible. Think of this reporting system as the mouth or opening of a funnel for all claims and actions of workplace harassment. The avenues should include ALL members of management, confidential reporting structures, ombudsmen, even hot lines.

In addition to assuring that targets have access to reporting incidents, management must also take steps to detect incidents on their own. Again, as the recent EEOC Report points out, managers should be trained in their additional duties in order to eliminate workplace bullying. These duties should include detecting ongoing harassment in their work areas and then assuring that the harassment is dealt with through the employer's policy. My recommendations for employers in this area have always included requiring that first managers and supervisors consistently engage in Management by Wandering Around. They should be out in their work areas and seeing what is going on. I have worked in many places where supervisors would rarely leave their offices during work hours, except for lunch and breaks. These work areas tended to have the highest rates of workplace bullying and harassment. Second, in order to assure that supervisors are aware of their work areas, I have recommended harassment audits. These include audits of the physical working areas (looking for anything inappropriate in the physical environment) as well as interviews and confidential surveys of those in the working area.

The reporting process is the first step to detecting, remedying and eliminating harassment. It is also a limiting step. Employers cannot eliminate harassment and bullying that they do not know about. However, keep in mind that employers do have an obligation not only to eliminate unlawful harassment that they know of, but also harassment that they should have known of.[19] This same standard should be applied to all forms of harassment and workplace bullying.

The investigation process

The investigation process is a critical element to a bullying policy. The investigation must lend confidence to the target, but it also must be a neutral, fair, fact-finding investigation.

The goal of the investigation must be to detect and determine whether the complainant's dignity has been harmed and whether workplace bullying has occurred. The investigation should be conducted by trained investigators who have no real or perceived biases or conflict of interest. The investigators should match the diversity of the parties to the complaint. This should include traditional demographics (race, color, gender, etc.) but also the diversity in the workplace (laborers, bargaining unit members, supervisors, etc.). Each investigation should include two investigators working together as a team. This type of investigation is necessary for practical as well as substantive reasons. First, from a practical standpoint, this will allow one investigator to take notes while the other asks questions. Second, this will help to overcome any potential biases that might arise during the course of an investigation by any one investigator.

In order to be able to do this, the employer must have a cadre of trained investigators available to investigate and claim. Many use external sources to do this. However, in my experience, too often employers select their defense counsel as investigators and the investigation turns into a series of depositions to establish a defense. I would suggest instead that employers develop an internal harassment committee. The members of this committee will need extensive training on how to investigate claims as well as on the harassment policy. The investigators should be trained to engage in a neutral, fact-finding investigation. They should be trained to avoid leading questions and interjecting their own opinions or asking for conclusions of law. Make sure that they do not judge the person, but merely act as finders of fact.

The committee should also be as diverse as possible. For each complaint or investigation, pick a team that matches the diversity of the parties involved. The team should be two members. During each interview, one should ask questions, and one should write down answers.

Under EEO laws, the employer has an obligation to keep any investigation as confidential as possible.[20] This same tact should be taken with investigations of general harassment or bullying. In order to maintain this confidentiality, the investigators should first interview the complainant. They should gather all of the facts of the alleged events from the complainant at this time as well as explore the requested remedies from the complainant. Investigators should ask the complainant for a list of potential witnesses. Then the investigators should interview the accused. Remember this is a fact-finding investigation and if at this point the facts from both parties are the same, there is no need to go further into this specific investigation (there may indeed be reasons to investigate to see if the alleged bully has engaged in similar behaviors in the past or toward other workers). There would be no need to breach confidentiality any further in that instance. However, in most cases, the investigators will then need to interview witnesses. The accused should also be asked for a list of witnesses. At this point, the employer should also implement their retaliation process and inform the complainant that retaliation against the complainant and/or anyone else involved in the complaint is strictly prohibited. The third step is talking to witnesses. Investigators again need to focus on a fact-gathering process. They should avoid asking the witnesses about their opinions or asking them to engage in any form of legal analysis. Legal terminology, leading questions and filling in the blanks should all be avoided by the investigators. We should have each interviewer and interviewee sign the collected notes from each interview. Document each step. After the interviews are done, make a list of the facts, assess credibility and determine next steps. Then take the list of facts back to the committee without using the names of the parties. Decide if inappropriate behavior occurred and if so what remedy is needed.

The retaliation policy

Employers will also need to address retaliation. The very real fear of retaliation is one of the main reasons that targets make the very reasonable decision to not report harassment to their employers. Retaliation suits continue to be a large part of the EEOC's workload and retaliation against targets who report and even bystanders who support targets who report workplace bullying is extremely common.[21] To prevent retaliation, the retaliation policy should be clear to all members of the organization. Just as reports of bullying will need to be taken extremely seriously, so must complaints of retaliation. However, these must be addressed in an even more expeditious manner.

Because retaliation is such a large issue, the employer should adopt a separate retaliation policy that is included along with the anti-harassment policy. The retaliation policy should include examples of retaliation and a strong statement against any form of retaliation. The penalties for retaliation must be strong in order to deter retaliatory actions. Further, the policy should include a clear, broad and easy-to-follow reporting system for targets of retaliation. Investigations of retaliation should occur immediately. Finally, the employer should take steps to assure that retaliation has not occurred and not been reported. These steps should include a follow-up process to each and every complaint filed under the harassment policy. At a minimum, the individual in charge of the investigation or the investigators should follow up with the complainant and witnesses within one day, two days, one week, one month, three months, six months and one year after the conclusion of the investigation to assure that no retaliation has occurred and to assure that any harassing behavior has ceased.

Dissemination and training

Both the harassment policy and the retaliation policy should be disseminated in complete form to all workers in the organization. Each and every employee should be trained on the policies at least once every two years and at the beginning of their employment (for example as part of the orientation). Employee-wide training should also take place at any point where it becomes clear that harassment or bullying is occurring throughout the workplace. This training should be used to inform all employees about the policy, about behaviors that are unacceptable as well as acceptable behaviors. The training should include bystander training to inform bystanders about how they can help to eliminate harassment/bullying in the workplace and how they are protected in taking reasonable steps to prevent, detect and report harassment. The training should include supervisory training and explain their heightened responsibilities under the policy. The employers should show a commitment to this training to further signal their commitment to a harassment-free workplace. This should include a commitment to engage in face to face interactive training for all forms of harassment training. Again, this form of training is encouraged by the recent EEOC report.[22]

While strong policies with strong and consistent enforcement can be an important step to addressing workplace harassment and bullying, employers simply too often do not implement these types of policies. As we can see by the cases in Chapter 5 of this volume, employers often implement narrow reporting structures rather than the broad structures needed to increase reporting rates and to detect the majority of workplace bullying. Exacerbating this problem, employers too often treat the investigation process as a way to cover themselves from legal liability rather than as a path to eliminating the workplace harassment and bullying. Too often, employers begin the process from a position of defending themselves rather than engaging in a neutral, fact-finding investigation. Often, employers will even bring in defense counsel to engage in the investigation, and, rather than gathering the facts from the complainant, the counsel will engage in an interrogation. I have seen employers engage in entire investigations where it was clear the purpose was to build a defense. These investigations often entail investigators asking leading questions to convince witnesses to take positions about legal standards. Rather than taking effective steps to prevent retaliation, employers far too often allow retaliation to occur and even participate in the retaliation.

In my experiences and research, I have found no meaningful support for employer-based policies amongst targets of workplace bullying. Vanessa suggested that reporting her experiences to her employer would have been career suicide. John suggested that his employer definitely knew about the bullying and could have eliminated it, so it made no sense to report it to him/her. Numerous other research participants suggested that the very people they would have to report the harassment to were the people supporting the harassment, allowing for the harassment or even engaging in the harassment and bullying. Hopefully, the recent report from the EEOC will spur employers to implement more effective policies to address unlawful harassment. However, even if this occurs, this will leave the targets of non-status-based harassment without adequate protections. Further, the reality is that, as of today, employer policies are an ineffective remedy for any form of harassment – unlawful or otherwise.

Employer ADR programs

Employer-implemented alternative dispute resolution plans present a second possible avenue for employers to eliminate general harassment/workplace bullying. Estreicher suggests that employer-implemented ADR programs that include mandatory arbitration are a benefit to employees and employers.[23] Estreicher suggests that these systems can provide the very important access that is needed for all targets of workplace bullying, access that the legal system does not provide even where the harassing behavior may be unlawful. This is particularly the case for low wage workers (a growing segment of the American workplace) who may be unable to "attract the attention of private lawyers because the stakes are "too small."[24] Seeber and Lipsky suggest that the employment arbitrators as actors in this system may be at least in part a substitution for the loss of collective action we see in the American workplace.[25]

Complaints that would not fall under any statutory or common law provision are often heard under these employer ADR systems. Bullying could be one such type of complaint. As discussed earlier, employees who have been the victims of bullying will not get a chance to have their case heard in a courtroom unless they can show such bullying was based on a protected status and that it led to an adverse job effect, or that such bullying was intentional and extremely outrageous. However, perhaps in arbitration or even in an employer-mandated mediation program, claims of bullying may be addressed.

Leader and Burger suggest that ADR has the potential to "revolutionize employment law." They point out that in employment litigation, many complainants can never get to the courtroom because they cannot afford an attorney, and even when employees get into the courtroom, their success rate at trial is less than 15%. They suggest that the greater access to employer-sponsored ADR systems than the courtroom will better help employees to bring their statutory claims.[26] In addition to allowing employees to have a better opportunity to bring statutory claims, these systems may also allow employees to bring claims such as workplace bullying. However, my own research, as well as research by Fox and Stallworth, suggests that there is limited support for internal employer-based dispute resolution systems as a means to address workplace bullying.[27] There clearly has not been a revolution of the employment environment as a result of ADR, at least not in terms of eliminating harassment and bullying. Instead, much like the investigations undertaken by many employers, ADR has been an effective tool to keep employers out of the courtroom and to minimize their legal liability and expenses. As of today, ADR is nothing more than another dead end.

A healthy workplace climate

The third and most promising way for employers to take steps to prevent, detect, remedy and eliminate workplace harassment and bullying is by creating a culture that does not support workplace bullying and instead supports a climate of civility. As discussed in Chapter 4 of this volume, in order for workplace bullying to occur, there must be an organizational culture or system that either supports or allows the bullying. An employer who is truly dedicated to preventing, detecting, remedying and eliminating bullying and harassment can look to develop an organizational culture that is built around respect and civility for all members of the organization. This theme of the need for a culture of diversity and inclusion was echoed throughout the meetings of the EEOC Select Task Force by members, experts and the EEOC Commissioners. This has also consistently been a key component of any harassment system I have helped employers to implement. Where the organization has a culture that allows for bullying or harassment, the employer will have the more difficult step of changing the culture. Not only will a culture have to be established, but first the culture must be changed. While this is not an easy task, it can be done.

In order to engage in this culture change, there must again be a commitment from the top of the organization, but this commitment alone will not be enough. The leadership of the organization will need to engage in a number of steps to truly change the culture. The leaders of the organization must be aware of the messages they send. As discussed in the policy section of this chapter, the leaders must be consistent and must be committed to not only eliminating harassment and bullying, but they must also be committed to a positive working environment of kindness, caring and acceptance. Employers will need to be aware of the ceremonies, symbols, rituals and rewards in their workplace. Employers should have events that celebrate inclusion and diversity. Managers and workers should be rewarded for positive behaviors, supervisors for addressing and preventing harassment and bullying. Performance management systems should include a focus on a positive working environment and healthy culture. Stories of success in terms of diversity and inclusion should be shared. Consistency will be a key.

In organizations where there is a need for culture change rather than just the building of a culture, as Dr. Bies suggested to the EEOC Select Task Force, the employer can follow Kotter's 8-Stage Process to organizational change. Employers will need to establish a sense of urgency that harassment and bullying must be eliminated. They can do this by sharing stories about the destructive nature of bullying, by sharing the benefits to all of eliminating bullying. They will need to bring informal and formal leaders together as a coalition to drive the change. They will need to develop an inspiring and motivating vision of where the organization can be when the change takes place and develop strategies about how to make the change happen. The organization must empower broad-based action as long as it is aligned with the goal of creating this positive, bullying-free culture. They should look to generate and promote short-term wins to increase buy-in to the change and to consolidate these wins to further convince stakeholders. Finally, they will need to anchor organizational systems to this new culture – reward systems, training, budgets, promotions all must be explicitly linked to the types of behaviors that fit the new culture.

Avoiding potential conflict with the NLRA

The issue of avoiding conflict with the National Labor Relations Act is not one that really caught my attention until I became a member of the EEOC Select Task Force on the Study of Workplace Harassment. As an HR and Employee Relations Manager, I implemented harassment programs in both union and non-union settings. I have also consulted with union and non-union employers in the development of anti-harassment programs and have worked with numerous unions to address workplace harassment and bullying. In those efforts, I have never run into any problems with a conflict with the NLRA or a conflict with the union members or leaders. The concerns about this conflict seem to have mainly arisen out of the *Cooper Tire & Rubber* case.

The *Cooper Tire & Rubber* case is an unfair labor practice charge case decided by the NLRB in 2015. The case came about as a result of Cooper Tire & Rubber terminating the employment of a union member for conduct on the picket line. Cooper Tire & Rubber and the Local 207L of the United Steelworkers were engaged in heated contract negotiations from late 2011 through the early part of 2012. The negotiations broke down and Cooper Tire & Rubber locked out the Steelworkers and brought in replacement workers beginning on November 28, 2011. On January 7, 2012, Anthony Runion was engaged in picketing with fellow locked-out steelworkers. As vanloads of replacement workers drove by Runion and into the plant, Runion and fellow USW members "flipped off" the vans. Approximately seven minutes after the van passed Runion, he turned to other picketers and yelled "Hey did you bring enough KFC for everyone?" and 20 minutes later possibly yelled "Hey, anybody smell that? I smell fried chicken and watermelon." These statements are clearly racially derogatory and have no value in the workplace. Based on these statements (at least according to Cooper Tire) the company terminated Runion's employment. Runion and the USW filed an 8(a)(3) (Discrimination and/or retaliation for union activity) unfair labor practice charge against Cooper Tire. In this case, the NLRB found in favor of Runion and the USW. Applying the *Clear Pine Mouldings* standard to this case, the board determined that words on a picket line, during a strike or lockout would not normally be enough to remove the actions of the picketer from protections under the National Labor Relations Act. The Board found that Runion's words were not enough to "coerce or intimidate" the replacement workers in their rights under the NLRA and did not raise a reasonable likelihood of imminent physical confrontation. The board explained there is a clear recognition that the picket line is different than the workplace. The Board agreed that the language was reprehensible, but that does not mean it was not protected activity under the circumstances.

The concerns over this case have been overblown by HR practitioners and employer-side attorneys. *Cooper Tire* is a unique case, with unique circumstances. The board made its determination based on clear precedent that sets a different standard for behavior and especially language on the picket line. Employers should be aware that the policy that they apply to picket line activity should be markedly different than the policy they apply in the workplace. In order to find behavior to be unacceptable on the picket line, it must clearly intimidate or coerce employees or must lead to an imminent likelihood of violence. The picket line is different from the workplace and anybody who has ever worked or really experienced a unionized setting in any way understands this difference. The picketers in Cooper Tire, just like other strike and lockout picketers, were picketing for their livelihoods. Picketers in these circumstances are out of work and watch others take their work on a daily basis. The picket line is a heated environment as is recognized by the NLRB and not too terribly difficult for employers to likewise recognize.

While the conflict from Cooper Tire can be reasonably resolved, employers have also been concerned with potential conflicts between harassment and bullying policies and NLRB General Counsel guidance. This concern is over conflict in two main areas. The first is the conflict between confidentiality requirements under EEO laws and limits on confidentiality under the NLRA. Again, this conflict is fairly easily resolved. The EEO requirement is that management investigators maintain confidentiality.[28] They should not share the details of an investigation with anyone who does not have the need to know. They should be careful in how much information they share with potential witnesses and what witnesses they should interview. While investigators should assure that interviewees during an investigation maintain a reasonable level of confidentiality, there should be nothing that restricts any complainant, accused or witness from obtaining assistance with the investigation including discussing their concerns with a representative or co-workers for their mutual aid or protection. Such a restriction would violate the worker's Section 7 rights under the National Labor Relations Act.[29] The employer is not liable in any way for this "breach" of confidentiality.

Perhaps the biggest real potential conflict with the NLRA comes about in the types of behaviors that can be prohibited. The NLRB has found that overly broad limitations on speech or conduct can indeed be a violation of an employee's Section 7 rights under the National Labor Relations Act – the right to engage in concerted activity for mutual aid or protection.[30] However, the NLRB General Counsel's position is clear that even language that appears on its face to be too restrictive will be read in context. The General Counsel has recognized that the engagement in Section 7 rights often requires a certain level of conflict with management and this conflict is protected under Section 7. It is perhaps most imperative that the policy does not limit these rights to criticize and contest management decisions and policies. One possibility is to develop a separate policy concerning employee-to-management relations. Concerted activity also leads to potential conflict with other employees, so again employers must be sure that the policy does not prohibit this type of activity. The General Counsel has indeed recognized the employers' right, if not obligation, to have a harassment-free workplace, but the prohibitions under such a policy should not limit "vigorous debate" amongst employees or the right to criticize management or the organization. Specifically, the conduct prohibited must be more specific than simply "disrespectful," "negative," "inappropriate" or "rude."[31] Generally, the NLRB has supported rules against harassment (especially unlawful) harassment and there is no reason to expect that a rule applying the definition of workplace bullying developed here would be found to violate Section 7. However, the more detailed an employer can be the better. In fact, the NLRB recognized that employers should avoid broad policies without "further clarification."[32] As a result, the employer might want to add as part of the definition of workplace bullying, what actions do not entail workplace bullying from an NLRA standpoint. Language could include:

This policy does not and should not be interpreted as limiting an employee's right to criticize management or the organization, nor does it in any way prohibit concerted activity that an employee might engage in for the mutual aid or protection of workers in this organization. This policy also does not prohibit vigorous debate amongst employees or between employees and members of management.

While the NLRB does not provide a safe harbor for these types of policies a best practice would be to work with the union leadership in any unionized facility. I have done this on several occasions and have had no problems implementing effective anti-bullying policies. The NLRB is also clear that the more detailed you can be about the prohibited behaviors (and how these differ from Section 7 activity) the better. Avoid ambiguous terms and focus on the rights of workers rather than taking the negative rights approach of focusing on prohibited behaviors. Also, engaging in meaningful training around the policy will also assure that employers can explain that the policy is not meant to limit Section 7 rights.

Employers can take steps to prevent, detect, remedy and eliminate workplace bullying. They can implement strong anti-bullying policies with wide reporting structures and an effective investigation process, they can implement effective and truly neutral ADR systems to assure that policies are effectively enforced and they can create cultures of diversity and inclusion that do not allow for harassment and bullying. The major problem with employer-based systems is that employers seldom do what they "can do" to address this problem. Instead, employers by and large continue to allow harassment and bullying to occur. This was the very reason for the need for the EEOC Select Task Force to Study Workplace Harassment. Rather than addressing workplace harassment and bullying effectively, employers too often allow targets of harassment to suffer, provide inadequate reporting avenues, engage in investigations to cover the employer from liability rather than to eliminate the harassment and allow, support and even engage in retaliation against targets and the bystanders who stand up for the targets. It is clearly understandable why targets of workplace bullying do not have any faith in the idea that employer-based systems will solve the problem of bullying in the American workplace and it is clear that we must explore and push for other more meaningful remedies to this problem.

Notes

1 (Burlington Industries, Inc. v. Ellerth, 1998); (Faragher v. Boca Raton, 1998).
2 (Kolstad v. American Dental Association, 1999).
3 (Clark v. UPS, 6th Cir. 2005, pp. 349–351).
4 (Feldblum & Lipnic, 2016).
5 For instance, in 1986, the Supreme Court first held that workplace harassment could definitively be considered a form of discrimination under Title VII, Meritor Savings Bank v. Vinson, 477 U.S. 57 (1986); further standards for employer liability were established under Harris v. Forklift Systems Inc., 510 U.S. 17 (1993), Oncale v. Sundowner Offshore Services, Inc. 118 S.Ct. 998 (1998), Faragher v. The City of Boca Raton, 524

U.S. 775 (1998) and Burlington Industries, Inc. v. Ellerth 524 U.S. 742 (1998). See Anne Lawton, "Operating in an Empirical Vacuum: The Ellerth and Faragher Affirmative Defense," 13, *Columbia Journal of Gender and Law* 197 (2004) for an analysis of the incentives for employers to simply construct policies rather than to truly attempt to eliminate harassment.

6 (Carroll, 1991).
7 (Marshall, 2005).
8 (Marshall, 2005).
9 (EEOC v. Xerxex, 4th Cir. 2011).
10 (Carroll, 1991).
11 (Coleman, 2004).
12 (Cowan, 2011).
13 (Fusilier & Penrod, 2015).
14 (Pierce, et al., 1997).
15 (Feldblum & Lipnic, 2016).
16 (Feldblum & Lipnic, 2016).
17 (Fusilier & Penrod, 2015).
18 (Feldblum & Lipnic, 2016).
19 (Burlington Industries, Inc. v. Ellerth, 1998); (EEOC v. CRST Expenditure, 8th Cir. 2012); (Faragher v. Boca Raton, 1998).
20 (Feldblum & Lipnic, 2016).
21 (Feldblum & Lipnic, 2016); (Gaffney, et al., 2012); (Namie & Namie, 2009).
22 (Feldblum & Lipnic, 2016).
23 (Estreicher, 2001).
24 (Estreicher, 2001, p. 563).
25 (Seeber & Lipsky, 2006).
26 (Leader & Burger, 2004, p. 88).
27 (Fox & Stallworth, 2004).
28 (Feldblum & Lipnic, 2016).
29 NLRB Office of the General Counsel Memorandum GC 15–04, March 18, 2015.
30 NLRB Office of the General Counsel Memorandum.
31 NLRB Office of the General Counsel Memorandum GC 15–04, March 18, 2015.
32 (Triple Play Sports Bar & Grille, August 22, 2014, p. 7).

10 Concerted activity as a solution

Sara knew what she was experiencing would not fall under the definition of harassment under any of the EEO laws. In fact, she had been told this by several attorneys. Her supervisor's behavior was simply not based on any protected status. However, Sara also knew that she deserved respect in the workplace and had a right to dignity at work. As a union member, she felt sure that her union leadership would help her to address the behaviors by her supervisor. She was shocked when the union leaders brushed her complaints aside, even at times telling her the dean was well within his powers to take such actions (ignoring that he was using the policies to wreak havoc on Sara's career).

Just as employers can play a role in preventing, detecting, remedying and eliminating workplace bullying, unions and union leaders can also take steps to do so. Concerted activity has traditionally led to the greatest protections and gains for working people in the United States. In one way or another, concerted activity has led to the eight-hour day; the five-day work week; workers' compensation; workplace safety laws; protections against discrimination based on race, color, national origin, religion, age status and disability; the minimum wage and protections against child labor. Specifically, concerted activity in the form of unionization has led to health care and pension protections for workers, safer working conditions, procedural due process, job protections and a decreased wage gap for female and minority workers.[1] So it makes sense to consider the potential role for concerted activity in protecting worker dignity and preventing, detecting, remedying and eliminating workplace bullying. In the final two chapters of this book, I will look at the role of concerted activity in two different ways. First, in this chapter, I will explore the role of traditional concerted activity and unions in protecting workers' dignity. In the next chapter, I will explore the role of concerted activity to bring about legislative protections for worker dignity and legislation to remedy workplace bullying.

Concerted activity in the labor relations process, or the union/labor movement, can potentially provide a solution through three different paths. First, they can directly address workplace bullying for their own members in three arenas – organizing around workplace bullying issues, collectively bargaining for protections against workplace bullying and/or the day-to-day management of the CBA. Second, they could help to address bullying by what is known as the threat effect or the union spillover effect. Third, workers, the labor movement and unions can play a role as a leader of the social movement that will be necessary to transform how we view work and workers' rights and to provide the impetus for meaningful legislation to address workplace bullying (this third route will be discussed in detail in the next chapter).

Preventing, detecting, remedying and eliminating bullying of union members

The purpose of a union is to make the lives of workers better.[2] This is the very heart of unionism and concerted activity. According to Yates, it is this concerted activity that can and often does protect the dignity of workers.[3] This same dignity is stripped from workers who are targets of workplace bullying.[4] Further, the workplace bully requires a power imbalance in order to be able to torment their targets.[5] This is the very type of imbalance that concerted activity is meant to eliminate.[6] Targets of bullying are also stripped of their voice in the workplace,[7] a voice that again is protected and secured through the labor relations process of concerted activity.[8] The causes, precursors and outcomes of workplace bullying all suggest that unions and concerted activity can be a path to eliminating the workplace bullying of union members. Based on my research and experience, unions can play an important role in protecting members from bullying. However, in order to do so, they must truly be committed to ending bullying in the same way employers must be committed if their policies are to have any meaningful impact. Unions and their leadership can help to reduce or even eliminate workplace bullying in all phases of the labor relations process – the organizing phase, the collective bargaining phase and/or the day-to-day management of the CBA phase.

Organizing phase

Unions and concerted activity can help to prevent, detect and eliminate workplace bullying as early as the organizing phase. However, in order to do so, the union organizers will need to make workplace bullying and worker dignity themes of the organizing drive. The first step is simply to understand that workplace bullying is indeed a serious issue for all workers. Organizers should be aware of the pervasiveness of workplace bullying as well as how seriously workplace bullying impacts the targets. A second step is to have a specific plan as to how concerted activity or collective bargaining can indeed address the issues and the incidents of workplace bullying. To develop this plan, it makes sense to go back to exploring the bullying tactics discussed earlier in this book and to develop plans that could address these specific tactics.

One organizing drive I was involved in at a public university demonstrated that, even in this early stage, a union can indeed help to address workplace bullying and in particular a workplace bully. In this drive, the union leadership readily recognized the bullying environment in the workplace, as well as the bullying nature of the President of the university. It clearly helped that the drive was led by an internal organizer who saw this bullying on a daily basis. The union organizers realized that not only did the university President engage in bullying and promote an atmosphere of bullying, but he also did very little to address faculty and staff concerns with state legislators. The union did try to get the President to engage in meet and discuss, but he refused. The union held day events, appeared at trustee meetings, wrote op-eds and letters to the editor and represented faculty members in disputes with the President where they were able to fit the dispute under the state employee grievance process. The union demonstrated Brofenbrenner's position that unions are more successful in organizing workers when they act as a union from day one.[9] The union leaders both internal and external took steps such as those suggested by Brofenbrenner – offering legal support, direct action or helping workers to utilize internal conflict resolution processes – to address worker concern. In this case, the members were availed of a state worker grievance process via state statute. At first, the union was hesitant to use this grievance process because they viewed it as a process to be used only when one feels they are going to win. However, eventually the process was used as more of a signaling and nuisance process. The union engaged in external pressures on the bully through a community campaign while also exerting internal pressure through complaints and formal grievances. The drive began to center at least in part on the bullying behaviors engaged in by the President as well as the bullying behaviors he supported and even promoted from staff members. The union leadership consistently called him out on these behaviors in press releases, grievances and meetings of the university Trustees. Eventually the bully left the organization. While there was no direct statement that the union pressure led to his leaving, the timing suggests that there was indeed a link. Further, even before he left the organization, the union activity was able to at least in part curtail his bullying behavior.

The collective bargaining phase and workplace bullying

Once a union has successfully organized a workplace, the next phase of the labor relations process is to negotiate a contract. In this phase of the labor relations process, unions can address workplace bullying in three ways. First, the union could indeed negotiate a direct anti-bullying clause. Second, the union could make bullying in the organization or even a specific bully the focus of negotiations and their willingness to engage in the process in a productive manner. An example of this tactic will be shared later. Finally, a union can look to understand bullying prior to negotiations, identify the tactics of bullies and eliminate the potential bully's control over these tactics by negotiating clauses that address these specific tactics or take these tactics out of the hands of potential bullies.

Workplace bullying can and should be a topic of collective bargaining. There is little doubt that a bullying atmosphere has an impact on working conditions, it is a term or condition of employment. As discussed in Chapter 3 of this volume, the impact of workplace bullying on targets is severe and can have more impact on workers than nearly any other term or condition of employment. Because of this impact on working conditions, workplace bullying is a mandatory topic of collective bargaining. However, bargaining over this issue is not common (although it does seem to be gaining some momentum).

Negotiating an anti-bullying clause

The language of a direct collective bargaining clause would have to meet the same type of requirements that we would see in any form of legislation. First, the clause should set out the positive right of the members that is being protected:

> Every member of the XYZ Bargaining Unit has a right to be treated with dignity in the workplace. Any violation of this right shall be a violation of this collective bargaining agreement and as such any member whose right to dignity has been violated will have the right to bring a grievance through the process as outlined under this CBA.

However, as we see with clauses that protect legal rights such as the right to be free from harassment, the language should avoid limiting these legal rights in any way:

> Nothing under this clause should be viewed as limiting such members' rights under any local, state or federal law, and the corresponding right to seek redress for such violations outside of the parameters of this CBA.

The language should set out the types of violations of this right:

> Workplace Bullying defined as the unwanted abuse of any source of power that has the effect of or intent to intimidate, control or otherwise strip a target of his/her right to esteem, growth, dignity, voice or other human rights in the workplace and is clearly a violation of the dignity of the targets of such behavior. Workplace bullying may take the form of harassment, incivility, abusive supervision, violence, aggressions and other types of objectionable behaviors. Further, these behaviors may take the form of interpersonal interactions or organizational practices. The behaviors may come from any level of the organization – supervision, co-workers, customers and even direct reports. The source of power shall not be considered as limited to formal organizational power or authority.

Avoid pitfalls – intent, level of severity, harm, and the problems with the *Faragher* defense:

> Nothing under this policy should require the target of the harassing/ bullying behavior to prove the intent at any level of the bully/harasser.

Where bullying/harassment has occurred, the target of such behavior(s) shall have the right to be fully remedied for any harm endured. The employer shall take every feasible measure to protect all employees' right to dignity in the workplace and to eliminate bullying/harassing behaviors from the working environment. The employer bears the absolutely responsibility to prevent, detect, remedy and eliminate bullying and harassment at XYZ.

The language should place the obligation on the employer:

XYZ employer is responsible for taking all steps to assure that the working environment at XYZ is free from workplace bullying and that the dignity of all members of the XYZ bargaining unit is protected. XYZ shall have the responsibility to take all feasible measures to prevent, detect, remedy and eliminate workplace bullying.

The language should provide an appropriate remedy:

If an XYZ bargaining unit member has been the target of workplace bullying, then XYZ shall be liable for all damages as a result of such bullying, including but not limited to lost work days, lost promotions and raises, physical and psychological damages. Such harmed employees shall have the right to demand that the bully be removed from their working area.

The language should include the Union and Employees as a decision maker under the policy:

The XYZ Union and its members will be represented in all functions under this policy. They will have equal representation to XYZ management on the team that develops the internal procedures under this policy and shall enjoy proportional representation on each committee, task force, etc. under this policy. This shall include membership on any committee that investigates and/or decides whether bullying/harassment has occurred and determines the remedies for such behavior.

Protecting the Right to Engage in Concerted Activity:

Nothing under this clause shall be construed as limiting the XYZ Union leadership and members from engaging in concerted activity for their mutual aid and protection. The standards of reasonableness of behaviors when engaging in such concerted activity shall be the standards as determined by the NLRB and under the interpretations of the NLRA (or state level labor law) by the courts having jurisdiction over XYZ Company and its employees.

Negotiations for an anti-bullying clause should easily take place under a mutual gains bargaining approach. Union leaders should understand what is referred to as the "business case" to eliminate workplace bullying. This in essence is the benefit to the employer of eliminating workplace bullying. There is a strong business case to eliminate workplace bullying. As discussed in Chapter 3 of this volume, bullies cost organizations millions of dollars per year, harm productivity and morale, lead to turnover and absenteeism and provide no meaningful organizational benefit. However, despite this case being readily available to all employers, employers for the most part have not taken steps to eliminate workplace bullying and to implement anti-bullying policies. So union leaders and members should expect the bargaining over such a clause to require leverage and hard bargaining. Negotiators must not forget the pervasiveness and severity of bullying in the workplace. Keep in mind that the vast majority of workers – your members – are impacted in a negative way by workplace bullying during their careers. These negative effects can be severe, including PTSD-type symptoms, engaging in violent retaliation and even suicide. Union leaders should be as ready to stand strong to secure an anti-bullying/harassment clause as they are for any other clause under a CBA.

While a direct, anti-bullying clause would be an ideal way to address the issue through collective bargaining, unions can also address workplace bullying through other substantive or even procedural measures. First, unions can negotiate broader clauses protecting worker dignity or worker safety (including psychological and emotional safety) to provide remedies to the harms often caused by workplace bullying. Unions can also negotiate rights to access for potential ameliorative measures. Unions can also simply craft a general harassment clause. Again, in this case, the necessary language to prevent any limitation on legal rights would be needed. However, such clause could simply state that members have a right to be free from workplace harassment. Harassment is defined as unwanted, objectionable behavior that is severe and/or pervasive enough to unreasonably interfere with the working environment and/or to create an intimidating or hostile environment.

Unions can also address the specific tactics of bullying during collective bargaining. For instance, many of the forms of bullying discussed in Chapter 4 of this volume could be addressed through collective bargaining. Clauses can address specific job requirements and the limitations on these. Clauses can address the formation of committees and assignment of jobs or tasks. Clauses can protect members against one-on-one meetings (even if they are non-disciplinary). Clauses should address work tasks and assignments, specific job duties and the power (limitations on the power) for supervisors to call employees to meetings. Clauses could also be implemented to protect bystanders and those who would stand up against workplace bullying.

Yet another possibility is to make workplace bullying that is current in the workplace a topic of the collective bargaining. During my time as an HR professional, I saw this occur in one unionized facility. While this facility had a long history of intimidating supervision and bad relationships between workers and supervisors, one particular supervisor was considered to be the biggest bully in the facility. This supervisor had many grievances filed against him. Many of these complaints fell outside of the CBA language, but the union decided they would address these anyway. They did so in the day to day by filing these grievances as well as taking other measures, but they also assured us they would address these during the collective bargaining phase. In fact, they had stated that they would not even sit down at the table until we took steps to address the bullying behavior. For that reason, as well as other more positive reasons, the management at this facility did indeed address the behaviors well ahead of the collective bargaining sessions.

Day-to-day CBA management

Unions can also protect members from workplace bullying via the day-to-day management of the collective bargaining agreement – whether the agreement has a direct workplace bullying clause "The workplace is where union members have power – real and potential."[10] By dealing with workplace bullies on a day-to-day basis, unions can make members' lives better. Unions can do so by enforcing direct anti-bullying clauses, enforcing indirect clauses that could address workplace bullying and/or by engaging in other forms of direct action when bullying occurs in the workplace.

If a union has succeeded in negotiating a direct anti-bullying clause, they should take the enforcement of such clause very seriously. While enforcing a hard-won clause would seem to be obvious, such measures are not always taken by union leaders. Instead, the day-to-day operations, especially in terms of the working environment, are too often ceded to management oftentimes to protect some form of partnership with management.[11] This concern about splintering such a relationship might be even stronger when the union is called upon to accuse the management of engaging in bullying. Rather than focusing on this relationship between union leaders and management, the leaders will need to focus on the rights of the members to adequately enforce the anti-bullying clause.

The leadership must take every claim of bullying, harassment, general harassment, abusive supervision and so on seriously. While union members are often more willing to bring claims forward, taking such a step is still a very hard step to take. Union leaders should be aware of this. They must also be aware of some of the effects of being bullied and how this might be perceived as something else (i.e. anxiety, paranoia, etc.). The leadership must understand that a weak response to the bullying is likely to be seen as support of the behavior, allowing the behavior to become worse. The target will see this response as being non-supportive, and they, as well as other bystanders and targets, will be less likely to bring a claim forward.

Likewise, unions should also look to enforce indirect clauses with just as much vigor. Winning an anti-bullying clause is not easy. However, when bullying leads to the violation of other clauses, pursuing these claims can bring to light the problems with workplace bullying. Union leaders and activists can look for dignity clauses, health and safety clauses, or respect type clauses in the contract to grieve acts of workplace bullying. One union I worked with in the Midwest had a great deal of success grieving workplace bullying as a violation of the employer's general duty under the CBA's health and safety clause.

Further, unions, stewards and even activist members can create disincentives for specific bullies to continue their bullying behavior. In other words, they can eliminate bullying behavior via punishment (the behavior being followed by a negative stimuli) or negative reinforcement (only taking away a negative stimulus when the behavior truly stops). The union I worked with in the deep south did just this to the bullying supervisor. They assured that workers refused to work voluntary overtime in his areas, they helped workers to bid out of his area and they helped workers in his area get on FMLA, driving the absenteeism in his area well above the plant average. Another union explained how they used the nuisance grievance approach to send a message to bullying managers by writing a flurry or storm of grievances against that bully.

The dangers of the weak response

While unions can help to eliminate workplace bullying of their members throughout the labor relations process, they also must be aware of how their actions or inactions can promote and exacerbate the problem of workplace bullying. Just as a lack of commitment by management to address workplace bullying sends the signal that such behavior is accepted or even promoted, unions can send these same signals. While I have worked with many unions who have helped to address workplace bullying, I have also seen unions who have failed to address the problem and created a culture of bullying for their members.

In one local professional union, I saw a weak and disjointed response to workplace bullying signal to members that the union would likely not take their side in addressing workplace bullying and signal to management that they were free to engage in such bullying. This union failed to address the concerns brought forward by numerous members concerning bullying behaviors on the part of management. While they did step in when the management attempted to discipline the targets of their bullying by showing up for the potential disciplinary meeting and forcing the management to revoke formal discipline because they had failed to follow the process, they continued to refuse to address the bullying. Further, they even conceded to allowing one manager to keep his own disciplinary file about a target of his bullying, when the organization had been forced to pull the record of discipline from the target's file.

Because the union leadership failed to address the bullying behavior, numerous targets turned to informal leaders to assist them and to represent them during meetings with management. Rather than support this concerted activity, the local union President decided to issue a cease and desist order directed at one of these informal leaders and then to request a legal memo from the statewide union attorney supporting his letter. There was no concern that the members felt they were being bullied by management and that the union leader was doing nothing to address this. Instead, the union leadership attempted to prevent their own members from engaging in protected concerted activity. While this union could have taken numerous steps to address the workplace bullying through the formal grievance process, informal meetings and complaints, publication of the bullies' behaviors and concerted action, they instead chose to do nothing other than to engage in the bare minimum representation of members at meetings. These weak and ineffective responses indicated a form of tacit approval of the bullying behavior or at least signaled such behavior would go unpunished. The response led to an increase in the bullying behavior, followed by the resignation, retirement and medical leave by several of the targeted employees.

In addition to the potential for weak responses by union members, we also cannot ignore another limiting factor on union activity as a solution to workplace bullying and that is union density. Just over 1 in 10 U.S. workers are currently represented by a union. That means that 9 out of 10 workers will not have any chance to have a union address workplace bullying at the collective bargaining table or in the day to day of working. Further, this union density number has been on a consistent decline, indicating that those who might be assisted in addressing their bullying during a union organizing drive is not even keeping up with the number of U.S. workers losing the protections at other phases of the labor relations process. A solution that leaves out nearly 90% of potential targets is not an acceptable solution. However, for those that are members of unions, these steps to address bullying should clearly be taken by union leaders and demanded by union members.

Benefits to unions of addressing workplace bullying in all three phases

Not only does concerted activity present a potential path for targets, but bullying presents a potential path for union revitalization. Addressing workplace bullying can be a benefit to specific unions and to the labor movement in general. Addressing workplace bullying can lead to increased union power, increased perception of union efficacy by members and presents a potential path to organizing success and potentially labor revitalization.

In the United States, current union density stands at right around 12% overall and 7% in the private sector.[12] No serious labor researcher, advocate or leader can deny that labor is in trouble of becoming what is often phrased too small to matter.[13] This low union density rate is in stark contrast to the high rates of workplace bullying that are so devastating to the targets. Brofenbrenner found that a key to successful organizing is focusing on "issues that resonate in the workplace . . . focusing on two or more of the following during the campaign; dignity, fairness, quality of service, power, voice or collective representation."[14] The reality is that a focus on bullying addresses all of these issues. Unions that address or propose that they will address workplace bullying can achieve the love, hope and saliency that has been critical to successful organizing.[15] I have seen this love, hope and saliency lead to a class consciousness even amongst research participants and I have also seen how addressing bullying helped to spur on at least one organizing drive.

Workplace bullying can lead to the deprivation of dignity that often leads to a desire for an employee to take action,[16] and the fact that there is no current remedy and there are no perceived effective individual paths to remedy workplace bullying suggests that targets of workplace bullying may indeed take the second step of the process of looking to collective action to resolve the issue. However, even if targets take this path, there is still the possibility of them taking other action, for example quitting or retiring. In order to take the step to concerted activity, the conditions of love, hope and saliency must exist.[17]

During the course of my initial research on workplace bullying, I saw how love, hope and saliency were all built in the course of half-day focus groups. By the end of the focus groups, the targets of workplace bullying who participated had, in each case, built a form of class consciousness amongst their class of eight. Love in this case is defined as "people caring for each other to act together and share good interrelationships."[18] During these focus groups, participants became very defensive for each other. On several occasions when a research participant would express that he/she was not sure if his/her experiences were truly at the level of bullying, it was others who stepped in and stated that they were. For instance, Julie, after sharing her story, stated (as she had during the initial interview) that she still felt like perhaps she was just complaining and should just be tougher. The other group members immediately responded by explaining she was not to blame and what happened to her was unacceptable. In one case, a university faculty member expressed that she was not bullied because she would not be controlled. However, another member of the focus group suggested that the attempt to control her was just as much bullying as if she had been controlled and that if this were done to a different faculty member it would have been bullying. Each time a target would attempt to minimize his/her experiences, other participants expressed their anger over what the target had experienced. By the time each target had shared an experience with other members in the group, there seemed to be a legitimate concern for each other that permeated the group.

We might also see this "love" in the case of bystander interventions. Gaffney and colleagues found that that nurses do make attempts to interject to protect other nurses who are being bullied.[19] This could be the result of nursing having a high rate of bullying and these bystander protectors also feeling this type of class consciousness with their bullied co-workers. This consciousness would clearly rise to the level of "love" in Weikle and colleagues' organizing model. However, love is not enough, there still must be hope and saliency to create a class consciousness and willingness to engage in concerted activity.

Saliency is defined as "the recognition that problems exist and are commonly perceived by members of the work group."[20] On several occasions during the course of interviews, research participants shared their belief that they were the "only ones experiencing their problems." One research participant mentioned to me that even if others were experiencing what she defined as an uncivil atmosphere that she felt like she was probably simply being a "whiner" to even bring it up in the course of this research. Another participant (this one outside of the university setting) mentioned that his experience had occurred in his first real exposure to the working world (he mentioned he had previously worked at a fast food restaurant). He expressed that perhaps what he was going through was just part of the normal process of work. While this participant as well as others mentioned that the initial survey on workplace bullying had made them think about their working environment in a different light, it was not really until the focus group that the participants really began to show this saliency. However, at this stage, the saliency went beyond the walls of the university and really seemed to spur a form of working class consciousness – the idea that all workers were in the same boat and even if they were not experiencing workplace bullying, they were susceptible to bullying. It was from this class consciousness that the members of the focus groups became interested in working together to solve their problems of workplace bullying. It would be very easy for a union organizer to engage in this same type of consciousness to raise the saliency of the issue of workplace bullying. Given the prevalence of workplace bullying, convincing potential members that it is occurring should not be an onerous task. However, given the reaction by many targets of both bullying and even unlawful harassment of justifying the behaviors in some way, the key would be to show that these behaviors are unacceptable and detrimental.

Finally, the potential members must have hope. They must believe that the union will be able to address the problem that they share, that concerted activity can indeed be a solution.[21] In order to achieve this hope, unions can take a number of steps. First, they can and should represent the workers who are being bullied. Second, they can teach members how to engage together to address the workplace bullying. Finally, they can achieve successes for members on other issues.

This potential for organizing success not only played out in the research, but it also played out in the university organizing drive referenced earlier in this chapter. For one bargaining unit member, the lack of "hope" kept him from joining the union. Because the state had no collective bargaining rights for state employees and this was a state school, he felt that organizing without these rights would simply lead to more frustration rather than any effective resolution. He stated that if the state were to pass collective bargaining rights, he would immediately join the union. However, other targets engaged in my research as well as many other bargaining unit members did see the love, hope and saliency that the organizing drive offered. Many of the bargaining unit members viewed the President as a bully. His bullying behavior was often discussed in union meetings and in the hallways. The bargaining unit members also saw how the union organizing drive demonstrated hope that concerted activity could address the bullying. They saw the union progressively addressing the issue – first through discussions, then in union events, then to the trustees, then in the grievance process and in the press. They also saw how these actions began to impact the bullying President and many of the bullies around him. It was the success of these early steps that led to hope amongst bargaining unit members that led to a successful organizing drive.

Union spillover/threat effect

Union activity not only benefits the members of unions, but also has a spillover effect (or threat effect) for non-union workers.[22] In concept, non-union employers will implement common union worker protections, rights or benefits in order to avoid unionization (threat effect) or to be able to recruit and retain workers (spillover effect). For instance, we see this effect with wages because there is a wage premium for unionized workers; where union density is high, there is a spillover and non-union workers also receive higher wages.[23] This same threat or spillover effect applies to all of the wages, benefits and terms and conditions of employment, including protection from workplace bullying and protection of dignity in the workplace. Of course, as the labor movement has weakened, this spillover effect has also weakened. However, this spillover effect can still have at least some impact. If unions demand a workplace free from generalized harassment or bullying and this becomes the norm in collective bargaining agreements and unionized workplaces, this norm will spread to other employers.

Intra-union bullying

In addition to protecting members from harassment and bullying from managers and customers, union leadership must also play a role in addressing harassment and bullying amongst its members. The *Cooper Tire & Rubber* case discussed in Chapter 9 in this volume exemplifies this issue, and the national reaction to the *Cooper Tire & Rubber* decision exemplifies this need. While the Cooper Tire & Rubber strike should have been a focus on corporate greed at the expense of workers, much of the attention instead was directed at racially charged language by locked out workers. During picketing in response to the lockout, at least one USW picketer yelled racially charged comments at a van of replacement workers (from several seconds to minutes after they had actually passed the picket line). There is little doubt that the environment on the picket line was heated and emotionally charged. This was readily recognized by the NLRB. However, this fact did little to prevent employer-side attorneys and HR organizations from suggesting that the NLRB, this union and unions in general supported racial harassment and bullying and left employers unable to fully address such bullying.

This inflammatory, hostile and bullying language by the protestor was understandable given the situation (locked out work, concessions being thrust upon the union and replacement workers being bussed in), but it does not mean the behaviors were entirely excusable or that the union should not itself have taken steps to address this type of bullying and to, in the future, prevent such bullying and harassment. Unions should most assuredly address bullying amongst union members. They should clearly take steps such as those outlined for employers to prevent, detect, remedy and eliminate bullying in their organizations. This should not only apply to the staffers employed directly by the organization, but should also apply to members. First, unions have an instrumental reason to prevent this type of bullying. Their power is based on solidarity. They cannot afford to lose the hearts or minds of members who have become targets of other union members. Second, they may indeed have a legal obligation to take measures to remedy and even prevent the bullying of their members. Unions have a duty of fair representation. Their responsibility is to protect their members and to take steps to make their work lives better. Given the terrible outcomes to targets of workplace bullying, it would seem nonsensical to suggest that their advocate in the workplace could simply turn the other way to such behaviors. Finally, unions have a clear moral responsibility to address these behaviors. Workplace bullying and harassment does not benefit anyone. No members of a union should ever be subjected to such behaviors, whether the bully is a member of management or another bargaining unit member.

Given these practical, moral and even legal responsibilities, unions should address workplace bullying of fellow union members in their by-laws. These by-laws should include the type of bullying policies that I have suggested here for employers. They should provide a reasonable reporting system for members who have been bullied by other members, there should be an avenue for a prompt, fair and impartial fact-finding investigation, and, where bullying is found to have occurred, there should be remedies available to make the target whole, to stop the current bullying and to deter future bullying.

Labor movement's role in bringing about legislative change

The final way for unions and concerted activity to play a role in eliminating workplace bullying in the United States will be discussed in more detail in the final chapter of this book because it entails the role of the labor movement and concerted activity in general to support and pass anti-bullying legislation. As Harthill pointed out, a coalition of the labor movement and activists worked together to change the focus on the employment relationship in the United Kingdom.[24] They forced policy makers and employers to recognize the right to dignity in the workplace, and it was only once this focus was established that any measures to address workplace bullying in a meaningful way became possible. Not only was the coalition important, but so was the broader social movement that this coalition helped to spur. As will be discussed in Chapter 12 of this volume, this type of social movement is needed to force policy makers to implement the very necessary step of strong, anti-workplace bullying legislation with strong enforcement. Unions have been a part of these social movements on numerous employment issues. Unions fought for and eventually won the eight-hour day, the five-day work week, prohibitions against child labor and nearly every piece of legislation protecting workers. Unions should be willing to take this same step to eliminate workplace bullying.

Unions and concerted activity in general offer a clear path to preventing, detecting, remedying and eliminating workplace bullying. Union leaders and activists can take steps to address workplace bullying at every phase of the labor relations process. Organizers can build organizing drives around address-ing bullying behaviors in the workplace. Union organizers can act as employee advocates throughout the organizing phase and help them to address work-place bullying through formal and informal complaints and direct action. In the collective bargaining phase, union leaders can bargain for clauses that directly address workplace bullying. They can also bargain for indirect clauses that address the forms and outcomes of workplace bullying, such as clauses granting workers more control over their work or health, safety and dignity protections in the workplace. Union leaders and members can also help to eliminate work-place bullying by enforcing these clauses in a strong, meaningful and consist-ent manner. Where clauses protecting targets do not exist, union leaders and members can and should support direct, concerted action to respond to bul-lying behaviors. However, union leaders must be sure that they do indeed take this issue seriously and that they address it effectively, as weak, ineffective and inconsistent responses to workplace bullying will only exacerbate the problems for targets and empower the workplace bullies. By taking strong actions against workplace bullying, unions can increase their own organizing and mobilizing. By creating bullying-free working environments, unionized workplaces will also benefit non-union workers via the spillover effect. However, given the cur-rent level of union density, these direct actions by the labor movement are not enough. The labor movement and its leaders must also play a role in pushing for strong legislation with strong enforcement. A labor coalition is also a critical component of pushing for meaningful national legislation to address workplace bullying and such legislation is a necessary step to eliminating workplace bully-ing and protecting workers' right to dignity in the workplace.

Notes

1 (Budd, 2013); (Rosenfeld, 2014); (Yates, 2009).
2 (Moody, 2007).
3 (Yates, 2009).
4 (Carbo & Hughes, 2010).
5 (Carbo, 2009).
6 (Budd, 2013).
7 (Carbo & Hughes, 2010).
8 (Budd, 2013); (Yates, 2009).
9 (Broefenbrenner & Hickey, 2003).
10 (Moody, 2007, p. 177).
11 (Moody, 2007).
12 (Budd, 2013).
13 (Brofenbrenner, 2005).
14 (Broefenbrenner & Hickey, 2003, p. 10).

15 (Weikle, et al., 1998).
16 (Wheeler, 2002).
17 (Weikle, et al., 1998, p. 199).
18 (Weikle, et al., 1998, p. 199).
19 (Gaffney, et al., 2012).
20 (Weikle, et al., 1998, p. 199).
21 (Weikle, et al., 1998).
22 (Budd, 2013); (Rosenfeld, 2014).
23 (Yates, 2009).
24 (Harthill, 2008).

11 The need for a strong law and strong enforcement

When Bill came into my office, he had already been turned away by a dozen attorneys. He told me that when he informed the attorneys that he made $9 an hour, the majority had no interest in even meeting with him. Others turned him away when he told them that he was being harassed by an African-American general manager. Bill was also African-American and so these attorneys seemed to think he had no chance of proving a claim of racial harassment. The few remaining attorneys told him that his manager's behaviors were not severe enough to raise a claim. By the time Bill came to my office, he was completely dejected and resigned to having to simply give up and leave his job.

Bill did not belong to a union, so like 85% plus of American workers, he had no true advocate to stand up for him. Bill had gone to HR, but like most targets of workplace bullying, the HR department did not believe Bill. After all, Bill was the first to complain about his manager and his manager had turned around Bill's store from losing money to being one of the most profitable in the region. None of Bill's co-workers would stand up for him. In fact, most ended up engaging with the GM in bullying Bill. Finally, Bill had attempted self-help remedies, but nothing seemed to work – from ingratiation, to conceding, to medication. For Bill as well as the vast majority of others, these remedies were simply not available or helpful. Unfortunately for Bill, his chance of getting any effective remedy through the U.S. legal system was tenuous at best.

While individual solutions, employer solutions and union-based solutions all offer potential paths to eliminate at least some workplace bullying, all of these solutions are far from ideal. They leave too many targets, like Bill, susceptible, put bystanders at risk, fail to fully address workplace bullying or have proven to be inadequate. If we are truly going to address workplace bullying in the United States, then we must develop a strong national law with strong enforcement. However, we must be careful about how we develop this bill. The reality is that there is not likely to be a second chance and an ineffective bill in the long run is worse than no bill at all.

One of the few benefits of the United States lagging behind much of the rest of the industrialized world in addressing bullying is that there is no need to start from a blank slate. As mentioned in Chapter 6 of this volume, there are many lessons we can take from international laws such as those in France, Belgium, the United Kingdom, Sweden and the Province of Quebec. We also should not ignore the lessons from application of our own laws dealing with bullying types of behaviors as discussed in Chapter 5 of this volume. In this chapter, I will first build a proposal for legislation that will meet the goals of preventing, detecting, remedying and eliminating workplace bullying. Second, I will present a number of steps that will need to occur to be able to pass such legislation.

The legal solution to workplace bullying must effectively address all potential acts of bullying. The solution must provide all targets of workplace bullying a path to end their bullying and to be made whole. The legislation must also take steps to prevent and eliminate bullying. This will require protections for those who report bullying, those who protest bullying and those who engage in actions to protect targets of workplace bullying. The legislation must also provide an incentive for employers to take steps to eliminate all forms of bullying and then to prevent any future acts.

Coverage of all forms of workplace bullying defining the prohibited behavior

The first key to an effective piece of legislation addressing workplace bullying is that it must address all forms of workplace bullying. As discussed in Chapter 7 of this volume, this means that the definition of bullying must go beyond the current definitions in the bullying-specific research and it must go further than the definition (or quasi definition) used in the most commonly proposed bill to address workplace bullying – The Healthy Workplace Bill (HWB). The HWB, as proposed by David Yamada, goes well beyond any current protection offered through the U.S. legal system to targets of workplace bullying. However, the Healthy Workplace Bill is flawed and does not provide the protections necessary to eliminate the workplace bullying that strips targets of their right to dignity in the workplace. The reality is that the Healthy Workplace Bill, if passed in its current form, will leave many targets of workplace bullying with no legal recourse simply as a result of defining the phenomena of bullying too narrowly. The HWB fails to cover the full range of bullying behaviors by focusing on too narrow a list of behaviors, placing too much emphasis on a repetitive nature of bullying behaviors, requiring targets to prove not only general but specific intent and requiring targets to prove too high of a level of harm in order to have an actionable claim. However, this should not be viewed as a critique of the HWB. In fact, I recognize that the HWB has led to the first serious discussions of addressing workplace bullying in an effective manner in the United States. Instead, the HWB will be used as a starting point to develop a more comprehensive and effective suggested piece of anti-workplace bullying legislation. My hope would be that even the bill suggested here would be made better and stronger by other advocates and researchers.

The Healthy Workplace bill if enacted would not cover all of the acts of workplace bullying. The bill does not use the term "bullying," but instead uses the term "abusive conduct." The HWB does list a number of different behaviors that would be considered abusive, but also these all tend to fall under the personal type of bullying – derogatory remarks, insults, epithets, verbal, non-verbal behaviors, undermining behaviors.[1] The vast majority of the organizational forms of bullying I defined in Chapter 2 of this volume, which harmed so many targets during my research and career, could be interpreted as falling outside of this proposed bill. As we see in the Swedish Ordinance on Victimisation at Work, as well as the interpretations of the laws in Quebec, France and Belgium, there is no reason to eliminate organizational practices from possibly being viewed as workplace bullying. The Swedish bill specifically includes harmful supervision and administrative penal actions as potential forms of abusive action.[2] In France, the Court of Cassation has extended the definition of moral harassment to align closely with concept of "suffering at work" which could be the result of poor administrative or managerial policies and practices.[3] In both Australia and Quebec, the language of any behavior would seem to include organizational-level bullying.[4] The experiences in these countries and the experiences of targets suggest that administrative or managerial practices should not be excluded from the definition of bullying or the coverage of any effective anti-workplace bullying law. Unfortunately, not only does the HWB fail to include organizational practices as potentially abusive behavior, it also provides an added affirmative defense for many managerial practices and decisions – "reasonably made for poor performance, misconduct, or economic necessity" as well as a reasonable performance evaluation or an investigation of illegal or unethical activity.[5] This language would allow employers to argue many of the actions that impacted the targets of bullying discussed throughout this book to be legitimate business practices.

We also must assure that the definition we use in the bill that is eventually passed covers all forms of interpersonal behaviors that could arise to the level of bullying by harming the target's dignity, esteem and/or other human rights. First, the HWB places too much emphasis on the requirement that the behaviors be repeated or repetitive. The bill states "a single act normally shall not constitute abusive conduct," only making exceptions for behaviors that might meet the definition of IIED "an especially severe and egregious act."[6] This is an error that perhaps started early on in the research literature on workplace bullying. As Hershcovis points out, the repetitive nature is one of the elements often found in the construct of workplace bullying. It is quite possible that this limiting language is in response to concerns from employer-side advocates. However, this response along with others makes the bill largely ineffective.[7] However, this does not mean that this construct has any less or more of an effect on individuals than do constructs that do not address or include this element of repetitiveness.[8] As Cox and Lerouge have each found, single incidents have indeed made up a large percentage of actionable claims in the laws of Quebec, France and Belgium.[9] There is no need for a focus on or requirement of repetitiveness in a bill addressing workplace bullying. The emphasis instead must be on the protection of the dignity of the workers. In France and Quebec, similar language was used in terms of addressing single acts of bullying. However, now that these laws have been in place for a decade or longer, it has become apparent that single acts of bullying are extremely common and should not be treated differently than repetitive behavior.

The HWB would also leave out some of the less obvious or perhaps less severe forms of personal bullying including the types of low-grade incivility discussed as clear forms of bullying in Chapter 2 of this volume. Bullying can take many different forms. The form of the bullying is largely irrelevant, as Raver and Nishii found in their research;[10] as I have seen throughout my career as a researcher, advocate and even manager and as is recognized in many of the laws across the globe. A wide array of behaviors both personal and organizational can indeed harm targets' right to dignity in the workplace. Cortina has found that not only can this low-grade incivility rise to the level of bullying, to a large extent, it may indeed be a new form of unlawful harassment or discrimination in the workplace.[11] Again, as I have seen in my research and in my career as an advocate and manager, what is often thought of as low-grade incivility can have an extremely damaging impact on the targets of such behaviors, causing severe harm emotionally, psychologically, economically and even physically. It makes little sense to exclude these behaviors from a law meant to protect the dignity of workers. The categorization of bullying or abusive behavior or whatever term we use for workplace bullying must strive to be inclusive rather than exclusive. The terminology and its definition must assure that all acts or behaviors that harm the human rights of targets are addressed.

As discussed in the analysis of current U.S. law in Chapter 5 in this volume, one of the most egregious errors we could make in drafting a bill would be requiring the target to show intent. This impossible burden on the target of such behavior is recognized in the burden shifting analysis of disparate treatment (or intentional discrimination) claims, and this error is one of the major reasons that IIED claims are so untenable. The laws in France are clear that harassment can indeed occur in the absence of any form of intent.[12] In fact, there is a strong presumption that anytime there is moral harassment in the workplace, that there was intent.[13] Similarly, in Quebec, the focus is on whether there was the creation of harmful working environment, not whether there was intent to create such harm (Cox, 2010). Following the lead of these laws, there is no reason that we cannot avoid the mistakes of requiring intent that we see in the current U.S. legal system. The goal of a bill addressing workplace bullying is not to place blame, it is to stop the harassing behavior, to make the target whole and to prevent future harassing/bullying behavior directed at the specific target or other targets in the workplace. Unfortunately, the HWB again places a heavy burden of proving intent on the part of targets of workplace bullying – protecting them only from behaviors where an employer or "one or more of its employees [is] acting with intent to cause pain or distress".[14] Not only does this require the general intent of the bully intending to act, but it requires the even higher burden of showing specific intent to cause harm. Comparing this language to the French Social Modernization Act, which has language that states that "moral harassment [is that] which intentionally or unintentionally deteriorates their working condition," it becomes clear that the French Social Modernization Act is much more encompassing and much more likely to address the types of bullying I have discussed throughout the earlier chapters of this book.[15]

Level of harm/rights protected

Perhaps the key to any effective anti-workplace bullying legislation is the harm that such legislation looks to prevent. As discussed in Chapter 5 of this volume, the Supreme Court recognized that targets of harassment based on their gender, race, color, national origin or other protected status should not have to prove psychological harm or physical harm to have an actionable claim. Unfortunately, lower courts often seem to ignore this standard. However, there is no reason that targets of a more general harassment should have to show any heightened level of harm. Much like the Supreme Court focused on a hostile environment (in other words, the enduring of the harassing behavior itself) giving rise to a cognizable claim, we should apply the same standard for targets of general harassment or bullying. We should not require a showing of psychological or physical harm as we see in the HWB. Instead we could again follow the lead from some of the international laws: the French law – "deteriorates their working conditions . . . likely to violate their rights and dignity,"[16] the Belgian law – "the purpose or consequence that the personality, dignity, or physical or psychological integrity of an employee . . . is affected,"[17] the Quebec law – "[behavior] that affects an employee's dignity or psychological or physical integrity."[18] What becomes clear is that the international laws protect more than just physical or psychological harm (particularly when we consider under the HWB the target would have to establish such harm by "competent evidence"). What emerges is a focus on workers' positive right to dignity in the workplace and that such a positive right should be protected. This is why the international laws do not place a strong emphasis on defining prohibited behaviors, the typical negative rights approach to U.S. laws. This focus on dignity and positive rights will also allow us to draft a sensible bill that will protect the human rights of all workers.

Employer responsibility/duty versus employer defense

The HWB also provides too broad of a defense to employers. Rather than requiring effective remedial measures of employers, the Healthy Workplace Bill makes the same mistakes we see from the *Faragher* defense and allows employers to escape responsibility for their working environments and requires employees to jump through hurdles to file a claim.[19] The French law, Belgian law and Quebec law all place a much stricter burden on the employees and do not provide the type of broad defense we see in the *Faragher* defense (or at least its interpretation in the lower courts) as discussed in Chapter 5 of this volume. Instead, these laws place complete responsibility for the organization and its working conditions on the organization. Under French law, employers have an obligation to assure a respect for human rights, to assure the "integrity of the employee as a human being" and to take ALL necessary steps to prevent harassment.[20] In Belgium, there is a strict obligation for employers to protect against workplace harassment.[21] In Sweden, one of the shortcomings of the law is recognized that there are not enough requirements on the employer to prevent bullying in the workplace.[22] It is imperative that we not make this same mistake in any anti-bullying legislation passed in the United States. The HWB in its current form provides language identical to the *Faragher* defense, providing a defense for employers where there is no "adverse employment action" as long as the employer took "reasonable care to prevent and correctly prompt any actionable behavior and the complainant employee unreasonably failed" to take advantage of the employer's system.[23] This defense simply provides too many ways for employers to escape liability and excuses the employer from responsibility over the working environment he/she controls. There is simply no reason not to hold employers accountable for their working environment.

Enforcement

The HWB also fails to offer a clear path of enforcement for many targets of workplace bullying. Access to employment attorneys is already limited for many targets of discrimination and other unlawful employment actions. I have met many clients and targets like Bill who were unable to find an attorney to take their case on a contingency due to the low level of damages (as a result of the low wages they were receiving) and were unable to afford an attorney on an hourly rate. As discussed in Chapter 9 of this volume, under the possibility of ADR as a solution, there is a very real problem with access to the judicial system for victims of employment abuses. Fortunately, in many areas of employment law, there are administrative remedies that allow workers some access to remedies even without an attorney. For instance, in unlawful harassment claims, the EEOC and many state human rights agencies will investigate and even represent complainants (although this representation only happens in very limited circumstances). Likewise, the Department of Labor investigates and can litigate wage and hour violations, OSHA inspects claims of safety violations and the General Counsel's office of the National Labor Relations Board will litigate unfair labor practice claims. Because of the heightened standard for damages and the fact that there is only a private cause of action under the healthy workplace bill, many workers will be left unable to secure representation. This gap must be closed in some way. First, the potential for damages should be increased to give private attorneys incentives to bring claims for targeted employees. Second, the compensable harm must be expanded. Finally, just as we see with harassment and wage and hour claims, targets should have the option of turning to an administrative agency to represent them in their claim.

I do not pretend to have crafted the perfect law. There are many things that are most likely lacking in this proposed legislation, and issues that should still be addressed. However, this proposed bill provides a starting point that addresses the lessons learned from the current U.S. legal system as well as the anti-bullying laws in other countries.

The dignity at work act

An act which addresses, prevents, remedies and eliminates workplace bullying, moral, psychological and general harassment and other forms of abusive behavior in the workplace by assuring workers' right to dignity and other human rights.

I. Findings and Purpose

1   *Generalized workplace harassment and bullying is a severe and pervasive problem in the American workplace. Workplace harassment leads to a loss of esteem, dignity and self-worth for targets and witnesses of workplace bullying. Workplace bullying leads to severe emotional, psychological, economic and physical harm to targets of workplace bullying. Such harms include job loss, prescription addiction, PTSD-like symptoms, suicide ideation, heart disease, stress-induced illnesses, suicide and workplace violence. Generalized workplace harassment/bullying costs American employers millions of dollars in lost productivity, turnover, absenteeism, workers' compensation and medical and legal costs. There is no place for workplace bullying in the American workplace.*

2   *Workplace bullying and general harassment has been studied in the United States for at least the past 30 years. A multitude of employer systems have been made available to address workplace bullying. Despite these decades of work and awareness, employer policies alone have been ineffective in preventing, remedying and eliminating workplace bullying.*

3   *In order to protect workers' right to dignity in the American workplace, legislation must be passed protecting such right and providing for recourse for targets of workplace bullying, psychological, moral and/or general harassment and other abusive behaviors in the workplace.*

4   *It is the purpose of this Act to*

    a   Prevent, detect, remedy and eliminate workplace bullying, moral, psychological and general harassment and other abusive behavior from the American workplace in order to protect workers' right to dignity at all times in the workplace.

    b   Provide a remedy for workers who are targets of workplace bullying, moral, psychological or general harassment and/or other forms of workplace abuse in order to make whole such targets of workplace abuse.

    c   Provide an incentive for employers to prevent, detect, remedy and eliminate workplace bullying, moral, psychological and general harassment and other forms of abuse in the workplace in order that such behaviors shall be addressed and eliminated before they cause harm to the targets of such behaviors.

II. Definitions

1   *Employer – Employers shall be defined as any organization or individual employing an individual to engage in any work on their behalf or on behalf of their subsidiaries,*

customers or clients. This shall include non-profit agencies employing volunteers. This shall also include organizations hiring workers through a temporary agency or other such organization to perform work on their behalf. Employers who exert control over the means, methods, payroll or personnel practices of their suppliers shall be considered joint employers with said supplier for the purpose of this act. Where more than one organization or individual meets the definition of employer under this act, for the purpose of a claim by a targeted employer, such organizations shall have joint and several liability as co-employers.

2   *Employee – One who engages in work for another, whether such work is paid or unpaid and whether such other directly employs said employee.*

3   *Bullying – Workplace bullying shall be defined as the unwanted abuse of any source of power that has the effect of or intent to intimidate, control or otherwise strip a target of his/her right to esteem, growth, dignity, voice or other human rights in the workplace. Workplace bullying may take the form of harassment, incivility, abusive supervision, violence, aggressions and other types of objectionable behaviors. Further, these behaviors may take the form of interpersonal interactions or organizational practices. The behaviors may come from any level of the organization – supervision, co-workers, customers and even direct reports. The source of power shall not be considered as limited to formal organizational power or authority.*

4   *Moral, Psychological or General Harassment – Unwelcome, objectionable conduct that a reasonable person would find to create an intimidating, hostile or abusive working environment.*

III. Worker Right to Dignity in the Workplace

Every worker in the United States shall have the right to a workplace environment that affords them the dignity to which all human beings are entitled, free from all forms of harassment and bullying.

IV. Prohibition against Bullying, Moral, Psychological and General Harassment and other Abusive Behaviors

1   *It shall be unlawful for any individual to engage in workplace bullying, moral, psychological or general harassment of a co-worker or other employee in the working environment.*

V. Employer Responsibility to Assure Worker Dignity and Protect against Workplace Bullying, Moral, Psychological and General Harassment and Other Abusive Behaviors:

1   *Employers shall have a general duty to provide a workplace free from bullying and moral, psychological or general harassment.*

2   *Any employer who allows such behavior to occur in his/her workplace or does not take the steps necessary to prevent, detect and eliminate such behavior in his/her workplace shall be in violation of this law.*

3   *Employers shall have a general duty to provide a workplace free from such behavior and to provide a workplace that protects each employee's personal integrity, dignity and human rights.*

4   *Any employer who allows bullying in his/her workplace or does not take all steps necessary to prevent, detect and eliminate such behavior in his/her workplace shall be in violation of this law and shall be liable for damages to make the targets of such bullying whole, including but not limited to economic damages, damages for pain and suffering and equitable relief.*

5   *Employers shall be required to post notice of employees' rights under this law and to distribute the employer's anti-bullying policy, including an explanation of reporting measures, investigation process and remedial processes.*

6   *Employers shall take all necessary steps to assure that there be no retaliation against any complainant who has filed a complaint under this act in good faith.*

7   *Employers shall take all necessary steps to assure that there be no retaliation against any individual for participating in a complaint as a witness, or for taking action as a bystander to prevent or eliminate bullying of a target.*

VI.   Individual Liability:

Any individual who engages in workplace bullying or moral, psychological or general harassment shall be jointly and severally liable along with his/her employer.

VII.   Remedies:

1   *Targets of workplace bullying shall be entitled to all remedies necessary to make such targets whole. Such remedies shall include the following:*

   a   *Economic damages for lost wages, both back pay and front pay and any expenses related to treatment related to the bullying.*
   b   *Compensable damages to compensate for the pain and suffering, emotional and psychological damages resulting from such workplace bullying.*
   c   *Punitive damages as deemed necessary to deter future acts of workplace bullying.*
   d   *Injunctive relief.*

2   *Courts may also require employers to implement effective anti-bullying policies, including investigation and training policies, and require bullies to engage in training and other remedial measures.*

VIII.   Cause of Action:

1   *The Department of Labor shall establish a division to address workplace bullying and to enforce this act. Such division shall have the right to investigate claims of workplace bullying, represent claimants in the federal court system and during the ALJ process. At the conclusion of the DoL investigation they may bring the complaint in front of an ALJ to litigate the DoL determination, recommend appropriate penalties against an employer and/or engage in mediation between the claimant and employer or issue the claimant a right to sue letter to bring a private claim of action.*

2   In addition claimants shall have the right to litigate such claims via a private cause of action.

3   Statute of Limitations:

    a   Claimants shall have one year from the last act of bullying or moral, psychological or general harassment to either file a complaint with the DoL or to file litigation.

    b   If a claimant files a complaint with the DOL, the statute of limitations for filing a private cause of action is tolled.

    c   Claimants who file with the DOL shall have 90 days to file a private cause of action after the DoL issue a right to sue determination or one year from the last act of workplace bullying whichever is later.

IX. Conflict with Laws

1   Nothing in this law should be construed as limiting employee rights under any other law including rights under Title VII of the Civil Rights Act, The Americans with Disabilities Act, the Age Discrimination in Employment Act and state EEO laws.

2   Nothing in this law should be construed as limiting employee rights under the National Labor Relations Act and/or State Labor Rights laws. Concerted Activity/Section 7 activity under the NLRA as interpreted by the NLRB shall not be construed as workplace bullying or moral, psychological or general harassment.

Moving toward passage of the dignity at work act: The need for a social movement

There is no denying that passing legislation against workplace bullying, particularly in the current pro-business and anti-regulation of commerce environment, is a difficult task, to say the least. As Yates suggests, we (the United States) have "bent over backwards to implement what amounts to a full-scale assault on working people."[24] Even arguments for the most basic protections such as the right to a living wage and maternity leave, neither or which is assured to working Americans, cause great controversy in the United States. We see the same types of reactions to passing anti-workplace bullying legislation, both by the employer-side advocates and even by researchers. For instance, Sanders, Pattison and Bible argue that we should not pass bullying legislation out of fear of frivolous suits. They also argue that we would be legislating nice.

Addressing the naysayers

These arguments against workplace bullying legislation are baseless. First, they ignore the reality that we are talking about protecting a **basic human right**. It is a far cry from protecting the right to dignity to legislating nice. Anti-workplace bullying legislation is NOT about legislating nice. As discussed in Chapters 2, 3 and 4 in this volume, bullying behavior goes well beyond simply not being nice and the impacts of such behaviors are severe. In fact, nobody wins from bullying behavior – not the target, not the organization, not the family of the target, the target's community or society at large. There is simply no justification not to take effective steps to eliminate workplace bullying. Further, there is no public policy argument that we allow individuals to be harmed because we do not want to overburden a court system. If this were a legitimate public policy argument, it is hard to imagine how any employment legislation from the Fair Labor Standards Act, the Wagner Act to the Civil Rights Act could have ever been passed, considering the potential for the rush of litigation under each of these acts at the time of their passage. Further, consider the slippery slope of this argument. If anti-trust, criminal, personal injury, medical malpractice, consumer safety litigations were to become so common as to overburden the court, would this same argument not apply? This argument would suggest that by violating a law enough and increasing the costs of enforcement, the bad actors could in essence override the law by assuring that it would not be enforced. We would never allow that argument in these cases; it makes no sense to support this argument in terms of workplace bullying.

Perhaps the real concern is not the possibility of an overload of lawsuits, but the possibility of frivolous lawsuits. Yamada mentions this same concern and this is why he suggests a heightened standard of harm and behavior for workplace bullying claims.[25] Lueders suggests that even the Healthy Workplace Bill with these heightened standards of behavior and harm would open up too many potential claims.[26] Again, this concern is unfounded. There is simply no evidence that frivolous lawsuits create a problem under the EEO laws, or that frivolous IIED claims are clogging up the state courts and causing employers great distress. In fact, as mentioned in Chapter 5 of this volume, the real concern is that the great majority of complaints are never brought forward in any manner. Further, we already have methods to assure against frivolous suits and to address frivolous suits, including 12(b)(6) of the Federal Rules of Civil Procedure. States also can have similar measures. So the argument about concerns of frivolous suits in reality is a moot point or a baseless argument.

Second, these pundits and researchers ignore the reality that we already have statutes protecting against bullying behavior, but only when such behavior is based on a protected status. Even if these types of harassing behaviors do account for only 25% of the bullying incidents, the reality is that it does not create some onerous burden. Just as when an employer implements a strong anti-harassment policy, there may indeed be an initial flood of claims. However, if the law is correctly written and implemented, the employer will take steps to prevent, detect, remedy and eliminate workplace bullying, thus eliminating the need for litigation. It is hard to imagine that anyone would be against a target of workplace bullying having a legal remedy available when his/her employer has failed to provide an adequate remedy. We address unlawful harassment in the U.S. (although we do not always address it adequately), we can address status blind harassment as well. Further, we see other countries such as France, Canada, Australia, Belgium and Germany all addressing workplace bullying or general harassment. We need to stop making American exceptionalism about being the only country that cannot protect human rights. This is not the way we want to be exceptional. Instead, we should join the rest of the advanced economies around the world and take steps to protect workers' human rights including the right to be free from workplace bullying and harassment.

The right to dignity is one of the foundations of all human rights. According to Rene Cassin, a French legal scholar and Nobel laureate, "dignity, liberty, equality and brotherhood," form the foundation of human rights.[27] According to the Vienna Doctrine, "all human rights derive from the dignity, and worth inherent in the human person."[28] Dignity "plays an important role in ensuring a standard for the protection of civil and political rights and social and economic rights in Europe."[29] Human rights are rights one has by virtue of the simple fact of being a human. These rights apply to all humans regardless of race, color, gender, national origin, immigration status or any other status or position. These rights go beyond the mere ability to survive, and instead include those things needed to live the life of a human being. The key to human rights is of course the enforcement and protection of these rights for all. Enjoyment of these rights are what make us human in the first place. Human rights exist not only as the requisites for health, but to fulfill those needs for a life worthy of a human being.[30] Under the UDHR, it is recognized that to uphold this right to dignity, employees must be assured safe, just and favorable working conditions – clearly this includes the right to be free from bullying in the workplace.

Building the movement

These steps will indeed be a profound change. As is suggested by Bachman, such a change requires a social movement.[31] In order to involve masses of people in such a movement, according to Chong, it becomes necessary that individuals be able to identify social and psychological benefits from their participation.[32] Much in the same way that one makes a decision to participate in the collective action of forming a union, I would suggest that individuals must be able to identify a benefit of such movement (or a detriment of the status quo) and believe that the movement will be able to produce such a benefit.[33]

First, there needs to be an education of workers to inform them that bullying does not have to be a part of work and that their human rights in the workplace could be afforded legal protections, as in the laws of Sweden, France, Quebec and the United Kingdom. Workers are often unaware of what few legal protections they currently have in the workplace, especially in comparison to other industrialized countries. My experiences in teaching employment law to undergraduate students have been that many students believe employers in the United States can fire them only for good cause, that the United States must have the most employee-friendly leave laws, vacation time and other benefits of any country around the world. Students are often shocked and outraged when they learn about the state of employment law in the United States, and especially when I cover comparative laws. If the average worker is like my average student, they have no reason to be outraged, because they believe the laws in the United States are much more protective of their rights than they actually are. Targets of bullying also may not be aware of their own working conditions. One research participant stated that she could not be bullied because she would not allow it to happen to her. During the course of one focus group, in response to other participants' stories, she decided that she had indeed been bullied and became angry about the bullying. Another participant said she never thought of her situation as bullying until she filled out the initial survey. After that, she explored her working situation in more detail and began to notice all of the negative effects from her work that were spilling over into her home life.

Education about the current legal system in the United States and about workplace bullying is the first step to establishing this social movement. Activists and advocates for workers from various areas should play a role in this education. Activists in the labor movement; labor unions; labor union education departments; organizations such as the Labor and Employment Relations Association, the United Association of Labor Education and the Labor Research Action Network and non-profits such as the National Workplace Bullying Coalition should all participate in educating current and future workers about their legal rights or lack thereof in the workplace, the pervasiveness and severity of bullying and the methods taken in other countries to address workplace bullying.

Second, more needs to be done to convince workers that collective action can be successful and to convince individuals that only through such collective action will there be any benefit. Chong suggests that individuals will get a social benefit from participation when they have some sort of moral sense of requirement to participate,[34] for instance, if they believe that their participation is important to benefit those with whom they have social ties. The sharing of stories of targeted employees may be one way to create such feeling of obligation. Chong also suggests that the potential to play the Good Samaritan and the potential feeling of accomplishment in engaging in a social movement can also spur individuals to participate.[35] It is critical to spur such a movement. Without this social movement, there is little reason to expect that laws to protect employees will be passed, and without such laws it is unlikely that bullying will ever be eliminated from the workplace. Worker educators should share stories of past successes – such as those in the Fight for $15 and the array of successes of the labor movement throughout history. Activists should also fight for small successes to support the potential for longer term, larger success. For instance, union leaders and activists should be willing to defend bullied employees in their workplaces. They should be willing to assist these workers in filing complaints or engaging in concerted activity to address their bully. Activists will need to take creative steps to help this movement to gain traction.

In the current pro-employer environment, a meaningful anti-bullying piece of legislation will not be passed without a movement that forces such passage. Very few elected officials will be willing to stand up to the corporate lobby and expend political capital on this issue. However, passing a bill that is acceptable to the employer lobby will not address workplace bullying in a meaningful and effective manner. If we are to address workplace bullying and protect workers' human rights to dignity, esteem and well-being, then we must spur the movement that will lead to a meaningful and effective anti-workplace bullying law.

The only true solution to workplace bullying is a strong law with strong enforcement. Such a law must protect all targets of workplace bullying and must afford such targets access to a remedy that will make them whole. The law must also provide a meaningful incentive for employers to address workplace bullying – to take steps to prevent workplace bullying before it happens, to detect all acts of workplace bullying, to eliminate these acts from their workplaces and to remedy the damages to targets and bystanders. This law will need to first and foremost protect workers' right to dignity. It will need to broadly define workplace bullying in order to capture the currently divided definitions of various workplace abuses. The law will need to provide access to the remedies for all targets, including those who may struggle to gain access to the courts due to financial reasons. The law must hold employers accountable for their workplaces.

Such a law is not pie-in-the-sky type of thinking. We have seen steps taken internationally, such as in Sweden, Canada, Germany, Belgium and France, to effectively address workplace bullying and to protect workers' right to dignity. The failure to do so in the United States is simply a failure to develop the political will to defend workers and a capitulation to the various employer lobbies who oppose such a law. In order to overcome this inertia towards the employer interest, activists and advocates must help to create a social movement around workplace bullying. This will require informing workers and the public about the very real, pervasive and devastating problem of workplace bullying. This will also entail informing the workers and public about the very real possibilities for addressing workplace bullying, such as those taken in other countries. If we are ever to effectively prevent, detect, remedy and eliminate workplace bullying, these steps must be taken.

Notes

1 (Story & Flanagan, House Docket 2072, No 1771, 2015).
2 Swedish Ordinance on Victimisation at Work, as posted at http://bullyonline.org/old/action/victwork.htm, visited January 13, 2017.
3 (Lerouge, 2010, p. 124).
4 Quebec Law on Psychological Harassment at Work (Squelch & Guthrie, 2010).
5 (Story & Flanagan, House Docket 2072, No 1771, 2015, Section 6[a] & [b]).
6 (Story & Flanagan, House Docket 2072, No 1771, 2015, Section 2).
7 (Herschcovis, 2011).
8 (Herschcovis, 2011); (Raver & Nishii, 2010).
9 (Cox, 2010); (Lerouge, 2010).
10 (Raver & Nishii, 2010).
11 (Cortina, 2008).
12 (Lerouge, 2010).
13 (Lerouge, 2010).
14 (Story & Flanagan, House Docket 2072, No 1771, 2015, Section 2).

15 (Lerouge, 2010, p. 112).
16 (Lerouge, 2010).
17 (Lerouge, 2010).
18 (Cox, 2010).
19 (Story & Flanagan, House Docket 2072, No 1771, 2015).
20 (Lerouge, 2010, p. 115).
21 (Lerouge, 2010).
22 (Hoel & Einarsen, 2010).
23 (Story & Flanagan, House Docket 2072, No 1771, 2015, Section 4[b][1] & [2]).
24 (Yates, 2009, p. 132).
25 (Yamada, 2004).
26 (Lueders, 2008).
27 (Ishay, 2004, p. 3).
28 (The United Nations, 1993).
29 (Toth, 2008, p. 276).
30 (Donnelly, 2003).
31 (Donnelly, 2003).
32 (Chong, 1991).
33 (Weikle, et al., 1998).
34 (Chong, 1991).
35 (Chong, 1991).

12 Conclusion

Workplace bullying is a devastating and pervasive problem in the American workplace. Millions of workers are targets of workplace bullying each and every day they enter their workplaces. This bullying strips targets of their most fundamental human rights. Targets are stripped of their dignity, esteem and self-worth. They are stripped of the fundamental rights in the workplace assured under the Universal Declaration of Human Rights, including the right to just and favorable working conditions. Targets of bullying suffer economic, psychological, emotional and even physical harm. Targets of bullying are often forced to leave their employment, turn to pharmaceuticals or self-help medication to deal with their bullying, and even consider suicide and attempt to kill themselves to escape the bullying.

Targets of bullying also do not suffer alone. Bystanders, families and communities all suffer. Witnesses to workplace bullying often suffer from depression in the same way as the targets. They also often feel forced to leave their employment. Families suffer the fallout from the damaged targets as do communities. Workplace bullying also damages organizations and is extremely costly to organizations from a financial standpoint. Organizations that allow for bullying see increased turnover and absenteeism and decreased morale. Organizations lose billions of dollars in direct and indirect costs as a result of bullying.

Not only is workplace bullying extremely damaging, it is also extremely pervasive. Millions of American workers suffer from workplace bullying and millions more are targeted throughout the globe. At any one time, even with a narrow definition of workplace bullying, upwards of one in three workers in the United States are being targeted for workplace bullying. It is simply unacceptable to consider that 50+ million workers are stripped of their human rights when they enter a workplace as a result of a problem that can indeed be prevented, detected, remedied and eliminated.

In order for this bullying to even occur, society, organizations and bullies must all engage in steps to allow for the bullying. As the U.S. system of advanced capitalism has progressed to a complete profit focus, society has become more and more accepting of the behaviors that bullies use to torment their targets. We even see high-rated television programs that glorify workplace bullying and the workplace bullies. The same organizations that oppose meaningful legislation either allow or support workplace bullying, as without one or the other, bullying would not occur. Organizations allow the bullying by turning the other way and by failing to address complaints of bullying in any effective manner. They support bullying by promoting and rewarding workplace bullies.

The current U.S. legal system is not effective at addressing workplace bullying in any meaningful way. The EEO laws which prohibit status-based harassment do not address the majority of incidents of workplace bullying. The status-based requirement, the sexualized nature of court interpretations of harassment, the severe AND pervasive standard often applied by courts and the overly broad *Faragher* defense all leave millions of targets of bullying with no protection under the EEO laws. Likewise, targets have no real common law claim. While IIED comes closest to addressing workplace bullying, the standard of severity, the intent requirement and the standard of harm leave the vast majority of targets with no real avenue of recourse.

While the U.S. legal system has not addressed workplace bullying that does not mean it cannot be addressed from a legal standpoint. Statutory, administrative and common laws have been used to address workplace bullying in Sweden, France, Belgium, Canada, the United Kingdom, Australia and Germany, as well as a host of other countries. While many of these laws have flaws, they all present targets with better options than what we see in the United States. Further, we see efforts in all of these instances to make these laws better by better protecting targets and by taking steps to provide incentives for employers to prevent, detect, remedy and eliminate workplace bullying.

In order to fully address workplace bullying, we must have a full and complete understanding of workplace bullying and we must have a definition that will capture all of the different potential forms of workplace bullying. Bullying comes in many different forms, from all different levels of any organization. Targets' experiences with workplace bullying demonstrate that many of the narrow definitions of workplace bullying fail to address the very real abuses they endure in the workplace. By understanding the experiences of targets, we can close the gaps in the definitions of workplace bullying and develop a more comprehensive and effective definition of workplace bullying that can be used in legislation as well as by proactive employers to prevent and eliminate workplace bullying. Workplace bullying is the unwanted abuse of any source of power that has the effect of or intent to intimidate, control or otherwise strip a target of his/her right to esteem, growth, dignity, voice or other human rights in the workplace. Workplace bullying may take the form of harassment, incivility, abusive supervision, violence, aggressions and other types of objectionable behaviors. Further, these behaviors may take the form of interpersonal interactions or organizational practices. The behaviors may come from any level of the organization – supervision, co-workers, customers and even direct reports. The source of power shall not be considered as limited to formal organizational power or authority.

There are steps that can be taken at the individual and organizational level to address workplace bullying. Targets often take self-help such as ameliorating the stress of workplace bullying through medications, self-medication or other stress-relief methods. Targets also often look to avoid the bullying by avoiding work through absences, leaves or quitting. Targets sometimes even look to end the bullying by confronting their bullies or the ingratiation of their bullies. However, none of these self-help methods truly effectively address workplace bullying. Bystanders might also intervene on the target's behalf. These bystanders may try to deflect or change the bullying behavior or even help the target to file a formal complaint. Unfortunately, this bystander intervention has been largely unsuccessful; the helpful bystanders often find themselves the targets of retaliation from the bully and other organizational actors.

Employers are indeed in the position to prevent, detect, remedy and eliminate workplace bullying. Employers can effectively address workplace bullying by implementing effective policies and creating workplace cultures which do not allow for workplace bullying. Effective policies need to provide targets with reasonable avenues to report their workplace bullying, fair and effective investigations and effective remedies to make them whole. To create an anti-bullying workplace culture, employers must send the right signals, reward the right behaviors, prohibit the wrong behaviors and engage the entire organization from top to bottom in the process. Unfortunately, employers have not taken these steps. At this point in time, there is no excuse for employers. The bullying research is hardly new. Workplace harassment has been defined as a form of unlawful discrimination for 30 years and employers have failed to effectively address the narrower problem of unlawful harassment. While employers can address workplace bullying, the reality is that they do not.

Unions also offer potential solutions to workplace bullying. In all phases of the labor relations process, unions can play a role. Unions can address a bullying environment during an organizing campaign. Campaigns can center on the bullying or organizers can help targeted workers to effectively address the bullying in their workplaces. Unions can and should bargain over workplace bullying clauses. Workplace bullying clearly is a working condition and, through collective bargaining, unions can establish clauses to protect their members from bullying. Unions can also help to eliminate workplace bullying through the day-to-day management of the collective bargaining agreement (whether it has a direct bullying clause or not). Through the use of the grievance process and shop floor concerted activity, unions and their leaders can indeed address workplace bullying. Unfortunately, unions in the United States currently represent just over 1 in 10 U.S. workers, leaving the vast majority of workers without the potential for these protections. Further, too many unions and too many union leaders do not take bullying seriously and may even take steps that make the bullying scenario worse for the target.

If we are to truly prevent, detect, remedy and eliminate workplace bullying, the only real path to do so is through a strong national law, with strong enforcement. First and foremost, we must assure that any workplace bullying law is strong from day one. We cannot pass a weak law and hope it gets better. There will be little chance to improve such a law from a legislative standpoint and one of the lessons we see from court interpretations of Title VII is that courts are likely to take steps to water down the law. The law must protect all targets, it must afford access to all targets, the law must provide remedies that will make targets whole. The law must also provide meaningful incentives to employers to address workplace bullying. What I mean by this is that employers must be held responsible for their workplaces and employers must be required to take all steps necessary to prevent, detect, remedy and eliminate workplace bullying. Bullying will still occur in many workplaces, but in every situation, the employer is in the best situation to have prevented the bullying and he/she should be held accountable for failing to do so.

A true social movement will be needed to pass such legislation in the current pro-capitalist, pro-employer environment. Activists, advocates and workers (past, present and future) must be educated about workplace bullying, its devastating effects and what can be done to eliminate workplace bullying. Once educated, these individuals must be activated and mobilized to engage in the needed mass movement to force legislators to pass a strong law that assures strong enforcement against workplace bullying. These activists must be willing to and must engage in the lobbying, demonstrating, picketing and protesting needed to push such a law through. These activists should look to identify candidates who will support such legislation and to campaign and to support these candidates.

Workplace bullying is a pervasive and devastating problem in workplaces in the United States and throughout the globe. If you have been a target of workplace bullying, I hope that this book helps you to understand that you are not at fault and you are not alone. I hope that this book has also given you some hope about what you can do to address the workplace bullying you have endured. If you are a bully, I also hope this book has made a difference with you. I hope that you will understand the impact of your actions and why you must stop. If you are a bully, I hope this book has led you to an immediate change. For organizational and union leaders, I hope this book gives you a map of what you can and should do to eliminate the bullying of members of your organizations. Finally, for all of the readers of this book, I hope that I have convinced you of the need for strong legislation and for your participation in a movement to push for such legislation. I hope you will take that next step to begin this process. Lobby your elected officials, send letters and emails and call their offices. Push the leaders of the labor movement in your area to address this problem, bring together other workers in your workplace and community to inform them of the problem and to develop steps you can take to end workplace bullying. Join me in the National Workplace Bullying Coalition (www.workplacebullyingcoalition .org), contact me at *jacarbo@ship.edu* or start your own coalition or program to bring an end to workplace bullying.

References

29 C.F.R. § 1604.11 (1999).

Agervold, M. & Mikkelson, G. E., 2004. Relationships between Bullying, Psychosocial Work Environment and Individual Stress Reactions. *Work & Stress*, 18, pp. 336–351.

Anon., 2004. *Merriam-Webster Dictionary*. New ed. s.l.: Merriam-Webster.

Baldwin v. Blue Cross/Blue Shield (11th Cir. 2007) 480 F. 3d 1287.

Barker, J., 1993. Tightening the Iron Cage: Concertive Control in Self-Managed Teams. *Administrative Quarterly*, 38, pp. 408–437.

Baskerville v. Culligan Int'l. Co. (7th Cir. 1995) 50 F.3d 428.

Berry, P. A., Gillespie, G. L., Gates, D. & Schafer, J., 2012. Novice Nurse Productivity Following Workplace Bullying. *Journal of Nurse Scholarship*, 44(1), pp. 80–87.

Bracke v. County of L.A. (9th Cir. 2003) 60 Fed. Appx. 120, 2003 U.S. App. LEXIS 4204.

Brofenbrenner, K., 2005. What Is Labor's True Purpose: The Implications of SEIU's Unite to Win Proposals for Organizing. *New Labor Forum*, 14, pp. 19–26.

Broefenbrenner, K. & Hickey, R., 2003. Winning Is Possible: Successful Union Organizing in the United States – Clear Lessons, Too Few Examples. *Multinational Monitor*, June, pp. 9–14.

Budd, J. W., 2013. *Labor Relations: Striking a Balance*. 4th ed. New York: McGraw-Hill Irwin.

Burawoy, M., 1979. *Manufacturing Consent: Changes in the Labor Process under Monopoly Capitalism*. Chicago: University of Chicago Press.

Burlington Industries, Inc. v. Ellerth (1998) 524 U.S. 742.

Burns v. McGregor (1993) 989 F.2d 959.

Cabrera, C. M., 2012. Relationship of Teachers' Perceptions of Organizational Health and Workplace Bullying (Doctoral Dissertation). s.l.: Proquest LLC Database.

Carbo, J. A., 2009. Strengthening the Healthy Workplace Act: Lessons from Title VII and IIED Litigation and Stories of Targets' Experiences. *Journal of Workplace Rights*, 14, pp. 97–120.

Carbo, J. A., 2015. Workplace Bullying: Concerted Activity as Viable Solution. In: Michele A. Paludi, ed. *Bullies in the Workplace: Seeing and Stopping Adults Who Abuse Their Co-Workers and Employees*. Santa Barbara, CA: Praeger, pp. 9–30.

Carbo, J. A. & Hughes, A., 2010. Workplace Bullying: Developing a Human Rights Based Definition from the Perspective and Experiences of Targets. *WorkingUSA*, 13, pp. 387–403.

Carroll, A. B., 1991. The Pyramid of Corporate Social Responsibility: Toward the Moral Management of Organizational Stakeholder. *Business Horizons*, 34(4), p. 39.

Cheng Chu, S. J., 2014. The Workplace Bullying Dilemma in Connecticut: Connecticut's Response to the Healthy Workplace Bill. *Connecticut Public Interest Law Journal*, 13, pp. 351–386.

Chong, D., 1991. *Collective Action and the Civil Rights Movement.* Chicago: The University of Chicago Press.

Chow, J. C., 1999. Sticks, Stones, and Simple Teasing: The Jurisprudence of Non-Cognizable Harassing Conduct in the Context of Title VII Hostile Work Environment Claims. *Loyola of Los Angeles Law Review*, 33, p. 133.

Clark v. UPS (6th Cir. 2005) 400 F.3d 341.

Coleman, B., 2004. Pragmatism's Insult: The Growing Interdisciplinary Challenge to American Harassment Jurisprudence. *Employee Rights and Employment Policy Journal*, 8, p. 239.

Cortina, L. M., 2008. Unseen Injustice: Incivility as Modern Discrimination in Organizations. *Academy of Management Review*, 33(1), pp. 55–75.

Cowan, R. L., 2011. Yes, We Have an Anti-Bullying Policy, But . . . HR Professionals' Understanding and Experiences with Workplace Bullying. *Communication Studies*, 62(3), pp. 307–327.

Cox, R., 2010. Canada: Psychological Harassment Legislation in Quebec: The First Five Years. *Comparative Labor Law & Policy Journal*, 32, p. 55.

Cox v. Keystone Carbon Co., 861 F.2d 390, 395 (3d.Cir. 1988).

Davenport, N., Schwartz, R. D. & Elliot, G. P., 2002. *Mobbing: Emotional Abuse in the American Workplace.* Ames, IA: Civil Society Publishing.

David Baldwin v. Dep't of Transportation (July 15, 2015) EEOC Appeal No. 0120133080.

Donnelly, J., 2003. *Universal Human Rights: In Theory and Practice.* 2nd ed. Ithaca, NY: Cornell University Press.

Dussault, M. & Frenett, E., 2015. Supervisors' Transformational Leadership and Bullying in the Workplace. *Psychological Reports*, 117(3), pp. 724–733.

Dyer, C., 2005. When a Boss Turns into a Bully. *The Guardian*, 29 March.

EEOC v. CRST Expenditure (8th Cir. 2012) 679 F.3d 657.

EEOC v. Xerxex (4th Cir. 2011) 629 F.3d 658.

Ehrenreich, R., 1999. Dignity and Discrimination: Toward a Pluralistic Understanding of Workplace Harassment. *Georgetown Law Review*, 88, November, p. 1.

Ehrenreich, R., 2004. Global Perspective on Workplace Harassment Law: Proceedings of the 2004 Annual Meeting, Association of American laws Schools Section on Labor Relations and Employment Law. *Employee Rights and Employment Policy Journal*, 8, p. 151.

Ehrenreich, B., 2001. *Nickel and Dimed: On (Not) Getting by in America.* Metropolitan Books, New York.

Einarsen, S., 1999. The Nature and Causes of Bullying at Work. *International Journal of Manpower*, 20(1/2), pp. 16–27.

Einarsen, S., 2000. Harassment and Bullying at Work: A Review of the Scandinavian approach. *Aggression and Violent Behavior: A Review Journal*, 4(5), pp. 371–401.

Einarsen, S., Hoel, H., Zapf, D. & Cooper, G. L., 2003. *Bullying and Emotional Abuse in the Workplace.* New York: Taylor and Francis.

Emdad, R., Alipour, A., Hagberg, J. & Jensen, I. B., 2013. The Impact of Bystanding to Workplace Bullying on Symptoms of Depression among Women and Men in Industry in Sweden: An Empirical and Theoretical Longitudinal Study. *International Archives of Occupational and Environmental Health*, 86, pp. 709–716.

Estreicher, S., 2001. Saturns for Rickshaws: The Stakes in the Debate over Predispute Employment Arbitration Agreements. *Ohio State Journal on Dispute Resolution*, 16, p. 559.

Fahie, D. & Devine, D., 2014. The Impact of Workplace Bullying on Primary School Teachers and Principals. *Scandinavian Journal of Educational Research*, 58(2), pp. 235–252.

Faragher v. Boca Raton (1998) 524 U.S. 775.

Farrington, D. P., 1993. Understanding and Preventing Bullying. *Crime and Justice*, 17.

Feldblum, C. R. & Lipnic, V. A., 2016. *Select Task Force on the Study of Harassment in the Workplace.* Washington, DC: EEOC, pp. 381–458.

Fischinger, P. S., 2010. "Mobbing": The German Law of Bullying. *Comparative Labor Law & Policy Journal*, 32, p. 153.

Fox, S. & Stallworth, L. E., 2004. Employee Perceptions of Internal Conflict Management Programs and ADR Processes for Preventing and Resolving Incidents of Workplace Bullying: Ethical Challenges for Decision-makers in Organizations. *Employee Rights and Employment Policy Journal*, 8, p. 375.

French, J. R. & Raven, B., 2006. The Bases of Social Power. In: J. L. Pierce & J. W. Newstrom, eds. *Leaders and the Leadership Process: Reading, Self-Assessments and Applications.* New York: McGraw-Hill Irwin, pp. 146–152.

Frieman, J. M., 1976. The Development of the At-Will Rule. *The American Journal of Legal History*, 20(2), pp. 118–135.

Fusilier, M. & Penrod, C., 2015. University Employee Sexual Harassment Policies. *Employee Responsibilities and Rights Journal*, 27(1), pp. 47–60.

Gaffney, D. A., DeMarco, R. F., Hofmeyer, A., Vessey, J. A. and Budin, W. C., 2012. Making Things Right: Nurses Experiences with Workplace Bullying – A Grounded Theory. *Nursing Research and Practice*, pp. 1–10.

Gardner, S. & Johnson, P., 2001. The Leaner, Meaner Workplace: Strategies for Handling Bullies at Work. *Employment Relations Today*, Summer, pp. 23–36.

Gibson v. Potter (5th Cir. 2008) 2008 U.S. App. LEXIS 2111.

Gross, J., 1994. Jury Awards $7 Million in Sex Case. *The New York Times*, 2 September.

Gross, J. A., 2004. Incorporating Human Rights Principles into US Labor Arbitration: A Proposal for Fundamental Change. *Employee Rights and Employment Policy Journal*, 8(1), pp. 1–47.

Grubb, P. L., 2004. Introduction to the Symposium on Workplace Bullying: What Organizations Are Saying. *Employee Rights and Employment Policy Journal*, 8, p. 407.

Guerrero, M. I. S., 2004. The Development of Moral Harassment (or Mobbing) Law in Sweden and France as a Step Towards EU Legislation. *Boston College International and Comparative Law Review*, 27, p. 477.

Hansen, A. M., Hogh, A., Garde, A. H. & Persson, R., 2014. Workplace Bullying and Sleep Difficulties. *International Archives of Occupational and Environmental Health*, 87, pp. 285–294.

Harris v. Forklift (1993) 510 U.S. 17.

Harthill, S., 2008. Bullying in the Workplace: Lessons from the United Kingdom. *Minnesota Journal of International Law*, 17, p. 247.

Hartsell v. Duplex Products (4th Cir. 1997) 123 F.3d 766.

Hatton v. Sutherland (Court of Appeal Civil Division, Feb. 2002) [2002] EWCA Civ 76.

Herschcovis, S. M., 2011. Incivility, Social Undermining, Bullying . . . Oh My!: A Call to Reconcile Constructs within Workplace Aggression Research. *Journal of Organizational Behavior*, 32, pp. 499–519.

Hockman v. Westward Communication (5th Cir. 2004) 407 F.3d 317.

Hoel, H. & Einarsen, S., 2010. Shortcomings of Anti-Bullying Regulations: The Case of Sweden. *European Journal of Work and Organizational Psychology*, 19(1), pp. 30–50.

Hornstein, H. A., 1996. *Brutal Bosses and Their Prey: How to Identify and Overcome Abuse in the Workplace.* s.l.: Riverhead Books.

Ishay, M. R., 2004. *The History of Human Rights: From Ancient Times to the Globalization Era.* Berkeley, CA: The University of California Press.

Jefferson, T., 1776. The Declaration of Independence. In: *The Thomas Jefferson Reader.* s.l.: Konecky & Konecky, pp. 21–27.

Johnson, S. G. & Johnson, P., 2001. The Leaner, Meaner Workplace: Strategies for Handling Bullies at Work. *Employment Relations Today*, 28(2), p. 28.

Jones, G. R. & George, J. M., 2007. Chapter 9: Motivation and Performance. In: *Essentials of Contemporary Management*. s.l.: McGraw-Hill Irwin, pp. 329–331.

Keashley, L. & Jagatic, K., 2003. By Any Other Name: American Perspectives on Workplace Bullying. In: S. Einarsen, H. Hoel, D. Zapf & C. L. Cooper, eds. *Bullying and Emotional Abuse in the Workplace*. New York: Taylor & Francis, pp. 31–61.

Keashley, L. & Neuman, J. H., 2004. Bullying in the Workplace: Its Impact and Management. *Employee Rights and Employment Policy Journal*, 8, p. 335–346.

Kennedy, R. G., 2006. Corporations, Common Goods and Human Persons. *Ave Maria Law Review*, 4, Winter, pp. 1–32.

Kleiman, L. S., 2003–2004. Sexual Harassment and the Law: Court Standards for Assessing Hostile Environment Claims. *Journal of Individual Employee Rights*, 11(1), pp. 53–73.

Kolstad v. American Dental Association (1999) 527 U.S. 526.

Korkmaz, M. & Cemalugli, N., 2010. Relationship between Organizational Learning and Workplace Bullying in Learning Organizations. *Educational Research Quarterly*, 33(3), pp. 3–38.

Kouri v. Liberian Services (ED Va. 1991) 1991 U.S. Dist. LEXIS 4143.

Leader, L. & Burger, M., 2004. Let's Get a Vision: Drafting Effective Arbitration Agreements in Employment and Effecting Other Safeguards to Insure Equal Access to Justice. *Employee Rights and Employment Policy Journal*, 8, p. 87.

Lehman, B., 2000. Why Title VII Should Prohibit All Workplace Sexual Harassment. *Yale Journal of Law & Feminism*, 12, p. 225.

Lenihan v. Boeing Co. (S.D. Tex. 1998) 994 F. Supp. 776.

Lerouge, L., 2010. Moral Harassment in the Workplace: French Law and European Perspectives. *Comparative Labor Law Journal & Policy Journal*, 32, p. 109.

Liadis v. Sears, Roebuck & Co. (6th Cir. 2002) 47 Fed. Appx. 295.

Lieber, L., 2010. How Workplace Bullying Affects the Bottom Line. *Employment Relations Today*, Fall, pp. 91–101.

Linville v. Sears and Roebuck (8th Cir. 2003) 335 F.3d 822.

Love v. Georgia Pacific Corp (2001) 209 W.Va. 515.

Lueders, A., 2008. You'll Need More Than a Voltage Converter: Plugging European Workplace Bullying Laws into the American Jurisprudential Outlet. *Arizona Journal of International and Comparative Law*, 15, pp. 197–262.

Madray v. Publix Supermarkets, Inc (11th Cir. 2000) 208 F.3d 1290.

Majrowski v. Guy's and St Thomas's NHS Trust, House of Lords (12 July 2006) [2006] UKHL 34, [2007] 1 AC 224.

Marshall, A. M., 2005. Idle Rights: Employees' Rights Consciousness and the Construction of Sexual Harassment Policies. *Law & Society Review*, 39, p. 83.

McCarthy, P. & Mayhew, C., 2004. *Safeguarding the Organization against Violence and Bullying*. New York: Palgrave Macmillan.

McCown v. St. John's Health (8th Cir. 2003) 349 F.3d 540.

Meritor Savings Bank v. Vinson (1986) 477 U.S. 57.

Metoyer v. Chassman (9th Cir. 2007) 101 Fair Empl. Prac. Cas. (BNA) 1017.

Mikkelson, G. & Einarsen, S., 2001. Bullying in Danish Work-Life: Prevalence and Health Correlates. *European Journal of Work and Organizational Psychology*, 10(4), pp. 393–413.

Mintzberg, H., Simons, R. & Basu, K., 2002. Beyond Selfishness. *MIT Sloan Management Review*, 44(1), pp. 67–74.

Moody, K., 2007. *US Labor in Trouble and Transition: The Failure of Reform from Above, the Promise of Revival from Below.* London: Verso.

Namie, G. & Lutgen-Sandvik, P. E., 2010. Active and Passive Accomplices: The Communal Character of Workplace Bullying. *International Journal of Communication*, 4, pp. 343–373.

Namie, G. & Namie, R., 2009. *The Bully at Work*. 2nd ed. Naperville, IL: Sourcebooks, Inc.

Naughton, M., 2006. The Corporation as a Community of Work: Understanding the Firm within the Catholic Social Tradition. *Ave Maria Law Review*, 4, Winter, pp. 33–75.

Nielsen, M. B., Nielsen, G. H., Notelaers, G. & Einarsen, S., 2015. Workplace Bullying and Suicide Ideation: A 3-Wave Longitudinal Norwegian Study. *American Journal of Public Health*, 105(11), pp. e23–e28.

Noa Davenport, R. D. S. & Elliott, G. P., 2002. *Mobbing: Emotional Abuse in the American Workplace.* s.l.: Civil Society Publishing.

Oncale v. Sundowner (1998) 523 U.S. 75.

Pakenham-Walsh v. Connell Residential (Private unlimited company) and another (Court of Appeal – Civil Division, 21 Feb. 2006) [2006] EWCA Civ 90.

Parkes, D., 2004. Targeting Workplace Harassment in Quebec: On Exporting a Legislative Agenda. *Employee Rights and Employment Policy Journal*, 8, p. 423.

Pedroza v. Cintas (8th Cir. 2005) 397 F.3d 1063.

Pellegrino, K., Carbo, J. & Pellegrino, R., 1999. Sexual Harassment: Is the Media Manipulating the Facts? *Journal of Individual Employment Rights*, 8(1), pp. 1–14.

Pierce, E. R., Rosen, B. & Hiller, T. B., 1997. Breaking the Silence: Creating User Friendly Sexual Harassment Policies. *Employee Rights and Responsibilities Journal*, 10(3), pp. 225–242.

Powell, J. E., Powell, A. L. & Petrosko, J. M., 2015. School climate as a predictor of incivility and bullying among public school employees: A multilevel analysis. *Journal of School Violence*, 14(2), pp. 217–244.

Randall, P., 1997. *Adult Bullying: Perpetrators and Victims*. New York: Routledge.

Raver, J. L. & Nishii, L. H., 2010. Once, Twice or Three Times as Harmful? Ethnic Harassment, Gender Harassment, and Generalized Workplace Harassment. *Journal of Applied Psychology*, 96(2), pp. 235–254.

Rayner, C., Hoel, H. & Cooper, C. L., 2002. *Workplace Bullying: What We Know, Who Is to Blame and What Can We Do.* London and New York: Taylor and Francis.

Reed v. MBNA Mktg. Sys., Inc., (1st Cir. 2003) 333 F.3d 27.

Riley, D., Duncan, D. J. & Edwards, J., 2011. Staff Bullying in Australian Schools. *Journal of Educational Administration*, 49(1), pp. 7–20.

Riske v. King Soopers (10th Cir. 2004) 366 F. 3d 1085.

Rosenfeld, J., 2014. *What Unions No Longer Do*. Cambridge, MA: Harvard University Press.

Rothstein, M. A. & Liebman, L., 2011. *Employment Law: Cases and Materials.* 7th ed. New York: Foundation Press.

Sanders, D. F., Pattison, P. and Bible, J. D., 2012. Legislating "nice": Analysis and assessment of proposed workplace bullying prohibitions. *Southern Law Journal*, 22(1), p. 1.

Seeber, R. L. & Lipsky, D. B., 2006. The Ascendency of Employment Arbitrators in US. Employment Relations: A New Actor in the American System? *British Journal of Industrial Relations*, 44(4), pp. 719–756.

Sheehan, M., Barker, M. & Rayner, C., 1999. Applying Strategies for Dealing with Workplace Bullying. *International Journal of Manpower* 20(1/2), pp. 50–57.

Shoemaker v. Myers (Cal. 1990) 52 Cal.3d 1, 276 Cal. Rptr. 303, 801 P.2d 1054.

Simmons, R., 2002. *Odd Girl Out: The Hidden Culture of Aggression in Girls.* s.l.: Harcourt, Inc.

Sjoberg, G., Gill, E. & Williams, N., 2001. A Sociology of Human Rights. *Social Problems*, 48, pp. 11–47.

Squelch, J. & Guthrie, R., 2010. Australia: The Australian Legal Framework for Workplace Bullying. *Comparative Labor Law & Policy Journal*, 32, p. 15.

Story, E., Flanagan, J. L. & House Docket 2072, No 1771, 2015. *An Act Addressing Workplace, Mobbing, and Harassment without Regard to Protected Class Status*. Massachusetts: The House of the Commonwealth of Massachusetts.

Tindall v. Housing Auth. of the City of Ft. Smith (W.D. Ark. 1991) 762 F.Supp. 259.

Toth, M. A., 2008. The Right to Dignity at Work: Reflections on Article 26 of the Revised European Social Charter. *Comparative Labor Law Journal & Policy Journal*, 29, p. 275.

Tracy, S. J., Lutgen-Sandvik, P. & Alberts, J. K., 2006. Nightmares, Demons and Slaves: Exploring the Painful Metaphors of Workplace Bullying. *Management Communications Quarterly*, 20(2), pp. 148–185.

Triple Play Sports Bar & Grille (August 22, 2014) 361 NLRB No. 31.

The United Nations, 1948. The Universal Declaration of Human Rights. [Online] Available at: http://www.un.org/en/universal-declaration-human-rights/index.html [Accessed 24 August 2016].

The United Nations, 1993. *Vienna Declaration and Programme of Action*. s.l.: World Conference of Human Rights. [Online] Available at: www.ohchr.org/EN/ProfessionalInterest/Pages/Vienna.aspx

The United Nations General Assembly, 1966. *International Covenant on Economic, Social and Cultural Rights*. s.l.: s.n.

Velazquez, M., 2010. The Spanish Code of Practice on Work-Related Bullying: Reflections on European Law and Its Impact on a National Strategy for Labor Inspectors. *Comparative Labor Law & Policy Journal*, 32, p. 185.

Walsh, D. J., 2007. *Employment Law for Human Resource Practice*. 2nd ed. s.l.: Thomson Southwestern.

Walton v. Johnson and Johnson Services, Inc. (11th Cir. 2003) 347 F.3d 1272.

Weikle, R. D., Wheeler, H. N. & McClendon, J. A., 1998. A Comparative Case Study of Union Organizing Success and Failure: Implications for Practical Strategy. In: Kate Brofenbrenner, Sheldon Friedman, Richard W. Hurg, Rudolph A. Oswalk, & Ronald L. Seeber, eds. *Organizing to Win*. Ithaca, NY: Cornell University Press, pp. 197–212.

Wheeler, H. N., 2002. *The Future of the American Labor Movement*. Cambridge, MA: Cambridge University Press.

Wood, H. C., 1877. *Master and Servant*. s.l.: s.n.

Yamada, D.C., 2000. Workplace Bullying and the Need for Status-blind Hostile Work Environment Protection. *Georgetown Law Journal*, 88(3), pp. 475–536.

Yamada, D. C., 2004. Crafting a Legislative Response to Workplace Bullying. *Employee Rights and Employment Policy Journal*, 8, p. 475.

Yates, M. D., 2009. *Why Unions Matter*. 2nd ed. New York: Monthly Review Press.

Index

Note: page numbers in italic indicate a figure or table on the corresponding page.

activism, in support of anti-bullying legislation 155–7, 162
administrative remedies, for workplace harassment 65–6
advocates, creative 111–13
Age Discrimination in Employment Act 48
Agervold, M. 29
alternative dispute resolution (ADR) plans 122–3
Americans with Disabilities Act 48
anti-harassment policy: criteria for effectiveness 118; dissemination/ training 121–2; investigation process 119–21; overview of 117; reporting structure 118–19; retaliation policy 121; *see also* dignity at work act; U.S. Equal Employment Opportunity laws
Army, organizational bullying in 16
attorneys, as creative advocates 112
Australia, preventing workplace bullying in 66, 70, 79, 146
avoidance techniques 109–10

Baker and McKenzie law firm 8
Barker, J. 35
Baskerville v. Culligan International Co. 53–5
behaviors, bullying: overview of 37–8; severity vs. pervasiveness 96–7; types/outcomes of 93–6
Belgium, preventing workplace bullying in 78–9, 146, 149
Bergman, Mindy, Dr. 29, 30, 58
Brofenbrenner, K. 131, 137
bullies: behaviors of 37–8; demographic characteristics of 4–5, 11, 21; power of 36–7; types of 19–21
bully by proxy 18–19, *19*

Burawoy, M. 35
Burger, M. 123
Burns v. McGregor 7–8
business case, to eliminate workplace bullying 130–1
bystander interventions 110–11, 138, 161

Canada, preventing workplace bullying in 47, 76–8
Carroll, Archie 116
Carroll's Pyramid of Corporate Social Responsibility 116
Cassin, Rene 155
CBA *see* collective bargaining agreement (CBA)
Chong, D. 155, 156
Chow, J. C. 48
Civil Rights Act, Title VII 48, 51, 153, 154, 162
class consciousness, of targets 41–2, 138–9
Clear Pine Mouldings standard 125
Code of Federal Regulations 89
Coleman, B. 65
collective bargaining agreement (CBA): anti-bullying clause in 132–5; day-to-day management of 135–6; in preventing workplace bullying 131–2
collective consciousness *see* class consciousness, of targets
communities, effects of bullying on 26–7, *28*
confidentiality 120, 126
consequences, of workplace bullying 3–4, 22–4, 159–62
constructive discharge 77
control, of bullies 37–8

Cooper Tire & Rubber case 125–6, 140
Cornell University 12
Cortina, L. M. 30, 94, 95, 147
costs of workplace bullying 26, 159
Court of Cassation (France) 98, 146
co-workers, as bullies 19–20
Cox, R. 77–8, 89, 146
Cox v. Keystone Carbon Co. 61
culture change 123–4

Davenport, N. 4, 63, 64
defining workplace bullying: analysis
    of 87–8; current definitions 88, 151;
    level/type of harm 97–8; necessity of
    intent 98–9; overview of 85–7; power
    differential 100–2; repeated vs. single
    incidents 89–93; summary of 104–5;
    type/severity of attack 93–7;
    as "unwanted" 102–4
demographic characteristics, of bullies 4–5,
    11, 21
denial of leave, as bullying tactic 15–16
Department of Labor (DoL) 152–3
Devine, D. 11
dignity: as basic human right 151, 153–5;
    damage to 93–4, 97–8; discrimination
    vs. 49–51; effect of sexual harassment
    on 51–2; focus on 148; protection of 80,
    86–7; putting profits before 35–6
dignity at work act: activism in support
    of 155–7, 162; addressing arguments
    against 153–5; cause of action 152–3;
    conflict with laws 153; definitions
    150–1; employer responsibility 151–2;
    entitlement to remedies 152; findings/
    purpose of 150; individual liability 152;
    prohibition against abusive behaviors
    151; worker right to dignity 151
Dignity at Work Bill 75
discrimination: focus on 49–51; incivility
    as 95; sexual harassment and 51–2
DoL *see* Department of Labor (DoL)
Duncan, D. J. 29

education, regarding anti-harassment
    laws 156
Edwards, J. 29
EEOC (Equal Employment Opportunity
    Commission) 10, 42; *see also* U.S. Equal
    Employment Opportunity laws
EEOC Select Task Force on the Study of
    Harassment 10, 29, 51, 58, 115, 123, 124
Ehrenreich, B. 51
Einarsen, S. 29, 57, 73, 98, 100

emotional distress 24, 61–5
employee, definition of 151
employer-based solutions: ADR programs
    122–3; anti-harassment policy 117–22;
    avoiding conflict with NLRA 124–7;
    healthy workplace climate 123–4;
    overview of 114–17
employers: as complicit in bullying 7;
    definition of 150–1; ineffectual address
    to bullying 47–8; need to maintain
    control 34–5; responsibility of 71–3, 75,
    77, 148–9, 151–2
Employment Rights Act of 1996 75
Equal Employment Opportunity
    Commission *see* EEOC (Equal
    Employment Opportunity Commission)
Estreicher, S. 122
Ezekial v. The Court Service 75

fact-gathering process 120–1
Fahie, D. 11
Fair Labor Standards Act 154
family, effects of bullying on 25, *28*
Faragher and *Ellerth* rulings 8, 57, 114, 115
Faragher v. Boca Raton 53, 58, 93, 148–9
Farrington, D. P. 88
Federal Rules of Civil Procedure 154
Feldblum, C. R. 115
focus groups 138
formal power position 100
Fox, S. 123
France, preventing workplace bullying
    in 74–5, 94, 146–9
French, J. R. 100
friends, effects of bullying on 25, *28*
Fusilier, M. 115

Gaffney, D. A. 111, 138
gaining-of-consciousness experience 40–1
Gardner, S. 4
Gates, Bill 36
generalized harassment, unlawful
    harassment vs. 8–9, 29
Germany, preventing workplace bullying
    in 70, 79–80
Gibson v. Potter 103
Ginsburg, Justice R. 56

harassment, definition of 151
harm from bullying 97–8, 148, 159
Harris v. Forklift 49, 56, 97
Harthill, S. 66, 76, 80, 94, 141
Hartsell v. Duplex Products 54
Hatton v. Sutherland 75–6

health, impact of bullying on 3–4, 24
Healthy Workplace Bill 88, 97, 145–9
Hell's Kitchen 36
Herschcovis, S. M. 30, 86, 90, 94, 146
Hockman v. Westward Communication 56–7
Hoel, H. 73
hope, targets' experience of 139
Hornstein, H. A. 4
HR (human resources) department 7
Hughes, Amy 29

IIED *see* intentional infliction of emotional distress (IIED)
illness, workplace bullying and 3–4, 24
incivility 93–7, 147
individual bully level factors 33–4, 36–7
individual consciousness, of being bullied 40–1
individual liability 152
Industrial Relations Act (Australia) 79
intent *see* malicious intent
intentional infliction of emotional distress (IIED) 61–5
internal harassment committee 120
interpersonal communications, in personal level bullying 13–14
intra-union bullying 140–1
investigation policies 15
investigation process 119–21

Jagatic, K. 4
job exit, to escape bullying 23, 24
job performance, effect of harassment on 56–7
Jobs, Steve 36
Johnson, P. 4
Jordan v. Memorial Hermann Southeast Hospital 56
justification, for workplace bullying 108

Keashley, L. 4
Kleiman, L. S. 103
Kolstad v. American Dental Association 115
Kotter, John 124
Kotter's 8-Stage Process 124
Kouri v. Liberian Services, Inc. 102–3

Labor and Employment Relations Association 156
Labor Research Action Network 156
labor unions: benefits of addressing bullying 137–40; collective bargaining agreement 131–2; creative advocates in 112; dangers of weak response by 136–7; day-to-day

CBA management 135–6; intra-union bullying 140–1; negotiating anti-bullying clause 132–5; organizing phase of 130–1; preventing workplace bullying 75, 129–30, 161; role in legislative change 141–2; spillover/threat effect 140
Leader, L. 123
Lehman, B. 48
Lenihan v. Boeing Co. 54
Lerouge, L. 146
Leymann Inventory on Psychological Terror (LIPT) 29
Lipnic, V. A. 115
Lipsky, D. B. 123
love, targets' experience of 138
Love v. Georgia Pacific Corporation 63
low-grade incivility 93–7, 147
Lueders, A. 154

McCarthy, P. 55
malicious intent: as irrelevant 74, 81, 147; necessity of 98–9; showing of 62
managerial practices 61–2, 71–3
Marshall, Anne Marie 51, 52, 115–16
Mayhew, C. 55
Meritor Savings Bank v. Vinson 56, 115
Mikkelson, G. 29, 57
moral harassment 74–5, 90, 94, 98, 151
myths, regarding workplace bullying 1–2

Namie, G. 49, 111
Namie, R. 49, 111
National Labor Relations Act (NLRA), avoiding conflict with 124–7
National Workplace Bullying Coalition 156, 162
Negative Acts Questionnaire (NAQ) 29
negative reinforcement, for bullying behavior 136
Neuman, J. H. 4
Nishii, L. H. 30, 86, 90, 147
nuisance grievance approach 135–6

O'Connor, Justice S. 56
Oncale Ruling (1999) 49
operational method of measuring bullying 27, 29–31
Ordinance Concerning Victimisation at Work (Sweden) 71, 146
organizational level factors, antecedents for workplace bullying 33–5
organizational policy bullying 12, 15–18, *19*, 146

organizations: effects of bullying on 25–6, *28*; support of bullying 5, 159–60
OSHA (Occupational Safety and Health Act) 66, 79
outrageous conduct 61–2

Pakenham-Walsh v Connell Residential and another 75
Penrod, C. 115
performance evaluations, as bullying tactic 15, 17
personal level bullying 12, 13–14, *19*
physical intimidation 100–1
policies: anti-harassment (*see* anti-harassment policy); organizational bullying via 15–18
Posner, Justice R. 53–4
post-traumatic stress disorder (PTSD) 4, 22, 134, 150
power: of bullies 36–7; differential 100–2
preconditions, for workplace bullying 33–7
preventing workplace bullying: in Australia 79; in Belgium 78–9; in Canada 76–8; in France 74–5; in Sweden 71–4; in United Kingdom 75–6; outside United States 70–1
profits 25, 35–6
protected status: in Canada 77; focus on 49–51; as irrelevant 73; sexual harassment and 49–51
Protection from Harassment Act of 1997 (United Kingdom) 76
psychological effects, of workplace bullying 24
psychological harassment 77–8, 89, 151
punishment, for bullying behavior 136

Quebec, preventing workplace bullying in 77, 146–7
Queensland, preventing workplace bullying in 79

racial-based harassment 13
Randall, P. 88, 89, 98
rationalization, for workplace bullying 108
Raven, B. 100
Raver, J. L. 30, 86, 90, 147
repetitive acts, of workplace bullying 89–93, 146
reporting requirements, of EEO laws 57–60
reporting structure 118–19
Restatement of Torts, Second 61
retaliation policy 121
Revised Statutes of Quebec 77–8

Riley, D 29, 30
Riske v. King Soopers 50
rumors, as bullying tactic 13–14
Runion, Anthony 125

saliency, targets' experience of 138–9
School of Industrial and Labor Relations 12
SCOTUS *see* Supreme Court of the United States (SCOTUS)
Seeber, R. L. 123
self-blame, as target response 108
self-report method of measuring bullying 27, 29–31
severe or pervasive standard: of EEO laws 52–6; of IIED 61–5
sexual harassment: bullying as 13–14; definition of 49; loss of dignity in 51–2; minimization of 8; protected status and 49–51; severe or pervasive standard in 52–5; underreporting of 30
Shah v. Xerox Canada 77
shift assignment, as bullying tactic 15, 16–17
Shultz, Vicki 51, 52
Simmons, Rachel 95
single incidents, of workplace bullying 89–93
Social Modernization Law (France) 74, 147–8
social movement, supporting anti-bullying legislation 155–7, 162
society: antecedents for bullying in 33–5; effects of bullying on 26–7, *28*; support of bullying 5
Souter, Justice David H. 53
Spain, preventing workplace bullying in 80
spillover effect, for non-union members 140
Stallworth, L. E. 123
status-based harassment: focus on 49–51; as irrelevant 73; sexual harassment and 51–2
stealth monitoring 73
Stone v. Lancaster Chamber of Commerce 75
stress relief techniques 109
suicide, linked to workplace bullying 4, 22–3
supervisory bullies 19–20
Supreme Court of the United States (SCOTUS) 8, 49, 53, 56–8, 93–4, 114
Sweden, preventing workplace bullying in 71–4, 94, 146, 149
Swedish National Board of Occupational Safety and Health 71

target responses: attempts to stop bullying 108–9; avoidance/escape techniques 109–10; gaining class consciousness 41–2; individual consciousness of being bullied 40–1; justification/self-blame 108; outcomes of 42, 44; prior to consciousness of being bullied 39; range of 102–4, 107–8; stress relief techniques 109

targets: exploring experience of 87, 89–93; impact on 22–4, *28*, 38, *43*; lack of legal recourse 48; reactions of (*see* target responses); of workplace bullying 3–4

task assignment, as bullying tactic 15, 16–17

threat effect, for non-union members 140

top performers, as bullies 5, 9, 118

Tracy, S. J. 93, 94

training, in anti-harassment policy 121–2

trickle down bullying 19

uncivil behaviors 93–7

unemployment compensation, as inadequate remedy 65–6

United Association of Labor Education 156

United Kingdom, preventing workplace bullying in 75–6, 94

Universal Declaration of Human Rights (UDHR) 7, 159

unlawful harassment, generalized harassment vs. 8–9, 29

unreported bullying 102–4

unwanted actions, bullying as 102–4

U.S. common law 61–5, 160

U.S. Equal Employment Opportunity laws: focus on status-based harassment 49–52; gaps in 48; heightened standard of 52–6; as ineffectual 45, 60–1, 160; job-related outcomes and 56–7;

protection under 48–9; reporting requirements 57–60

U.S. legal system: access to remedies 149–50; addressing all forms of bullying 145–8; anti-bullying legislation 35; bullying ignored/exacerbated by 5, 7; employer responsibility 148–9; focus on protecting rights 148; need for strong legislation 144–5; possibility of overburdening 80–1, 154

Vienna Doctrine 155

Wagner Act 154

Walton v. Johnson 58

Weikle, R. D. 138

Whitting v. Winnipeg River Brokenhead Community Futures Development Corp. 77

Williams v. the US Dept. of the Navy 56

withholding information, as bullying tactic 17–18

workers' compensation 65–6

work overload, as bullying tactic 16–17

workplace bullying: attempts to stop 108–9; avoiding/escaping 109–10; bystander interventions 110–11; categories of (*see specific categories*); defining (*see* defining workplace bullying); as epidemic 27–31, 85–6; failure to deal with 5–7; life cycle of *43*; models for eliminating 10; pervasiveness of 31, 159; preconditions/antecedents for 33–7; prevention/elimination of (*see* preventing workplace bullying)

Yamada, D. C. 48, 75, 145, 154

Yates, M. D. 153